BUDDHAHOOD
WITHOUT MEDITATION

Dudjom Lingpa

Buddhahood Without Meditation

A Visionary Account Known as
Refining One's Perception
(*Nang-jang*)

REVISED EDITION

Dudjom Lingpa

Translated from the Tibetan under the direction
of His Eminence Chagdud Tulku Rinpoche
and Lama Padma Drimed Norbu
by Richard Barron (Lama Chökyi Nyima)
and Susanne Fairclough

PADMA PUBLISHING

Published by Padma Publishing
P.O. Box 279
Junction City, CA 96048-0279

© Padma Publishing 1994
Revised Edition 2002
Revised Edition, Second Printing 2006

Printed in the United States of America

Library of Congress Cataloging-in-Publication Data
Bdud-'joms-gliṅ-pa, Gter-ston, b. 1835.
[Raṅ bźin rdzogs pa chen po'i raṅźal mṅon du byed
pa'i gdams pa zab gsan sñin po. English]
Buddhahood without meditation : a visionary account known
as *Refining one's perception* (*Nang-jang*) / Dudjom Lingpa;
translated from the Tibetan under the direction of
Chagdud Tulku Rinpoche and Lama Padma Drimed Norbu
by Richard Barron and Susanne Fairclough.
p. cm.

ISBN-10: 1-881847-33-0
ISBN-13: 978-1-881847-33-5

1. Rdzogs-chen (Rñiṅ-ma-pa)   I. Title: Nang-jang.
II. Barron, Richard.   III. Title
BQ7662.4.B3422813   2002
294.3'4446—dc21   2002025261
CIP

THIS TEXT BELONGS to the category of atiyoga, the highest of the nine vehicles that constitute the Buddhist path. Moreover, it is from the short lineage of Dudjom Lingpa, a direct transmission of the Great Perfection approach so powerful that even hearing it read aloud ensures that the listener will eventually escape the suffering of samsara.

It should be remembered, however, that to benefit fully from the *Nang-jang*, one must receive empowerment, oral transmission, and teachings from a qualified Dzogchhen master.

Contents

Illustrations

Translators' Note to the Revised Edition

DURING THE COURSE of the transmission of the Buddha's teachings from India to Tibet, editions of translated texts evolved, often over many hundreds of years, before the texts that we now use as the standard came into being.

This revised edition of *Buddhahood Without Meditation,* though having evolved over only four years, is the result of significant changes that reflect the blessings of Lama Padma Drimed Norbu and his transmission of this text at his annual Dzogchhen retreats. Because Lama Drimed wished to make the terminology and meaning clearer to his Western students, we began a review of the text in 1998. Spurred by his insightful inquiries and in consultation with him, we continued to refine its language over the next three years, resolving questions with His Eminence Chagdud Tulku Rinpoche.

This process greatly benefited from refinements in terminology resulting from the work of the Padma Translation Committee on two other Great Perfection texts, Longchhenpa's *The Precious Treasury of the Way of Abiding* and *The Precious Treasury of the Basic Space of Phenomena.* These terms have been applied to the main body of *Buddhahood Without Meditation,* the Structural Analysis and Outline by His Holiness Dudjom Rinpoche, and the Glossary. Finally, to assist the reader we have included a pronunciation guide to the transliterated Tibetan terms.

May all those who encounter such a precious text have the good fortune to receive the lineage of transmission from a re-alized master and bring to fruition its incomparable blessings.

RICHARD BARRON
SUSANNE FAIRCLOUGH
March 2002

Translator's Note to the First Edition

THIS TEXT IS A TRANSLATION of an account compiled in the nineteenth century by Dudjom Lingpa, a great visionary and meditation master of the Nyingma school of Tibetan Buddhism who lived from 1835 to 1904. The full title of the text is *Buddhahood Without Meditation: Advice for Making Fully Evident One's True Face—Natural Great Perfection,* but the work is most commonly referred to among Tibetans as the *Nang-jang,* which might be rendered *Refining One's Perception.* It is one of the standard works now used to present the teachings of the Dzogchhen, or Great Perfection, approach, particularly those teachings that relate to the level of practice known as *t'hreg-chhod,* or "cutting through solidity."

Dudjom Lingpa's account is in the form of a journal describing a number of visions and dreams that he experienced throughout his life. Indeed, much of the text consists of Dudjom Lingpa quoting the deities and masters he encountered on these occasions. The knowledge he gained during his experiences spans the range of teachings on the "view" of the Great Perfection approach of the Nyingma school. His Holiness Dudjom Rinpoche, Jigdral Yeshe Dorje (1904–1987), who was the rebirth of Dudjom Lingpa, edited the original manuscript to ensure its accuracy. He also wrote an invaluable structural analysis and outline that organizes and elucidates the information received by Dudjom Lingpa. A translation of this outline has been included in this volume to serve as a study guide to the main text.

The initial drafts of the translation were prepared in the spring of 1988, following a six-week retreat under the direction of the Venerable Chagdud Tulku Rinpoche. Chagdud Rinpoche used the text of the *Nang-jang* as the basis for his explanations of the path of *t'hreg-chhod*. This course was my first in-depth exposure to the teachings of the Great Perfection. I recall that I was as enthralled with the magical quality of Dudjom Lingpa's style and Chagdud Rinpoche's presentation as with the information these conveyed. After the retreat, Chagdud Rinpoche's interpreter, Tsering Everest, requested that the text be translated into English. The translation project was undertaken by Padma Publishing, a branch of Chagdud Gonpa Foundation. As the project's translator, I produced a rough draft of the text over the next few months. This was reviewed in meticulous detail by Chagdud Rinpoche, whose corrections and suggestions were then incorporated.

The lengthy process of revision involved redrafting the English text a number of times, each successive version of which was reviewed by Chagdud Rinpoche, and then further redrafting to improve the accuracy of the translation. At several stages, the text was edited by the Translation Committee of Padma Publishing.

Over a period of five years, then, the translation has undergone extensive revision, and we now offer this publication with the hope that the meaning of Dudjom Lingpa's words is accurately conveyed and that some of the spirit of this extraordinary account has been preserved.

A note on the transliteration of Tibetan and Sanskrit terms and names: Tibetan is a difficult language to phoneticize for English speakers, and as many systems exist as there are translators. We have followed the system used by Padma Publishing, based upon an earlier system developed by Chagdud Rinpoche for his students. To accommodate those with some knowledge of Tibetan, there is a glossary with the terms in Tibetan script. For Sanskrit terms in the text, a modified version of transliteration has been used that omits the diacritical marks adopted by scholars; the entries in the glossary, however, provide full diacriticals. For the benefit of those who are familiar with the Tibetan language, or wish to become so, we have included the Tibetan for both the main text and the outline, arranged to correspond as closely as possible to the English translation on the facing pages.

I would like to acknowledge a deep debt of gratitude to Chagdud Rinpoche for providing the inspiration and guidance essential to understanding (and therefore translating) a text of such profundity. My thanks go also to the members of the Translation Committee for their constructive and illuminating criticism of my attempts to capture the sense of this text. I am also grateful to Phyllis Glanville for the original line drawings.

RICHARD BARRON
August 1993

Introduction

His Eminence Chagdud Tulku Rinpoche

Dharmakaya, the entire vast array of timeless purity;
sambhogakaya, the entire vast array of an unceasing
    display of peaceful and wrathful deities;
nirmanakaya, the entire vast array that tames any
    being in any way necessary:
I bow with devotion to Dudjom Lingpa, tamer of
    beings.
O lord protector, although your qualities cannot be
    adequately described,
I will write in brief of your life example in order to
    open the doorway for those of us with small minds
    to enter with faith
into the splendor of your excellent speech, nectar of
    profound spiritual advice.
Deities and gurus, grant me your blessings for my
    undertaking!

In the distant past, in order to bring benefit to the teachings and to beings, the great dharmakaya teacher Vajradhara manifested in the perceptions of those to be tamed, arising in the form of a lord among yogins known as Nüdan Dorje. This powerful yogin, who was empowered as a spiritual ruler of the three realms and who prayed with enormous aspiration to benefit beings, conferred empowerment on the one thousand future buddhas of this eon. He prayed, "Until the teachings of these one thousand buddhas of the fortunate eon have come to an end, may my emanations appear without interruption, accomplishing vast benefit for beings to be tamed!"

The power of this aspiration was such that hundreds of his emanations benefited beings whenever circumstances were right. Among these were the emanation of the shravaka Shariputra during the time of our teacher, the Buddha Shakyamuni, and following him the rigdzin Hungchhenkara, the translator Drogban Khye'uchhung Lotsawa, Dampa Desheg, who founded Kat'hog Monastery, Kharnagpa of the Drum clan, and Hepa Chhöjung, as well as Dudjom Dorje, Duddul Rolpatzal, and numerous other emanations who ensured the welfare of beings.

Most especially the master Padmakara, whose knowledge encompasses the three times, exhorted an emanation to appear as his own emissary, a lord protector for beings in times of spiritual degeneration. In accordance with his command, Dudjom Lingpa was conceived amid wondrous signs in the womb of a woman of the Nub clan. His mother felt great physical and mental well-being during her pregnancy, and there were marvelous portents when he was born without difficulty in a small felt tent. The entire dwelling was filled with and surrounded by rainbows and spheres of light, fragrant odors wafted about, and a rain of blossoms fell. In 1835, a sheep year, on the tenth day of the first month (which commemorates the Buddha's display of miracles), his form, marked with major and minor signs of perfection, appeared like a lotus blossoming. Everyone in the surrounding area spoke of an incarnation having been born. Many holy people, such as Lama Jigmed, praised him as an incomparably sublime nirmanakaya and prophesied that he would accomplish great things for the sake of others.

For the first three years of his life, he saw hosts of dakinis and protective deities carrying out their activities, guarding and looking after him while singing, dancing, and playing music. He also had various visions of hordes of obstructive maras battling with the gods whose function it was to guard him. Other people could sometimes see and hear what was taking place.

Later in his life, Dudjom Lingpa related an incident that occurred when he was three: "I saw my mother preparing to go out to gather edible roots and tried to go along, but she tied me to the main guy rope of our tent and left me. I began to cry and was close to fainting when I saw a white dakini, who said to me, 'Let's go be with your mother.' With that, I beheld the full array of a pure realm glowing with sapphire-colored light, many world systems to the north. In the center of that realm was a buddha, a transcendent and accomplished conqueror named Don Mizawai Gyalpo (King Who Does Not Hesitate), surrounded by a retinue of countless bodhisattvas. I prostrated to them with devotion and said:

> Homage!
> Sublime epitome of all buddha families and
>   mandalas,
> I pay homage to you, O transcendent and
>   accomplished victorious one!

Liberate me and others, all beings drifting in
samsara—
liberate us from the ocean of conditioned existence
and inspire us.

"When I had prayed with these words, rays of five-colored light shone from the heart of the victorious one and dissolved into my heart, whereupon I experienced timeless awareness as inseparable bliss and emptiness. From the mouth of the tathagata came the words, 'My son, I extol you as my regent. I confer upon you the empowerments of the secret mantra approach of the vajrayana. You have gained sublime and ordinary siddhis.' Saying this, he placed a crystal casket in my hands. Within it were the syllables *Om Ah Hung*, respectively white, red, and blue. He said, 'These are like an inheritance of your spiritual father's wealth, so you should swallow them without any reservations.' As I swallowed them, many topics of the Buddha's teachings and vivid memories of former lifetimes became clear to me, as did recollections of teachings I had heard, contemplated, and meditated upon.

"On another occasion a dakini led me to Oddiyana, the realm of dakinis, where I encountered Vajravarahi, foremost among the dakinis. From her hands emanated the four life force syllables of the dakinis (*Ha Ri Ni Sa*), and I donned protective armor made of light rays. As well, from the tip of her right breast came a *Bam* syllable, which dissolved into my heart and rendered me victorious over obstacles. I gained mastery over psychic powers and miraculous abilities. Dakinis revealed their faces to me, gave me nectar from their skull-cups, and uttered prophecies about my need to rely on spiritual mentors. All at once, hundreds of doorways opened for hearing and contemplating the teachings."

Avalokiteshvara, exalted and sublime bodhisattva of loving kindness, guarded Dudjom Lingpa while acting as a companion, taking the form of a fair-skinned boy, handsome and youthful. Manjushri, Lion of Speech, took him under his care, causing the powerful dynamic energy of sublime knowing to blaze within him. In addition, he was cared for and blessed by the timeless awareness embodiments of such deities and gurus as the Lord of Secrets Vajrapani, the great siddha Saraha, the eight great rigdzins, Longchhen Rabjam, Zurchhung Sheyrab Dragpa, and others.

He journeyed to the Mountain of Glory on the subcontinent of Ngayab. Though he spent only a day in human terms, for him his stay lasted twelve years. From the great Orgyan he received spiritual instructions that ripened and liberated him. This great master invested Dudjom Lingpa as his regent to act as a lord protector for beings in times of spiritual degeneration. Within every atom Dudjom Lingpa beheld oceans of enlightened embodiments and pure realms, and from each of these embodiments his limitless emanations heard spiritual teachings that the ordinary imagination could comprehend only with great difficulty.

With the arousing of his previous karmic propensities, Dudjom Lingpa gained consummate wisdom and realization, so that those who bore indications of learning and spiritual accomplishment showed him honor through their devotion. Hosts of dakinis, such as Yeshe Tsogyal, prophesied events to him and cared for him like a son. Oath-bound guardians, protectors of the Buddha's teachings, and guardians of hidden treasure teachings all accompanied him like a shadow does a body and heeded his injunctions to them.

He had no craving for the ordinary passions that lead to lustful behavior and a degenerate kind of bliss. Rather, he was free of all flaws of attachment that result from following a path of ordinary desire. He was a great spiritual practitioner in the true sense of the term, one who upheld the highest principles of pure conduct. He was so thoroughly motivated by love and compassion, and had cultivated sublime bodhichitta, the altruistic motivation to benefit others, over so many eons, that all who were connected to this great bodhisattva, this son of the victorious ones, found purpose in that connection.

In his pursuit of the supreme skillful means of the short path, the vajrayana, this great lord among yogins brought to its furthest limit the realization born of practicing the stage of development, so that he perceived appearances and sounds to be a state of purity, a mandala of timeless awareness. Timeless awareness became completely evident to him as bliss blazed in his body, potency in his speech, and realization in his mind. Men and dakas, women and dakinis, food, and possessions and wealth all gathered around him like clouds amassing. He was a great master of transformation, enacting activity for desirable ends, demonstrating mastery over the four kinds of activity and the eight spiritual attainments, such as moving through space or solid matter.

The phase of the stage of completion that involves effort is a marvelous approach. Through these forceful skillful means, this great spiritual hero thoroughly harnessed the subtle energies moving in the *roma* and *kyangma,* the lateral channels of skillful means and sublime knowing, so that these "passages of the sun and moon" were brought within the basic space of the *dhuti,* the central channel. With this, he triumphed over the machinations of confusion created by the impure subtle energy of karma. Stimulated by the subtle energy of naturally occurring timeless awareness, the play of the sublime warmth of *chandali* transformed his three channels and chakras, emptying and burning away the thought patterns of dualistic grasping within the vast expanse of nondual sublime knowing. The radiant brilliance of this intoxicated him with the sixteen degrees of joy—the apparently changing process of what is actually the most sublimely unchanging level of skillful means. This resulted in the brilliant and supreme bliss of equalness, and he thereupon adopted a mode of conduct that brought awareness's natural manifestations under his power and overwhelmed external appearances with the splendor of his realization. His conduct became a dance through which he aroused, in very direct ways, the supremely blissful aspect of timeless awareness in anyone who had the appropriate karma and good fortune.

The most special approach, the most secret of secret paths, is the swift path of utter lucidity, the vajra pinnacle. Untainted by considerations of good or bad, timeless awareness is the naked union of awareness and emptiness, atemporal in its original purity. This is the inherently and fundamentally unconditioned nature of mind itself, the enlightened intent of Kuntuzangpo, free of elaboration. This secret key point of view became completely evident to Dudjom Lingpa.

As for the process of effortless meditation, the fundamental nature of all phenomena is such that it is utterly effortless, free of any sense of "this is to be done" or "this is how to do it." Beyond ordinary concepts of meditation or nonmeditation, it is the uncontrived, genuine state. Free of the obscuring overlay of the nonrecognition of awareness, it is unobstructed. Free of the narrow confines of hope and fear, it is unrestricted. The "yoga of space" is the yoga concerned with this supremely vast expanse of being in which realization and freedom are simultaneous, in which there is nothing to meditate upon, yet neither is there any distraction. Inner lucidity is the unceasing "glow of being"—the nature of all qualities of the kayas and timeless awareness, effortlessly and spontaneously present. By gaining mastery over this through the key points of physical postures and gazing techniques on the path of "surpassing the pinnacle" (*t'hod-gal*), Dudjom Lingpa encountered the visionary appearances of the true nature of phenomena—that is, of basic space (*ying*), spheres of light (*t'hig-le*), and the radiance of awareness (*rig-dang*). Once he gained direct perception of these three, they were enriched and reached full expression as the visions of this path unfolded in what seemed the blink of an eye, like an ocean of marvelous qualities arising as the forms of peaceful and wrathful deities.

The dakinis of the basic space of timeless awareness conferred upon him their supreme treasury of unsurpassable profundity and secrecy, and extolled in prophecies the extensive and sublime goals he would accomplish in the future. They exhorted him to open the doorway to the treasury of the dakinis' secrets. Within the vision of timeless awareness that has no fixed frame of reference, he immersed himself in visions of the entire universe as a vast array of purity. Hidden treasure teachings of inexhaustible enlightened mind welled forth as a matter of course from the vast expanse of his enlightened intent. In releasing the dakinis' seal of entrustment and bringing forth these profound hidden treasure teachings, Dudjom Lingpa was a sublime revealer of such treasures, a great universal monarch among masters. He promulgated a treasure trove of gemlike hidden teachings as a banquet to be enjoyed by fortunate students to be tamed—teachings concerning guruyoga, the Great Perfection, the bodhisattva of compassion Avalokiteshvara, the stages of development and completion, primary practices and secondary techniques, as well as minor activity rituals for a multitude of purposes.

There are beings in these times of spiritual degeneration who prove difficult to tame through effortful spiritual approaches. Vajra prophecies extol the need to tame them through the effortless approach of ati, the Great Perfection, the secret heart essence of definitive truth. In accordance with these prophecies, for the sake of fortunate ones to be tamed, Dudjom Lingpa illuminated the lamp of these teachings of the pinnacle approach of supreme secrets.

His sublime and charismatic form, bringing liberation upon sight, was clad in white robes and weighted down with massive locks of hair. It could pass at will through ordinary tangible things. In his ears he wore large hoops of conch shell.

He could revive beings who had been slain. Rainbow light shimmered, showers of blossoms fell, and fragrant odors wafted about when he performed empowerments, intensive group rituals (*drubchhens*), and feast offerings. These signs of successful accomplishment were directly perceived by those present. Part of the benefit he brought derived from the melodious vajra songs of profound teaching and spiritual advice that flowed ceaselessly from his golden throat, and to hear these brought liberation. He freed the mindstreams of his students the moment he focused his enlightened intent on them, often accompanying this with sharp words or blows. Through the path of supreme passion without ordinary attachment, he led those women with whom he had a connection, dakinis of samaya commitment, to a destiny equal to that of his own as a glorious heruka.

He founded a lineage of accomplished siddhas through eight incarnate beings who carried on his blood lineage, thirteen excellent heart children who attained rainbow body, some one thousand of his students who gained the level of rigdzin, and others. In his dreams, a god-child named Dung-gi Zurp'hud and a nonhuman named Zurme, who was Dudjom Lingpa's sister, unraveled symbols for him and prophesied that the benefit to beings deriving from his profound hidden treasure teachings would go west, saying, "Those cities of human beings to the west hold those deserving of being tamed by you." They also said, "The sounding of the conch shell in the west is a sign of your fame increasing. The shining of rays of sunlight in pits in the ground is symbolic of those you will tame." In accordance with these prophecies, we have seen that the activities associated with Dudjom Lingpa's profound hidden treasure teachings have spread and flourished in regions near and far, especially in the Western Hemisphere.

It would be difficult indeed to describe accurately the significance of the inconceivable secrets of enlightened speech found in the profound hidden treasure teachings of such a king of the Buddha's teachings as the great revealer of treasures T'hrag-t'hung Dudjom Lingpa. Nevertheless, this translation has been undertaken by a translator who, because of previous aspirations and karma, is fluent in English and Tibetan. He is named Chökyi Nyima in the language of Tibet, the Land of Snows, and Richard Barron in the language of his Western homes of Canada and the United States. This fine translation was scrupulously edited over and over again for accuracy and to ensure a clear and readable version of the text. I myself contributed to the process of translating and editing throughout by offering my own services with heartfelt respect for these teachings.

As Dudjom Rinpoche notes in the Afterword, the words of this text are the "relics of the dharmakaya." They may be read by those who have received the teachings personally from a lama who holds this lineage; until such time the text should be kept as an object of worship on one's shrine. If this condition is met, there is no doubt that one will emerge victorious in the battle with counterproductive circumstances and obstacles, and that supportive circumstances will bring benefit immediately in this lifetime and on into the future.

> Although this lord protector's life example is difficult
>   to describe fully,
> I have spoken briefly of it with a noble attitude.
> Through the power of this, may the lord protector
>   guide me in all lifetimes,

and may my ability to benefit beings be as enormous
    as yours, my lord protector!
From the endless depths of his enlightened mind,
    secret and profound,
issued this profound advice, *Buddhahood Without
    Meditation,* making fully evident one's true face—
    natural great perfection.
With altruistic motivation, patrons have sponsored
    this project, a translator fluent in both tongues
has set forth this translation, and editors have
    polished away inaccuracies.
For all beings in the three realms, and foremost for all
    who show this teaching the respect it deserves,
may the distortions of the three obscurations be
    dispersed in the basic space of phenomena,
and may their fundamental nature—the enlightened
    intent of the three kayas—become evident!

༄༅། །རང་བཞིན་རྫོགས་པ་ཆེན་པོའི་རང་ཞལ་མངོན་དུ་བྱེད་པའི་

གདམས་པ་མ་བསྒོམ་སངས་རྒྱས་བཞུགས་སོ།།

Buddhahood Without Meditation

*Advice for Making Fully Evident One's
True Face—Natural Great Perfection*

༄༅། །ཁྲབ་བདག་གདོད་མའི་མགོན་པོ་ཡེ་ཤེས་སྐུ་འཕུལ་རོལ་པའི་གྲོང་ཁྱེར་མཆོག་ལ་མི་ཕྱེད་དད་པའི་སྒོ་ནས་ཕྱག་འཚལ་ལོ། །དུས་དེང་སང་སྐྱེ་བགས་མ་ལུ་བདོ་བའི་སྣབས་འདིར་སེམས་ཅན་དམུ་རྒོད་ལས་ངན་དབང་ཆེ་བའི་སྟོབས་ཀྱིས་མི་ཚེ་སྟེ་ལམ་གྱི་གནས་སྐབས་ཚམ་འདི་ལ་ཞེན་ཅིང་ལྷོ་ཐག་རིང་པོས་གཏན་དུ་སྤྱོད་གྲུབ་བྱེད་ཅིང་ཕྱི་མའི་དོན་གཉེར་རྒྱབ་ཏུ་བོར་བ་ཤ་སྟག་ལས་མེད་དེ། དེའི་ཕྱིར་ཐར་པ་དང་རྣམ་མཁྱེན་གྱི་གོ་འཕང་དོན་དུ་གཉེར་བ་དེ་ཉིན་མོའི་སྐར་མ་ཙམ་ལས་མ་མཐོང་། གལ་ཏེ་འཚེ་བ་དྲན་ནས་ཆོས་ཉམས་སུ་ལེན་པར་སྤྲོ་ཡང་ལུས་ངག་གི་དགེ་སྟོར་ཚམ་ལ་མི་ཚེ་ཟད་ནས་མཐོ་རིས་ལྷ་མིའི་གོ་འཕང་དོན་དུ་གཉེར་བ་དང་། ཡང་འགའ་ཞིག་གིས་ལྷ་བ་སྟོང་ཉིད་ཀྱི་ཕྱོགས་ཚམ་མི་ཤེས་པར་རང་སེམས་སྟོང་པ་རུ་ཐག་བཅད་ནས་རྣམ་པར་རྟོག་པའམ་ཤེས་པ་བཟོ་མེད་ཚམ་རོ་སྙོད་དེ་དེའི་ངང་དུ་ཁྲར་མེད་དུ་སྤྱོད་པས

WITH UNWAVERING faith I pay homage to the sublime citadel of the magical display of timeless awareness (*ye-shey*), the sovereign principle, the primordial guide.

These days, when the five kinds of degeneration are on the rise, ordinary beings are without exception rough, wild, and under the sway of very powerful negative karma. Fixated on the mere passing dream of this human lifetime, they make long-range plans as though they were going to live forever and turn their backs on the pursuit of something meaningful for future lifetimes. For this reason, it seems to me that those who earnestly seek liberation and omniscience are no more numerous than daytime stars. Even though people may be aware of their mortality and ardently wish to practice the Buddha's teachings, they spend their human existence simply engaging physically and verbally in spiritual endeavors and thus pursue higher rebirths as gods or humans.

Some, without the slightest understanding of the view of emptiness (*tong-nyid*), come to a decision that their own minds are empty. This introduces them to what is nothing more than a state of conceptualization (*nam-par tog-pa*) or passive consciousness. They remain in this state with nothing whatsoever to do and so are propelled toward rebirth among

༄༅། །འདོད་གཟུགས་ཀྱི་ལྷ་རུ་འཐེན་པ་ཚམ་ལས་རྣམ་མཁྱེན་གྱི་ལམ་
ལ་སྦྱུ་རྩེ་ཚམ་ཡང་རྗེ་བ་མ་ཡིན་ནོ། །དེའི་ཕྱིར་ན་བསྐལ་པ་དཔག་ཏུ་མེད་
པའི་གོང་རོལ་ནས་ཚོགས་རྒྱ་ཆེན་པོ་བསགས། སློན་ལམ་བཟང་པོས་མཚམས་
སྦྱར། དོན་དམ་པའི་ཚོས་ལ་ལས་འབྲེལ་བཞག་པའི་སྐྱེས་བུ་རེ་ཚམ་མཆིས་
ན་དེའི་དབང་སྐྱལ་དུ་རས་བསྟུན་པ་ཡིན། ང་དང་ལས་འབྲེལ་མེད་ཅིང་རྟོགས་
པ་ཆེན་པོའི་ཚོས་ལ་དབང་བྱེད་པའི་སྐལ་པ་མེད་པ་དག་གིས་བསྟུན་པ་འདི་ལ་
སྐྱོ་སྐྱུར་བྱེད་པ་ལས་སྨོ་འབྲོག་དགོན་པ་རུ་འབྲོས་པར་འགྱུར་པ་ཡིན། དེ་
ལྟར་མ་ཡིན་པའི་བདག་དང་སྐལ་པ་མཉམ་པའི་སྐྱེས་བུ་རྣམས་ཀྱིས་གདམས་
པ་འདིར་སྨོས་ལ་བརྟག་དཔྱད་གོམས་འཛིས་ཀྱི་སྨོ་ནས་འཁོར་འདས་སྟོང་ཉིད་
ཆེན་པོར་རོ་ཤེས་ཏེ་ང་རྟོགས་པར་མཛོད་ཅིག །འདིར་རང་བཞིན་རྟོགས་
པ་ཆེན་པོ་ལ་སེམས་སྐྱོང་མན་ངག་གི་སྟེ་གསུམ་དུ་ཡོད་པ་ལས། འདི་ནི་
གསང་བ་མན་དག་གི་སྟེ་ཞེས་བྱ་བ་ཡིན། འདི་ལ་ལྟ་བ་དང་། བསྒོམ་
པ་དང་། སྤྱོད་པ་གསུམ་དུ་ཡོད་པ་ལས།

the gods of the desire and form realms, but this does not bring them even a hair's breadth closer to the path of omniscience.

Therefore, if a few spiritual individuals have, for immeasurable eons, gathered the accumulations on a vast scale and, having joined these with noble aspirations, established some karmic connection to spiritual teachings concerning ultimate reality, I will teach them according to their acumen and good fortune. Those who lack both a karmic connection to me and the good fortune to make use of the Great Perfection teachings, and instead exaggerate or denigrate them, have banished their own minds to some lonely wilderness. You spiritual individuals who are not like this and whose good fortune is equal to my own, consider my advice. Through examination, analysis, familiarization, and acquaintance, recognize samsara and nirvana to be supreme emptiness and so realize their fundamental nature (*ngang*).

Three categories are found in the approach of natural Great Perfection: the Category of Mind (*sem-dhe*), the Category of Expanse (*long-dhe*), and the Category of Direct Transmission (*man-ngag-dhe*). This text pertains to what is termed the secret Category of Direct Transmission. There are three sections herein, concerning view (*ta-wa*), meditation (*gom-pa*), and conduct (*kyod-pa*).

Avalokiteshvara

༄༅། །དང་པོ་ལྷ་བ་གཏན་ལ་དབབ་པ་ལ། མེད་པ་དང་། གཅིག་
པུ་དང་། ཕྱལ་བ་དང་། ལྷུན་གྲུབ་རྣམ་པ་བཞིའི་སྒོ་ནས་གཏན་ལ་
ཕབ་སྟེ་རྗེ་ལྷ་བ་བཞིན་དུ་རྟོགས་པར་བྱ་བ་ནི་གནད་དམ་པ་ཡིན་ནོ། །དེ་ལ་
དང་པོ་མེད་པའི་ཚུལ་གཏན་ལ་དབབ་པ་ལ། གང་ཟག་གི་བདག་གཏན་ལ་
དབབ་པ་དང་། ཆོས་ཀྱི་བདག་གཏན་ལ་དབབ་པ་དང་གཉིས་ལས། ཡོད་པ་ལས།
དང་པོ་གང་ཟག་གི་བདག་ཅེས་བྱ་བ་ནི། ཉིན་སྐྱང་དང་། མི་སྐྱང་
དང་། བར་སྐྱེད་དང་། ཕྱི་མའི་དུས་རྣམས་སུ་བདག་ཡོད་པར་སྐྱང་ཚམ་
ཉིད་ལ་གང་ཟག་གི་བདག་ཅེས་བྱའོ། །དེ་མ་ཐག་ཏུ་ང་དུ་བཟུང་བའི་ཤེས་
པ་བག་ལ་ཉལ་བ་ལ་ཤེས་པ་ཕྱི་མའམ་རྣམ་པར་རྟོག་པ་ཞེས་བྱ་སྟེ། དེས་
གསལ་བཏབ་ནས་བཏུན་ཅིང་འཐས་པར་བྱས་པ་ཡིན། དེའ་ཕྱིར་ང་ཞེས་བྱ་བ་
དེ་དང་པོ་བྱུང་བའི་ཁུངས་ལ་བརྟག་ནས་བྱུང་ཁུངས་མེད་པའི་ས་ལ་གཏུག་གོ

F IRST, TO REACH a definitive conclusion (*tan la wab-pa*) regarding view, the sacred key point is to come to a definitive understanding through four topics—ineffability (*med-pa*), oneness (*chig-pu*), openness (*khyal-wa*), and spontaneous presence (*lhun-drub*)—and to realize these just as they are. In the first of these topics, the process of reaching a definitive conclusion regarding ineffability has two divisions: coming to a definitive conclusion about personal identity (*gang zag gi dag*) and a definitive conclusion about the identity of phenomena (*chhö kyi dag*).

Let us begin by defining "personal identity." The impression that an identity (*dag*) exists, whether in waking experience, dream states, the bardo—the intermediate state of conditioned existence between death and rebirth—or the next lifetime, is termed "personal identity." Immediately following this first impression, there is an underlying consciousness that takes this impression to be an "I" and that is termed "subsequent consciousness" or "conceptualization." As attention is given to this, it comes to seem stable and solid. For these reasons, by trying to locate the source from which this so-called I first occurs, you will arrive at the conclusion that it has no authentic source.

༄༅། །བར་དུ་གནས་པའི་ས་བཅལ་བ་ལ། ང་ཞེས་བྱ་བ་དེ་གནས་
ས་དང་གནས་མཁན་སོ་སོར་དོས་བཟུང་མཆན་མ་ཚན་དུ་ཡོད་དམ་མེད་འདི་ལྟར་
བརྟག་པར་བྱའོ། མགོ་ལ་ནི་མགོ་ཞིས་བྱ་སྟེ་ང་མ་ཡིན། དེ་བཞིན་མགོ་
ལྤགས་ལའང་ལྤགས་པ་ཞིས་བྱ་སྟེ་ང་མ་ཡིན། རུས་པ་ལ་རུས་པ་བརྗོད་
པ་ལས་ང་མ་ཡིན། དེ་བཞིན་དུ་མིག་ནི་མིག་ལས་ང་མ་ཡིན། རྣ་བ་
ནི་རྣ་བ་ལས་ང་མ་ཡིན། སྣ་ནི་སྣ་ལས་ང་མ་ཡིན། ལྕེ་ནི་ལྕེ་ལས་ང་
མ་ཡིན། སོ་ནི་སོ་ལས་ང་མ་ཡིན། རྐྱང་པ་ཡང་ང་མ་ཡིན། ཤ་
ཁྲག་རྒྱུ་སེར་རུ་རྒྱུས་རྣམས་ལའང་རང་རང་གི་མིང་ལས་ང་མ་ཐོག་པ་དེས་ཞེས།
ཡང་ལག་པ་ནི་ལག་པ་ལས་ང་མ་ཡིན། སོག་པ་ནི་དེ་བཞིན་ང་མ་ཡིན།
དཔུང་པ་ནི་མ་ཡིན། ལག་ངར་ནི་མ་ཡིན། སོར་མཛུབ་རྣམས་ཀྱང་མ་
ཡིན། ཡང་རྐྱལ་ཚིགས་ནི་རྐྱལ་ཚིགས་ལས་ང་མ་ཡིན། རྩིབས་མ་
ནི་ང་མ་ཡིན། བྲང་ནི་ང་མ་ཡིན། སྒྲོ་བ་ནི་ང་མ་ཡིན། སྙིང་ནི་ང་
མ་ཡིན། མཆིན་ཁྲི་ནི་ང་མ་ཡིན། མཆིན་པ་དང་མཚེར་པ་ནི་ང་མ་ཡིན།
རྒྱུ་མ་དང་མཁལ་མ་ནི་ང་མ་ཡིན། དེ་རྒྱུ་དང་འཕང་ལྤེ་ནི་ང་མ་ཡིན། ཡང་
རྐང་པ་ལའང་ང་ཡི་མིང་མི་གདག་སྟེ། བརྐ་ལ་བརྐ་ཞིས་གདག་པ་ལས་ང་
མི་གདག །དཔྱི་ཡང་དེ་བཞིན་དུ་ང་མ་ཡིན། རྗེ་ངར་ཡང་ང་མ་ཡིན།
བོལ་བ་ཡང་ང་མ་ཡིན། སོར་མཛུབ་ཡང་ང་མ་ཡིན། མདོར་ན་ཕྱིའི་

In searching for the place where this identity might dwell between its origination and its cessation, you should examine in the following way to determine whether, for this so-called I, a location and something located there exist as anything that can be individually identified and characterized.

The head is called "head"; it is not I. Similarly, the skin of the head is called "skin"; it is not I. Bone, in being referred to only as "bone," is not I. Likewise the eyes, in being only eyes, are not I. The ears, in being only ears, are not I. The nose, in being only the nose, is not I. The tongue, in being only the tongue, is not I. The teeth, in being only teeth, are not I. The brain is also not I. As for the muscles, blood, lymph, nerves, blood vessels, and tendons, in being referred to only by their own names, they are not labeled "I." From this you will gain understanding.

Furthermore, the arms, in being only arms, are not I. The shoulders are likewise not I, nor are the upper arms, the forearms, or the fingers. Moreover, the spine, in being only the spine, is not I. The ribs are not I, the chest is not I, the lungs are not I, the heart is not I, the diaphragm is not I, the liver and spleen are not I, the intestines and kidneys are not I, and urine and feces are not I.

As well, this label "I" is not applied to the legs. The label "thighs," not the label "I," is applied to the thighs. Similarly, the hips are not I. The shins are not I, nor are the insteps of the feet or the toes.

To summarize, the outer skin is not labeled "I"; the intermediate layers of muscle and fat, in being referred to as "muscle" and "fat," are not labeled "I"; the bones within, in

༄༄། སྐྱབས་པ་ལ་ང་མི་གདག །བར་གྱི་ཕ་ཚོལ་ལ་ཕ་ཚོལ་ཟེར་
བ་ལས་ང་མི་གདག །ནང་གི་དུས་པ་ལ་དུས་པ་ཟེར་བ་ལས་ང་མི་གདག།
གསང་བ་རྒྱང་ལའང་རྒྱང་ཟེར་བ་ལས་ང་མི་གདག །རྣམ་པར་ཤེས་པ་ལའང་
དེ་ལས་ང་མི་གདག །དེའི་ཕྱིར་བར་དུ་གནས་པའི་ས་དང་བདག་པོ་མེད་
པའི་སྟོང་པ་ཉིད་དུ་ངེས་པའོ། དེ་བཞིན་དུ་ཐ་མ་འགྲོ་བའི་ཡུལ་དང་བདག
པོ་ཐམས་ཅད་ལས་འདས་པ་ཉིད་དུ་ཐག་ཆོད་པར་བྱའོ། །དོན་ལ་མེད་བཞིན
ཡོད་པར་སྣང་བ་དེ་རབ་རིབ་ལྟ་བུའོ། མིང་བཏོད་པ་དེ་དག་ཀྱང་རེ་བོང་གི
རྭ་བཏོད་པ་ལྟ་བུའོ། གཉིས་པ་ཚོས་ཀྱི་བདག་མེད་གཏན་ལ་དབབ་པར་བྱ
བ་ལ་མིང་གི་གདག་གཞི་བཙལ་བ། དངོས་པོའི་རྟག་འཛིན་བཤིག་པ། ཐུན
གཏོད་ཀྱི་མཚང་ལ་ཀློལ་བ། རེ་དོགས་ཀྱི་རྫུན་ཕུག་བརྗེད་པའོ། དང
པོ་ནི། མིང་ཐམས་ཅད་བཏགས་དོན་བཙལ་ན་མེད་བཞིན་དུ་ཏོག་པའི་རང
མདངས་ཚམ་ལ་བཏགས་པར་ཟད་དེ། ཚོས་གང་ཡང་གདག་གཞིའི་སྟེང
ན་ཚུགས་ཐུབ་དུ་གྲུབ་པར་མི་སྲིད་པའི་ཕྱིར་རོ། །དེ་ཡང་མགོ་ཞིབས་བུ་ཙིའི
ཕྱིར་ཙི་ལ་བཏགས། ལུས་ཆགས་པའི་དང་པོ་ཡིན་པས་སམ། རྒྱམ
པོ་ཡིན་པས་སམ། སྟེང་དུ་བསྐུན་པ་ལ་བཏགས། ལུས་ཆགས་པའི

being referred to as "bones," are not labeled "I"; the innermost marrow, in being referred to as "marrow," is not labeled "I"; and even consciousness, in being so labeled, is not labeled "I." Therefore, you can be certain of emptiness in the absence of any location or something located between origination and cessation.

Similarly, you should come to the decision that all final destinations and anything going there are transcended. In actuality, as with impaired vision, there is the appearance that things are what they are not. Moreover, using all these labels is like speaking of the horns of a rabbit.

Second, to reach a definitive conclusion that phenomena lack any identity, you must search for some basis on which labels can be applied, abolish your concepts of the seeming permanence of things, confront the hidden flaws of benefit and harm, and collapse the false cave of hope and fear.

To begin with, if you search for something with ultimate meaning that underlies the application of all names, you will find that this amounts to nothing more than labels being applied to what, in being ineffable, is simply the natural glow (*rang-dang*) that underlies thought. This is because it is impossible for any phenomenon whatsoever to have ever existed as self-sustaining in terms of being a basis for labeling. For example, what does "head" refer to and why? Is the label applied because the head constitutes the first stage in the growth of the body, because it is round, or because it appears uppermost? In fact, the head is not the first stage in the growth of the body, the label "head" is not applied to everything that is round, and when you examine the concepts of "upper" and

༄༅། །དང་པོར་ནི་མགོ་མ་སྨྲེས། རྣམ་པོ་ཐམས་ཅད་ལ་ནི་མགོ་མི་
ཐོག །སྟེང་འོག་ཀུང་བཏགས་ན་ནམ་མཁའ་ལ་སྟེང་འོག་མེད། དེ་བཞིན་
དུ་སྨྲ་ནི་མགོ་མ་ཡིན། ཕྱགས་པ་ལ་ཕྱགས་པ་ལས་མགོ་མི་ཐོགས། རུས་
པ་ལ་རུས་པ་ཟེར་བ་ལས་མགོ་མི་ཐོགས། ཀུན་པ་ནི་མགོ་མ་ཡིན། མེག
དང་རྣ་བ་ནི་མགོ་མ་ཡིན། སྨྲ་དང་ལྕེ་ནི་མགོ་མ་ཡིན། དེ་ལྟར་སོ་སོར་
ཕྱལ་ན་མ་ཡིན་ཀྱང་ལྷུན་དུ་ཚོགས་པ་ལ་མགོ་ཟེར་བ་ཡིན་སྙམ་ན་སྲོག་ཆགས་
ཞིག་གི་མགོ་བཅད་དེ་རྡུལ་དང་རྡུལ་ཕྲན་ཚ་མེད་དུ་བཏགས་ནས་འཇོམ་བུ་སྐྱེང་
གི་མི་ལ་བསྐུན་ཀྱང་མགོ་ཞེས་མི་སྨྲ། རྒྱས་སྨྲས་ཀྱང་མགོ་མི་ཐོགས་པས་
མགོ་ཞེས་བྱ་བ་བརྟོད་པ་ཙམ་ལས་བརྟོད་གཞི་ཡུལ་མེད་དུ་འདུག་པའི་དང་ཚུལ་
ཤེས་པར་བྱའོ། །དེ་བཞིན་དུ་མིག་ལ་ཡང་ཆུ་བུར་རྦུང་དུ་ཡོད་པ་ལ་མིག་མི་
ཐོགས། ཕྱགས་པ་ནི་མིག་མ་ཡིན། རྒྱ་དང་རྩ་ཁྲག་རྣམས་ཀྱང་དེ་
བཞིན་དུ་མིག་མ་ཡིན། དེ་དག་སོ་སོར་ཕྱེས་ཀྱང་མ་ཡིན། ལྷུན་ཚིག
ཚོགས་པའི་རྡུལ་ཀྱང་མ་ཡིན། རྒྱས་སྨྲས་པའི་འདག་པ་ཡང་མ་ཡིན།
གཟུགས་མཐོང་མཁན་ཀྱང་ཤེས་པ་ཡིན་པ་ལས་རྒྱ་བྱར་མ་ཡིན་པ་རྟེ་ལམ་དང་
བར་དོའི་སྐབས་སུ་མཐོང་བྱེད་ཡོད་པ་དེས་སྟོན་ཏོ། །རྣ་བ་ཡང་དེ་བཞིན་
དུ་སྤུ་གུ་ནི་རྣ་བ་མ་ཡིན། ཕྱགས་པ་ནི་རྣ་བ་མ་ཡིན། ཤ་དང་ཚ་རྒྱས་
ཁྲག་དང་རྒྱ་སེར་རྣམས་ནི་རང་རང་གི་མིང་ལས་རྣ་བ་མ་ཡིན། དེ་རྡུལ་དུ

"lower," there are no absolutes of upper or lower in space. Similarly, the hair of the head is not the head. The skin, in being skin, is not labeled "head." The bones, in being called "bones," are not labeled "head." The brain is not the head, the eyes and ears are not the head, and the nose and tongue are not the head.

You might suggest that, if we isolate these parts individually, they do not constitute the head but that their collective mass is called "head." But if you were to cut off a creature's head, pulverize it into molecules and subatomic particles, and then show it to anyone in the world, no one would say that it was a "head." Even if the particles were reconstituted with water, this mass would not be labeled a "head." So you should understand the situation—that there is no object that is the basis for the expression "head," which is merely a figure of speech.

Let us take a similar case, that of the eyes. The label "eyes" does not apply to spheres that exist in pairs. The sclera is not the eyes. The fluids, nerves, vessels, and blood are likewise not the eyes. If you analyze these components individually, you will see that none of them is the eyes. Nor are the particles of their collective mass or the mass that would be obtained by reconstituting these particles with water. That which sees forms, in being a state of consciousness, is not the eyeballs, as is evidenced by the fact that it causes seeing to take place during dreams and the bardo.

Likewise in the case of the ears, the auditory canals are not the ears. The skin is not the ears. The cartilage, nerves, vessels, blood, and lymph, in being referred to by their own names, are not the ears. The powder that would result from

༄༅། ཐབ་པའི་ཕྱི་མ་ཡང་རྟ་བ་མ་ཡིན། སྐུན་ཚིག་སྐྱེས་པའི་འདག
པ་ཡང་རྟ་བ་མ་ཡིན། སྨྲ་བོས་མཁན་ལ་རྟ་བ་ཞེས་བཏགས་པར་སེམས་ན།
རྟེ་སྐྱང་རྙེན་སྐྱང་བར་དོའི་སྐབས་ཀྱི་སྨྲ་བོས་མཁན་ལ་ལྟོས། སེམས་ཡེ་གནས
ཀྱི་ཞེས་པ་དེད་ཡིན་ཏེ་རྟ་བ་མ་ཡིན། དེ་བཞིན་དུ་སྐྱ་ཡང་སྨྱུ་གུ་དང་སྦྱགས
པ་དང་རྫས་པ་ཕ་དང་རྩ་རྒྱས་ཐམས་ཅད་རང་རང་གི་མིང་ལས་སྐྱ་ཞིས་མི་གདག།
དེ་ཚོར་མཁན་ཡང་ཞེས་པ་དེད་ཡིན་པར་རྟྱེ་ལམ་དང་བར་དོའི་སྐབས་སུ་དེ་ཚོར
མཁན་ལ་བཏག་པར་བྱའོ། །སྐྱེ་ཡང་དེ་བཞིན་དུ་སོ་སོར་ཕྱེས་ན་ཕ་ལྷགས
ཁྱག་དང་རྩ་རྒྱས་ཐམས་ཅད་ལ་རང་རང་གི་མིང་ལས་སྐྱེ་ཞིས་མི་བྱ། དེ་དག
རྫལ་དུ་ཐབ་པའི་རྫལ་ལའང་སྐྱེ་ཞིས་མི་བྱ། རྒྱས་སྐྱས་པའི་འདག་པ་ལའང
སྐྱེ་མི་གདག་པ་བཞིན་ཞོག་མ་ཀུན་ལ་འགྲི་བར་བྱའོ། །དེ་བཞིན་དུ་ལག
པའང་སོག་པ་དེ་ལག་པ་མ་ཡིན། དཔུང་པ་དེ་མ་ཡིན། ལག་ངར་དེ
མ་ཡིན། སོར་ཚིགས་རྣམས་ཀྱང་མ་ཡིན། ཕ་ལྷགས་རུས་པ་ཀྱང་ཡང
མ་ཡིན། སོག་པ་ཡང་དེ་བཞིན་སྦྱགས་པ་དེ་སོག་པ་མ་ཡིན། ཕ་དང
རུས་པ་རྣམས་ཀྱང་མ་ཡིན། སྐུན་ཚིག་འཚོགས་པའི་རྫལ་ཡང་མ་ཡིན། རྒྱས
སྐྱས་པའི་འདག་པ་ཡང་མ་ཡིན་ཏེ། །སོག་པའི་མིང་གི་གདག་གཞི་ཡུལ
མེད་དུ་སྟོང་པའོ། །དེ་བཞིན་དུ་དཔུང་པ་དང་ལག་ངར་ལ་བཏག་པས་ཕ

pulverizing them would not be the ears. The mass that would be obtained by reconstituting them would not be the ears. If you think that the label "ears" applies to that which hears sounds, just observe what hears sounds during dreams, the waking state, and the bardo. It is ordinary mind as timelessly present consciousness, not the ears.

Similarly, all the component parts of the nose—nostrils, skin, cartilage, nerves, and blood vessels—in being referred to by their own names, are not labeled "nose." Since that which smells odors is a state of consciousness, you should examine what smells odors during dreams and the bardo.

In the same way, if you analyze the tongue's individual components—the muscle, skin, blood, nerves, and vessels—in being referred to by their own names, they are not called "tongue." The powder that would result from pulverizing them would not be called "tongue." Even the mass obtained by reconstituting them with water would not be labeled "tongue."

The same reasoning applies in all of the following cases: In the case of the arms, the shoulders are not the arms, the upper arms are not the arms, nor are the forearms, the fingers and knuckles, the flesh, skin, bones, or marrow. Likewise regarding the shoulders, the skin is not the shoulders, nor are the flesh and bones. Neither is the collective mass of molecules or the mass that would be obtained by reconstituting them with water. Any basis on which the label "shoulder" could be applied is empty in that it does not exist as an object. When you likewise examine the upper arms and forearms, in being referred to by their respective names—"muscle" for muscle,

༄༅། །ལ་ཧ། རུས་པ་ལ་རུས་པ། སྤྲུགས་པ་ལ་སྤྲུགས་པ།
རྐང་ལ་རྐང་ཞེས་རང་རང་གི་མིང་ལས་གདག་གཞི་རྡུལ་ཕྲན་ཚམ་ཡང་མ་གྲུབ།
ལུས་དང་ཕུང་པོ་ཞེས་བཏོད་པའི་གཞི་རྟ་ལ་བཏག་པས་རྐྱལ་ཚིགས་དང་རྩི་བས་
མ་ལ་ལུས་མི་བྱ། བྱང་དང་ཤ་སྤྱགས་རུས་པ་ལ་ལུས་མི་བྱ། སྙིང་དང་
གློ་བ་མཆིན་པ་མཆིན་ཁྲི་མཚེར་པ་མཁལ་མ་རྒྱ་མ་རྣམས་ལ་རང་རང་གི་མིང་
སོ་སོར་བཏོད་པ་ལས་ལུས་དང་ཕུང་པོའི་གདག་གཞི་ཡུལ་མེད་དུ་སྟོང་པས་སྟོང་
པ་ཉིད་དོ། །རྐང་པ་ལའང་དེ་བཞིན་དུ་བཏག་པས་དཔྱེ་ནེ་རྐང་པ་མ་ཡིན།
བརླ་ནེ་མ་ཡིན། རྗེ་ངར་ནེ་མ་ཡིན། བོལ་བ་ཡང་མ་ཡིན་ཏེ། དེ་
བཞིན་དུ་དཔྱེ་ནེ་ཁ་ལ་མི་བྱ། སྤྲུགས་པ་དང་རུས་པ་རྩ་རྒྱུས་རྣམས་ལ་མི་
བྱའོ། །བཀྲ་ཡང་སྤྲུགས་པ་དང་ཕ་རུས་རྩ་རྒྱུས་ཐམས་ཅད་ལ་མི་བྱ། རྗེ་
ངར་ཡང་དེ་བཞིན་ཏེ། དེ་དག་ཐམས་ཅད་ཧྲུལ་དུ་ཕབ་པའི་ཕྱེ་མ་ལ་མིང་དེ་
དག་མ་གྲུབ། རྒྱས་སྦྱར་པའི་འདག་པ་ལའང་མིང་དེ་དག་མི་བྱའོ། །ཕྱིའི་
རི་བོ་ཞེས་བྱ་བའི་གདག་གཞི་བཙལ་ན། ས་ནི་རི་བོ་མ་ཡིན། དེ་བཞིན་
རྡོ་དང་ཤེང་ནེ་མ་ཡིན། རྡོའི་མ་ཡིན། བྲག་དང་རྒྱུ་ནེ་མ་ཡིན། ཁང་
ཁྱིམ་གྱི་མིང་གི་གདག་གཞི་བཙལ་ན། ས་ནི་ཁང་པ་མ་ཡིན་པ་བཞིན་དུ་
རྡོའི་མ་ཡིན། ཤེང་ནེ་མ་ཡིན། རྩིག་པ་ལའང་རྩིག་པ་ཞེས་བྱ་བ་ལས་
ཁང་པ་མི་གདག་པ་དེ་བཞིན་དུ་ཕྱི་དང་ནང་གང་དུ་ཡང་ཁང་པ་ཞེས་མ་གྲུབ་པ

"bone" for bone, "skin" for skin, and "marrow" for marrow—none of these has ever existed as a basis on which labels could be applied.

By examining the fundamental basis of the expressions "body" and "physical mass," you can see that the spine and ribs are not called "body." The chest, musculature, skin, and bones are not called "body." The heart, lungs, liver, diaphragm, spleen, kidneys, and intestines, in being described by their own names, nevertheless constitute emptiness, in that any basis on which the labels "body" and "physical mass" could be applied is empty since it does not exist as an object.

When you examine the legs in a similar way, you will find that the hips are not the legs, nor are the thighs, shins, or feet. The muscles are not called "hips," nor are the skin, bones, nerves, vessels, or tendons. Moreover, the skin, muscles, bones, nerves, vessels, or tendons are not called "thighs." The same is true for the shins. Such terms cannot be found to apply to the powder that would result from pulverizing these tissues, nor are they used to refer to the mass that would be obtained by reconstituting the particles with water.

If you search for some basis on which the label "mountain" could be applied in the outer world, you will see that earth is not a mountain, nor are the grasses or trees, the rocks, cliff faces, or water. If you search for some basis on which the labels "building" or "house" could be applied, just as the earthworks are not the house, neither is the stone or the wood. Moreover, as for the walls, in being called "walls," they are not labeled "house." Thus, "house" has never existed anywhere, externally or internally.

ༀ༔ ཨིན། མི་རྟག་ཁྲི་ལ་སོགས་པའི་མིང་གི་གདགས་གཞི་བཙལ་

བས་ཀྱང་། མིག་དང་རྣ་བ་སྣ་དང་ལྕེ་དང་ཤ་ཁྲག་རུས་པ་རྐང་དང་རྩ་རྒྱུས་

རྣམ་པར་ཤེས་པ་དང་བཅས་པ་ལ་རང་རང་གི་མིང་ལས་མི་རྟག་ཁྲི་དང་བཅས་པའི་

གདགས་གཞི་ཡུལ་མེད་པ་སྤྱར་ཐབས་ཆད་དེས་སྟོན་ཏོ། །དཔེར་ན་ཚེས་རྣམས་

ལས་རྫས་སུ་བ་དེ་ཤིང་ལ་མི་འགྲུ། ཀོ་བ་ལ་མི་འགྲུ། ཕྱི་དང་ནང་ལ་མི་

འགྲུ་བ་དང་། གྱི་ཡང་ལྕུགས་ལ་མི་འགྲུ། སོ་དང་ལྕགས་པ་རྩེ་མོ་ཡུ་བ་ཀུན་

ཏུ་གྱི་ཞེས་གདགས་ཡུལ་མ་གྲུབ་པ་ཡིན་ནོ། །མིང་དོན་འགྱུར་བའང་དཔེར་

ན། གྱིས་སྐྱུང་བུ་བྲུས་ཚེ་མིང་འགྱུར་བ་དང་། །ཁབ་བྲུས་པའི་ཚེ་མིང་སྡུ་

མ་ཐམས་ཅད་ཡུལ་མེད་དུ་སོང་བ་བཞིན་ནོ། །གང་ཟག་གི་བདག་ཅེས་བྱ་

བ་དང་མིང་གི་གདགས་གཞི་བཙལ་བ་འདི་གཉིས་ཀ་བདག་གི་བླ་མ་འཕགས་

མཆོག་ཐུགས་རྗེ་ཆེན་པོས་རྩེ་ལས་ཀྱི་སྐབས་སུ་གསུངས་པ་ལ་བརྟེན་ནས་

ལེགས་པར་རྟོགས་པ་ཡིན་ནོ།

You might search for some basis on which such labels as "human being," "horse," "dog," and so forth could be applied. Eyes, ears, nose, tongue, flesh, blood, bones, marrow, nerves, vessels, tendons, and attendant consciousnesses are referred to by their own names, but no object exists as a basis on which the label "human being," "horse," or "dog" could be applied.

To take another example, among material objects "drum" does not refer to the wood, the leather, the outside, or the inside. Similarly, "knife" does not refer to the steel. None of the component parts—the blade, the back of the blade, the point, or the haft—has ever existed as an object that could be so labeled. Moreover, names and functions change, as when a knife is used as an awl and its designation changes, or when an awl is used as a needle, and these previous labels all turn out to refer to what have no existence as sense objects.

Relying on what my guru, the noble and sublime Supremely Compassionate One [Avalokiteshvara], said to me in a dream, I came to a thorough realization concerning two points—that which is called "personal identity" and the search for some basis on which labels could be applied.

Orgyan Tsokyey Dorje

༄༅། །སྐར་ཡང་ཡོ་རྒྱུན་མཚོ་སྙེས་རྡོ་རྗེ་ཡེ་ཤེས་སྐུ་མའི་སྐུ་དང་མཐའ་
ཚོ་གནན་བའི་སྐྱང་བ་སྒྱུ་མར་སྒྱུར་བའི་གདམས་པ་ནི། རྒྱུ་རྐྱེན་འཕྲད་པའི་
རྟེན་འབྲེལ་དུ་ངོ་སྤྲོད་པ་ལ། དེ་ཡང་རྒྱུ་གཞི་དབྱིངས་དངས་གསལ་ཅི་ཡང་
འཆར་རུང་གི་ནུས་པ་ཅན་དང་། རྐྱེན་ངར་འཛིན་གྱི་ཤེས་པ་གཉིས་འདུས་
པ་ལ་བརྟེན་ནས་སྣང་བ་ཐམས་ཅད་སྒྱུ་མ་བཞིན་དུ་སྣང་བ་སྟེ། དེ་ལྟར་གཞི་
དབྱིངས་དང་། དེའི་རྩལ་ལས་འཕར་བའི་སེམས་དང་། སེམས་དེའི་སྣང་
ཆ་ཕྱི་ནང་གི་ཆོས་ཐམས་ཅད་དེ་མ་དང་དེ་མའི་ཟེར་བཞིན་ལུ་གུ་རྒྱུད་དུ་འཕྲེལ་
བས་ན་རྟེན་ཅིང་འབྲེལ་བར་འབྱུང་བ་ཞེས་བྱའོ། །དེའི་དཔེ་ནི་རྒྱུ་ནས་མཁའ་
དངས་གསལ་ལ་བརྟེན་ནས་རྐྱེན་སྒྱུ་མའི་རྫས་སྔགས་དང་སྒྱུལ་སེམས་དུས་

O N ANOTHER OCCASION, when I encountered Orgyan Tsokyey Dorje—the embodiment of the magical illusion of timeless awareness—he bestowed advice for refining my perception of things so that I could see that they are illusory (*gyu-ma*). He said, "For me to introduce you directly to the interdependence of causes and conditions coming together, consider this: The cause is the ground of being as basic space (*zhi-ying*), which is pristinely lucid (*dang-sal*) and endowed with the capacity for anything whatsoever to arise. The condition is a consciousness that conceives of an 'I.' From the coming together of these two, all sensory appearances (*nang-wa*) manifest like illusions.

"In this way, the ground of being as basic space, ordinary mind (*sem*) that arises from the dynamic energy (*tzal*) of that ground, and the external and internal phenomena that constitute the manifest aspect of that mind are all interlinked (*lu-gu-gyud*), like the sun and its rays. Thus, we use the expression 'occurring in interdependent connection.'

"Here are some metaphors for this process: It is like the appearance of a magical illusion, which depends on the pristine clarity of space as the cause and manifests through the interdependent connection created by the synchronicity of the

༄༅། འཚོལ་བ་ལས་རྟེན་འབྲེལ་སྒྱུ་མ་སྣང་བ་ལྟ་བུའོ། །འདི་ལྟར་
སྣང་བའི་ཆོས་ཐམས་ཅད་མེད་བཞིན་དུ་རང་འཚོར་གྱི་དབང་གིས་སྣང་བ་ནི་ནམ་
མཁའ་དྭངས་གསལ་དང་དོད་གཞིར་དུས་འཚོལ་པ་ལས་སྐྱིག་རྒྱུ་སྣང་བ་ལྟ་
བུའོ། །ཞིན་སྣང་དང་རྨི་སྣང་བར་སྒྲིད་ཕྱི་མའི་སྣང་བ་ཐམས་ཅད་མེད་བཞིན་
དུ་སྣང་བ་ལ་བདེན་ཞེན་གྱི་དབང་གིས་འཁྲུལ་པ་ནི་དཔེར་ན་རྨི་ལམ་གྱི་དུས་སུ་
འདི་རྨི་ལམ་མོ་སྙམ་དུ་རྟེན་པར་མི་སེམས་ཏེ་གཏན་གྱི་གནས་ཡུལ་དུ་བཟུང་
ནས་ཞེན་པ་ལྟ་བུའོ། །ནང་ང་རུ་འཚོར་པའི་བདག་ཀྱེན་ལས་སྣ་ཚོགས་ཆོས་
ཁམས་གཞན་དུ་སྣང་བ་བྱུད་དང་མི་ལོང་འཕུད་པའི་རྟེན་འབྲེལ་ལས་གཟུགས་
བརྙན་སྣང་བ་ལྟ་བུའོ། །བདག་འཚོན་གྱིས་ཀུན་ནས་དཀྲིས་པའི་དབང་གིས་
གྲོང་ཁྱེར་དྲུག་གི་འཇིག་རྟེན་རེས་མོས་སུ་སྣང་བ་ནི་སེམས་འཚོར་གྱི་སྣང་ཉམས་
ཞིག་ཏུ་རུབ་ཁའི་ཐང་སྒོགས་ཡུལ་ལ་དྲི་ཟའི་གྲོང་ཁྱེར་སྣང་བ་ལྟ་བུའོ། །འདོད་
ཡོན་གྱི་སྣང་བ་གདོད་ནས་མ་གྲུབ་པ་ལ་མཐོང་ཐོས་སྐྱོང་ཚོར་སྣ་ཚོགས་བདག་
སྣང་གཞན་ལྟར་སྣང་བ་བྲག་ཅ་ལྟ་བུའོ། །སྣང་བ་ཐམས་ཅད་གཞི་ལས་མི་
གཞན་པར་གཞི་ཉིད་དུ་རོ་གཅིག་པ་ནི་རྒྱ་མཚོའི་གཟབ་ན་སྣར་ཐམས་ཅད་རྒྱ་མཚོ་

conditions—that is, magical substances, mantras, and the mind that creates the illusion.

"All phenomena, which manifest as they do, are ineffable, yet appear due to the influence of conceiving of an 'I.' This process is like a mirage appearing from the synchronicity of vividly clear space and the presence of warmth and moisture.

"All sensory appearances of waking consciousness, dream states, the bardo, and future lifetimes are apparent yet ineffable. Confusion comes about due to fixation on their seeming truth. This is like a dream that one does not consider false—thinking, 'This is a dream'—but instead reifies and fixates on as some enduring objective environment.

"Due to the predominant condition of the perception of an inner 'I,' the realm of phenomena manifests as something 'other.' This is like the appearance of a reflection through the interdependent connection of a face and a mirror coming together.

"Because one is thoroughly ensnared by concepts of identity (*dag-dzin*), the realms of the six states manifest one after the other. This is like the cities of the gandharvas appearing in one's environment—for example, on a plain at sunset—as visionary experiences reified by the ordinary mind.

"While sensory appearances are primordially such that they have never existed, the myriad appearances that are seen, heard, smelled, tasted, or felt are like echoes—subjective appearances manifesting as though they were something else.

"All sensory appearances are not other than the ground of being, but are of one taste with that ground itself, like the reflections of all the planets and stars in the ocean that are not other than the ocean, but are of one taste with the water itself.

༄༅། །ལས་མི་གཞན་པར་རྒྱུ་ཉིད་དུ་རོ་གཅིག་པ་ལྷ་བུའོ། །གཞི་དབྱིངས་
ཁྱབ་བརྟལ་རྣམ་མཁའི་ཁོར་ཡུག་ལ་ངར་འཛིན་གྱི་དབང་གིས་བདག་གཞན་
བདེན་གྲུབ་དུ་སྣང་བ་ནི་རྒྱ་ལས་ལྔ་བ་བརྟོལ་བ་ལྷ་བུའོ། །གཞི་དབྱིངས་སྟོང་
པ་དངས་གསལ་གྱི་ཆ་དེ་བདག་སྣང་ཡིད་ཤེས་སུ་གཅུན་ཏེ་བརྟན་པའི་སྟོབས་
ཀྱིས་འཁྲུལ་སྣང་སྣ་ཚོགས་སྣང་བ་ནི་དཔེར་ན་མིག་རྩ་བཙིར་བའམ་རྩ་ཁམས་
རྐྱང་གིས་བསྒྱུར་བ་ལས་མིག་ཡོར་སྣང་བ་ལྷ་བུའོ། །ངར་འཛིན་གྱི་ཤེས་
པའི་རོར་གཞི་ལས་སྣ་ཚོགས་སྣང་ཡང་གཞི་རང་ལས་མ་གཡོས་ཤིང་མ་བྱུང་
བ་ནི་དཔེར་ན་སྒྱུལ་བསྒྱུར་གྱི་ཏིང་ངེ་འཛིན་ལ་དབང་བསྒྱུར་བའི་སྐྱེས་བུ་སྒྱུལ་
བསྒྱུར་གྱི་ཏིང་ངེ་འཛིན་ལ་སྒྱོམས་པར་ཞུགས་ཚེ་སྒྱུལ་པ་སྣ་ཚོགས་སུ་སྣང་ཡང་
རོན་ལ་གཞི་རྩ་བྲལ་ཞིང་དངོས་ཡུལ་མ་གྲུབ་པ་ལྷ་བུའོ། །གྱི། ཁྲུ་
ཆུང་བསམ་དུ་མེད་པ་ཁྱོད་ཀྱིས་འདི་ལྟར་རིམ་བཞིན་དུ་བསྒོམ་དང་སྣང་བ་སྒྱུ་
མར་ཚོགས་པས་སྒྱུ་མའི་རྣལ་འབྱོར་དུ་འགྱུར་རོ། །ཞེས་གསུངས་ཤིང་མི་
སྣང་བར་གྱུར་ཏོ།

"Due to the concept of an 'I,' self and other manifest as though they truly existed within the panoramic sky of the ground of being, expansive basic space. This is analogous to bubbles forming on water.

"The pristine lucidity of the ground of being as empty basic space is forced into the narrow confines of the subjective perception of consciousness based on conceptual mind (*yid-shey*). The influence of this entrenched habit causes sensory appearances perceived in confusion to manifest in all their variety. This is like the appearance of a hallucination when pressure is applied to the optic nerve or when one's nervous system is disturbed by an imbalance of subtle energy (*lung*).

"Sensory appearances manifest from the ground of being in all their variety in view of a consciousness that conceives of an 'I,' yet they do not diverge from or occur outside of that ground. This is like the case of an adept who has gained mastery (*wang gyur-wa*) over states of meditative absorption (*ting-nge-dzin*) that permit the emanation and control of phantoms. Although a variety of phantoms manifest when such an individual is engaged in this process of emanation and control, in actuality these phantoms are free of any basis and have never existed as real objects.

"Ah, my incredible little child, meditate progressively in this way and, having realized that all sensory appearances are illusory, you will become a yogin of illusion."

Saying this, he vanished.

Rigdzin Duddul Dorje

༄༅། །ཡང་རིག་འཛིན་བདུད་འདུལ་རྡོ་རྗེས། རྡོ་རྗེ་ཐུག་པའི་རྡོ་རྗེའི།
རྡོན་དུ་ནམ་མཁའ་སྙིང་ལ་སྤྲོས། ཞེས་དང་། སྐྱར་ཡང་དེའི་དོན་བསྒྲོལ་
ནས་གསུངས་པ་ནི། ཀྱི་རྟོ་ནམ་མཁའ་སྟོང་པ་འདི་ནི་སྟོང་བཅུད་ཐམས་ཅད་
ཀྱི་འཆར་གཞི་ཡིན་ཏེ། དཔེར་ན་གཟུགས་བརྟན་འཆར་གཞི་མེ་ལོང་ཡིན་
ལ་མེ་ལོང་ལས་གཟུགས་བརྟན་གཞན་དུ་མ་གྲུབ་པ་དང་། རྒྱུ་སྒྲ་འཆར་གཞི་
རྒྱུ་ཡིན་ལ་རྒྱུ་ལས་རྒྱུ་སྒྲ་གཞན་དུ་མ་གྲུབ་པ་དང་། འཇའ་ཚོན་འཆར་གཞི་
ནམ་མཁའ་ཡིན་ལ་ནམ་མཁའ་ལས་འཇའ་ཚོན་གཞན་དུ་མ་གྲུབ་པ་བཞིན་ནོ། །
ནམ་མཁའ་དེ་ནི་རྣམ་མི་འགྱུར་བས་མི་ཚོད་པ། ནམ་མཁའ་ལ་གཟོ་མ་གཞིག་
ཐུབ་བས་མི་ཤིགས་པ། ནམ་མཁའ་སྣང་སྒྲིད་ཀྱི་མཆེད་གཞིར་གནས་པས་
བདེན་པ། ནམ་མཁའ་ལ་སྐྱོན་ཡོན་ཀྱི་བསྒྱུར་མི་འཇུག་པས་སྲ་བ། ནམ་
མཁའ་འཕོ་འགྱུར་བྲལ་བས་བཏན་པ། ནམ་མཁའ་རྡུལ་ཕྲ་རབ་ཡན་ཆད་
ཀྱི་ཁོངས་སུ་མ་ཞུགས་པ་མེད་པས་ཐམས་ཅད་དུ་ཐོགས་པ་མེད་པ། ནམ་
མཁའ་ལ་གཞན་གང་གིས་ཀྱང་གནོད་པས་མི་ཚུགས་པས་ཐམས་ཅད་ལས་མ་

O N ANOTHER OCCASION, Rigdzin Duddul Dorje said to me, "Vajra, the eternal vajra! For the actual meaning, look to space itself!" In revealing the meaning of this, he stated the following: "Ah! This empty space is the ground for the arising of the entire universe. For example, it is like a mirror being the ground for the arising of a reflection, which has never existed as anything other than the mirror. It is like water being the ground for the arising of the moon's image, which has never existed as anything other than water. And it is like the sky being the ground for the arising of a rainbow, which has never existed as anything other than the sky.

"This space, since it cannot be injured, is invulnerable. Since space cannot be conquered or destroyed, it is indestructible. Since space abides as the basis for the unfolding of the world of appearances and possibilities, it is authentic. Since space cannot be altered by flaws or positive qualities, it is incorruptible. Since space is free of transition or change, it is stable. Since space completely permeates even the tiniest subatomic particle, it is in all ways unobstructed. And since nothing whatsoever can damage it, space is in all ways invincible.

"Since all material substances can be damaged by weapons, they are vulnerable. Since they can be conquered or destroyed

༄༅། །ཕམ་པའོ། །རྫས་གཞན་གང་ལའང་མཚོན་གྱིས་རྨ་འབྱུང་
བས་ཆོད་པ། རྒྱན་གྱིས་གཟིམ་ཞིང་འཇིག་རྣམས་པས་ཤིགས་པ། གཅིག་
དང་དུ་མར་འགྱུར་བས་རྟེན་པ། གཞན་གྱིས་བསྐྱད་འཇུག་པས་མི་སྲུ་བ།
གཡོ་འགུལ་དང་བཅས་བརྟན་གནས་མེད་པས་མི་བརྟན་པ། གང་ལའང་
ཐོགས་པ་དང་བཅས་པ། རྒྱན་གཞན་གྱིས་སྟོང་པར་བྱེད་པས་ཕམ་པ་སྟེ།
བདེན་པར་མ་གྲུབ་པའི་མཚན་ཉིད་ཅན་དེ་དག་སྟོང་པའོ། །གཞན་ཡང་དངོས་
པོ་རགས་པ་རྡུལ་དུ་ཕབ་པས་རྡུལ། རྡུལ་དེ་བདུན་ཆར་བཏང་བས་རྡུལ་ཕྲན།
རྡུལ་ཕྲན་དེ་ཡང་བདུན་ཆར་བཏང་བས་ཆ་མེད་དུ་སྟོང་པ་ཡང་མ་གྲུབ་པའི་མཚན་
ཉིད་ཀྱིས་ཡིན་ནོ། །དེ་ཡང་བྱ་བྱས་པས་མེད་པར་བཏང་བ་ལས་དང་པོ་
ཡོད་པར་སེམས་ན། རྨི་ལམ་གྱི་སྣང་བ་སྣང་དུས་ཉིད་ནས་མ་གྲུབ་པ་ལ་
མཐོང་རེག་གི་བུ་བ་བུས་མ་བུས་དང་། མིག་འཕྱུད་བཙུམ་དང་གོམ་པ་འདེག་
འཇོགས་ཆམ་གྱིས་སྣང་བ་མཆེད་འགག་ཏུ་འགྱུར་བའི་ཆུལ་ལ་ལྟོས་ཤིག །འོན་
ཏེ་སྣ་མ་འགགག་ཅིང་ཡལ་ཏེ་ཕྱི་མ་ཕྱིས་མཆེད་པ་མ་ཡིན་ཏེ་སྣ་མ་ནས་གཞན་དུ་
འཕོས་ཚེ་སྣ་ཕྱི་ཐམས་ཅད་བདེན་གྲུབ་ཏུ་ཡོད་པར་སེམས་ན་རྨི་ལམ་གྱི་སྣང་
བ་ལ་ལྟོས་ཤིག །ཁྱད་པར་དུ་ཡང་རྒྱུ་འབྲས་ཕན་ཚུན་ལ་ལྟོས་ནས་བཏགས་
པ་མིན་པའི་ཆགས་ཐུབ་ཀྱི་ཌོ་བོ་ཞིག་ཡོད་མི་སྲིད་པས་དང་ཆལ་ཤིགས་པར

under certain conditions, they are subject to destruction. Since they can change into one thing or many, they are false. Since they can be altered by something else, they are corruptible. Since they involve movement and vacillation and have no permanent location, they are unstable. They are in every way obstructed. Since they can be reduced to nothingness under other conditions, they can be vanquished. Things characterized thus, as having never truly existed, are empty.

"In addition, coarse things can be reduced to fine powder, to molecules in fact. These molecules can be reduced by a factor of seven to atoms. These atoms can, in turn, be reduced by a factor of seven and finally reduced to emptiness, because their characteristics are such that they have never existed.

"If you think that these things originally existed but were reduced to nonexistence by your having gone through this process, just look at dream images, which even as they manifest have never existed, and determine whether or not these images can be seen or felt. Also, observe the way that sensory appearances arise or cease merely due to whether your eyes are open or closed, or whether your foot is lowered or raised in walking.

"You may contend, 'Well, it is not the case that an appearance at one point in time ceases and disappears, with another replacing it later. Rather, when the former moment is replaced by another, the sensory appearance is such that it truly exists throughout its entire duration.' If you think this is so, look again at dream images. Consider the matter well, for it is impossible for some essence to exist in its own right without be-

༄༅། སོམ་མཛོད། །འོན་ནམ་མཁའ་ལ་རྡོ་རྗེ་ཚོས་བདུན་ལྡན་པར་བཤད་པ་དེ་དག་ཀྱང་དངོས་མེད་ཡིན་པའི་རྒྱུ་མཚན་གྱིས་འཕོ་འགྱུར་མེད་ཚུལ་དཔེར་བཞག་ནས་ཚོས་ཉིད་ཀྱི་བཤགས་ཚུལ་སྟ་བསམ་བརྗོད་མེད་ཀྱི་ངོ་བོ་ལ་འགྱུར་བ་མེད་པར་སྟོན་པ་ཡིན་གྱི། དངོས་དང་དངོས་མེད་བདེན་བཟུན་གྱི་ཁྱད་འོང་བར་འཆད་པ་ལ་སྒྱུར་ན་ལེགས་པ་ཡིན་ནོ། །དེ་བས་ན་མཛད་པོས་རྣ་བ་སྟོན་པའི་བཟུ་ཐབས་ཕྱུས་ན་རྣ་བ་ལ་བལྟ་བར་བྱུ་ཨེ་མཛུབ་མོའི་རྟེ་ཚམ་ཞིག་བལྟ་བས་ཚོམ་པར་མི་བྱའོ། འདི་ལ་གོ་ཨིས་འདྲིས་ཡང་ཡང་བཏང་ནས་སྟོང་པར་ཐག་ཚོད་པ་ཞིག་མ་བྱས་ན་རྣམ་མ་ཁྱེན་གྱི་ལམ་དུ་ཕྱོགས་ཚམ་ཏེ་བར་མི་འགྱུར་རོ། །ཁྱུ་ཆུང་ཤེས་རིག་གི་རྗེ་མོ་ཁྱོད་ཀྱིས་འདིའི་དོན་ལ་རབ་ཏུ་ཕྱོས་ལ་སྤང་བ་ཐབས་ཚད་ནམ་མཁའ་ཉིད་དུ་རྟོགས་པའི་ནམ་མཁའ་གོ་འབྱེད་པའི་རྣལ་འབྱོར་པ་ཞིག་མཛོད་ཅིག །ཅེས་གསུངས་ཞིང་མི་སྨྲང་བར་གྱུར་ཏོ།

ing simply a conventional designation that relies on the relationship between cause and effect.

"In addition, the explanation of the seven vajra attributes of space makes use of metaphors to show how space is without transition or change because of its insubstantiality (*ngö-med*). This explanation demonstrates that there is no change in the indescribable, inconceivable, and inexpressible essence of the abiding mode of the true nature of phenomena (*chhö-nyid*). This is an ideal argument to apply in explaining the difference between what has substance and what does not, between truth and falsehood.

"So in employing the symbolic means of pointing a finger at the moon, look at the moon and don't be satisfied with looking merely at the tip of the finger. If you don't reach a decision concerning emptiness by familiarizing yourself with this point over and over again, you will not be the slightest bit closer to the path of omniscience.

"Ah, little one at the very pinnacle of understanding and awareness, you must look thoroughly into the meaning of this, becoming a yogin of the limitless potential of space who realizes all sensory appearances to be space itself."

Saying this, he vanished.

Longchhenpa Drimed Odzer

༄༅། །དེ་ལྟར་གཏན་ལ་ཕབ་པས་སྐྱོང་བ་ཐམས་ཅད་རང་ས་ཉིད་ནས་སྟོང་པར་ཤེས་ཀྱང་། ཕྱི་སྐྱོང་བ་སྐྱེད་ཀྱི་འཇིག་རྟེན་ནང་གཡོ་བ་བཅུད་ཀྱི་སེམས་ཅན་བར་འདོད་ཡོན་ལྔའི་ཡུལ་སྐྱོང་འདི་དག་ཐམས་ཅད་ཕྱལ་དུ་བོར་ནས་གནས་རིས་གཞན་དུ་འགྲོ་བ་དང་། སེམས་ཅན་ཐམས་ཅད་རང་རང་གི་རྒྱུད་ཅན་དུ་ཡོད་པར་སེམས་ནས་ཡོད་པའི་གནས་སྐབས་ན། རྩེ་ལམ་གྱི་སྐྱོང་དོ་ར་ངའི་རྣ་དུ་མེད་འོད་ཟེར་དང་ཞལ་མཇལ་ནས་དྲི་བ་རྡོད་ལན་གྱི་ཆུལ་དུ་དོ་སྟོད་འདི་ལྟར་གཏམས་སོ། །ཀྱི་རིགས་ཀྱི་བུ་ཕྱི་སྐྱོང་བ་སྐྱེད་ཀྱི་འཇིག་རྟེན། ནང་གཡོ་བ་བཅུད་ཀྱི་སེམས་ཅན། བར་འདོད་ཡོན་ལྔའི་ཡུལ་སྐྱོང་འདི་དག་སྒྱུ་མའི་འཕྲུལ་འཁོར་དབྱིངས་སུ་ཞིག་པ་བཞིན་དུ་ཀུན་གཞི་སྟོང་ཏུད་ཀྱི་ནམ་མཁར་ཐིམ་ནས་མཐར་ལས་རླུང་གཡོས་པའི་ཚོ་འཕུལ་གྱིས་བདག་ལུས་སྐྱོང་བ་ལས་རྩེ་ལམ་གྱི་སྟོང་བཅུད་འདོད་ཡོན་ཐམས་ཅད་མཆེད་པ་ལ་མཛོན་

HAVING COME TO such a definitive conclusion, I understood all sensory appearances to be empty in their own context (*rang-sa*). Yet regarding the sensory appearances of the outer world as a container, the animate beings contained therein, and the objects manifesting in between as the five kinds of sensory stimuli, I was still thinking in terms of these being left behind when one departs to another realm, and of all beings actually existing, each with an individual mindstream (*gyud*).

In a dream during this period, I met with my guru, [Longchhenpa] Drimed Odzer, who instructed me with a direct introduction in the form of questions and answers.

He said, "Ah, son of spiritual heritage, when you go to sleep, the outer sensory appearances of the inanimate universe as a container, the animate beings contained therein, and the objects manifesting in between as the five kinds of sensory stimuli dissolve into the space of the unconscious blankness of the ground of all ordinary experience (*kun-zhi*), just like the artifices of a magical illusion collapsing in basic space. Eventually, through the creative force of the subtle energy of karma (*lay kyi lung*) stirring, the sense of a self and the sensory appearance of a body manifest. A dream state—an entire

41

༄༅། །ཞེན་སྐྱེས་པས་འཁྲུལ་པ་དང་། སྒྱུར་ཡང་སྒྱུང་སྙིད་དེ་ཡང་

འཇའ་ཚོན་ནམ་མཁའ་ལ་ཡལ་བ་ལྟར་ཀུན་གཞི་སྟོང་དུད་ཀྱི་ནམ་མཁར་ཐིམ་

པ་ལས་ཡང་སྒྱུར་བཞིན་ཉིན་སྣང་མཆེད་པ་ཡིན། ཅེས་གསུངས་པ་ལ།

བདག་གིས་འདི་སྐྱད་ཞུས། བདག་གི་ལུས་འདི་ནི་སྣང་ཚམ་མ་ཡིན་པར་

ཌེས་པར་ཕ་མའི་རྒྱུ་རྐྱེན་ལས་བྱུང་བ་ཡིན་ནམ་སྙམ་ཞུས་པས། དེ་ལྟར་ཁྱོད་

ཀྱི་ལུས་ཕ་དང་མ་ལས་བྱུང་བར་སྙམ་ན། ཕ་མའི་ཐོག་མཐའ་བྱུང་གནས་

འགྲོ་གསུམ་གང་ལགས་སྟོས་དང་གསུངས་པ་ལ། བདག་གིས་ནི་ཡོད་

རྒྱང་མི་རྫུན་པ་ཡིན་སྣམ། ཕ་མ་མེད་པའི་ལུས་མི་སྙིད་པར་སེམས་ཀྱི་ཞུས་

པས། རྫི་ལམ་དང་བར་སྙིད་ཀྱི་ལུས་དང་དམྱལ་བའི་ལུས་སོགས་ཀྱི་ཕ་

མ་གང་ལགས་སྟོས་ཤིག་གསུངས་པས། ལུས་འདི་སྒྱུང་ཚམ་ལས་མ་

གྲུབ་པར་ཐག་ཆོད་པ་བྱུང་། ཡང་ཀྱི་བླ་མ་ལགས། བདག་གི་ལུས་མལ་

སར་གོས་ཀྱིས་གཡོགས་ནས་མི་ཡུལ་དང་བཅས་པ་མི་འགྱུར་བར་གནས་བཞིན་

རྫི་ལམ་ཀྱི་སྒྱུང་བ་འཁར་བ་ཡིན་པར་སེམས་འདུག་གི་ཞུས་པས། བླ་མའི་

ཞལ་ནས་ཕྱི་སྒྱུང་བ་སྟོང་ཀྱི་འཇིག་རྟེན་རྒྱུ་ཆེ་བ། ནང་གཡོ་བ་བཅུད་ཀྱི་སེམས་

ཅན་གྱང་ས་མང་བ། བར་འདོད་ཡོན་ལྔའི་ཡུལ་སྣང་བཀོད་ལེགས་པའི་རྫི་

ལམ་དེ་ལུས་ཀྱི་མགོ་དང་ཡན་ལག་སྟོད་སྨད་གང་གི་ནང་དུ་མཆེད་པའི་ཡུལ་

sensory universe—unfolds from this manifestation. Confusion occurs through overt fixation on this. Finally, that world of appearances and possibilities dissolves into the unconscious blankness of the ground of all ordinary experience, like a rainbow fading into the sky, and the sensory appearances of waking consciousness unfold as before."

To this I replied, "I still think that my body is not merely a sensory appearance, for surely it came from my parents, who were its cause and condition."

He said, "If you think that your body came from your father and mother, then what are the beginning and end of these parents? What are their source, their location, their final destination? Tell me!"

I answered, "I think that they exist, but I am not aware of what they are. It seems to me that a physical body without parents is not possible."

He retorted, "Consider this. Who are the parents of the body in a dream, in the bardo, and in the hell realms?" With that, I arrived at the decision that this body has never existed, being simply a sensory appearance.

I continued, "Ah, my guru, I feel that when my body is lying in bed covered with bedclothes, dream images arise while my body and the human realm remain unchanged."

The guru said, "Look for the location of the unfolding of this impressive array—these dream images of the outer appearances of a vast inanimate universe as a container, a multitude of beings contained therein, and the five kinds of sense objects manifesting in between. Is this location in the head, the limbs, or the upper or lower part of your body?"

༄༅། །ལ་སློས་ཤིག་གསུངས་པས། དེ་ཡང་མ་ཡིན་པའི་ཐག་ཆིས་
པར་ཆོད་པ་བྱུང་ཡང་ཪྒྱ་མ་ལགས། ཡུལ་གཞན་ཞིག་ཏུ་རྣམ་པར་ཤེས་པ་
སོང་བས་རྡི་སྒྱུང་འར། སྣར་ལུས་ནང་དུ་ལྷགས་ཚོ་ཉིན་སྒྱུང་འར་བ་ཡིན་
སྐམ་གྱི་ཞེས་ཞུས་པས། ཪྒྱ་མའི་ཞལ་ནས། འོན་དེ་ལྟར་ལགས་ན་ལུས་
འདི་གནས་ཁང་ལྟ་བུར་འགྱུར་བས་རྣམ་ཤེས་འབྱུང་འཇུག་བྱེད་པའི་གནས་ཁང་
གི་སྒོ་ལྟ་བུ་དེ་ངོས་ཟུངས་ལ་སློས་ཤིག །དིར་མ་ཟད་སེམས་ཀྱི་གནས་ས་
ཡང་ངོས་འཛིན་དགོས་ཏེ། སེམས་ལུས་ཀྱི་སྤྱོད་དུ་གནས་ན་སྐྱད་དུ་ཚོར་
མ་ཟུག་པ་ཚམ་གྱིས་ཟུག་ཏུ་ཅི་ལ་སྐྱོང་། སྐྱད་དུ་གནས་ན་དེ་བཞིན་སྦྱོད་དུ་
ཟུག་ཏུ་སྐྱོང་བའི་དོན་མ་མཆིས། དང་པོ་བུག་སྒོ་ནས་འབྱུང་འཇུག་བྱེད་པའི་
རྣམ་པར་ཤེས་པ་ཕྱ་མོ་དེ་ཡང་འཕེལ་ཏེ་ལུས་ཁྱབ་པ་དང་། ཡང་མར་འགྲིབ་སྟེ་
བུག་སྒོ་ཕྱ་མོ་ནས་ཐོན་པ་ཚམ་དུ་ཚེ་ཆུང་བྱེད་པ་མི་རིགས། དེ་ལྟར་ན་བེམ་རིག་
བྲལ་བའི་རྣམ་པར་ཤེས་པ་དེ་ཕྱི་བའི་དུས་སུ་ཡང་སྣར་བེམ་པོར་ཚིས་མི་འཇུག །
ཡུལ་གཞན་དུ་སོང་བའི་རྣམ་ཤེས་ཀྱི་ཡུལ་དེ་སྟེང་འོག་ཕྱོགས་མཚམས་གང་དུ་
ཡོད། ཉིན་སྣང་གི་སྤྱོད་བཅུད་དང་གཅིག་པར་འདོད་དམ་ཐ་དད་དུ་འདོད།
གཅིག་ཏུ་འདོད་ན་གཉིད་ཀྱིས་མཚམས་བཅད་དམ་མ་བཅད། བཅད་ན་ནི་
ཉིན་སྣང་མ་ཡིན་ལ། མ་བཅད་ན་ནི་སྨི་སྣང་མ་ཡིན། ཡང་ན་སྣང་བ་

44

Although I decided with certainty that there was no such location, I persisted. "My guru, I suppose then that dream images arise once my consciousness has gone to some other place and that the sensory appearances of the waking state arise when it reenters my body."

The guru replied, "If this were the case, then the body would become something like a hotel, so identify and describe to me what is, as it were, the door by which consciousness leaves and reenters this hotel. Not only that, you must also identify the place where the mind abides.

"If it resides in the upper part of the body, how is it that you feel pain with the slight prick of a thorn in the lower part? If it resides in the lower part, then there would likewise be no reason for feeling pain in the upper part. It is illogical to think that it assumes different sizes, with a tiny consciousness entering through an orifice only to expand to pervade the body and shrinking again only to exit through a tiny orifice. If that were the case, once awareness had separated from the body, why would consciousness not reenter the corpse after death?

"This environment of dream images, this other place to which you might go, where does it exist? Above? Below? In which cardinal or intermediate direction? Do you hold it to be identical to the universe you perceive in the waking state or to be something distinct? If you hold it to be identical, does sleep define the boundary between waking and dreaming or not? If sleep does define the boundary, your dream perception cannot be your waking perception; if sleep does not define the boundary, there can be no dream perception. Furthermore, it is not valid to hold that any sensory appearances exist, assign-

༄༅། །དེ་ཉིད་སྟེང་འོག་གམ་ཕྱི་ནང་བྱས་ནས་ཡོད་པར་འདོད་པ་ལས་

འོས་མེད་པ་ཡིན་ནོ། །ཞེས་གསུངས། །ཡང་བདག་གིས་བླ་མ་ལགས།

དེས་ན་ཐག་གང་ལ་གཅོད། ས་གང་གིས་འཛིན། བླ་མ་མཆོག་ཉིད་

ཀྱིས་བསླན་དུ་གསོལ་ཞུས་པས། བླ་མའི་ཞལ་ནས། ཚོ་རབས་ཐོག་

མ་མེད་པའི་དུས་ཀུན་ཏུ་སྐྱེ་མ་མྱོང་ཡང་སྐྱེ་སྲུང་ཚམ་དུ་ཟད། འཆི་མ་མྱོང་

ཡང་སྲུང་བ་གནས་འགྱུར་ཚ་དུ་དཔེར་ན་རྨི་སྲུང་དང་ཉིན་སྲུང་ལྟ་བུར་ཟད། མིག

དང་རྣ་བ་སྣ་དང་ལྗེ་དང་ལུས་རྣམས་སུ་གཟུགས་སྒྲ་དྲི་རོ་རེག་བྱར་མཐོང་ཐོས་

ཚོར་མྱང་མྱོང་བ་ཐམས་ཅད་རང་སྲུང་རང་ལ་འཁར་བ་ཚམ་ལས་གཞན་དུ་སྨྲ་རྩ་ཚམ

ཡོད་མ་མྱོང་། གལ་ཏེ་མཚན་སུམ་མིག་གིས་མཐོང་། དོན་ལག་པས་

ཟིན། དབང་པོའི་སྐོར་མྱོང་བས་གཞན་རང་རྒྱུད་པར་ཡོད་དོ་སྙམ་ན་རྨི་ལམ

གྱི་གཟུགས་བླ་དེ་རོ་རེག་བྱ་ཐམས་ཅད་དེ་དང་དེའི་དུས་སུ་བདེན་པར་སྲུང་ཡང་

སད་དུས་ཉིད་ནས་ཡུལ་མེད་ལ་ཡོད་མ་མྱོང་བ་དེས་སྟོན་ཏེ། །ཚོ་འཁོར་བ་ཐོག

མ་མེད་པའི་དུས་ནས་གནས་འཕོ་ཞིང་འགྲོ་མ་མྱོང་། ཡུལ་གཞན་དུ་སྟོང

མ་མྱོང་བའི་ཆུལ་ནི། །སྤྱི་ལམ་གྱི་སྲུང་བ་དང་མཚུངས་སོ། །སྤྱི་སྲུང

དང་ཉིན་སྲུང་གི་བདེན་རྟེན་མི་མཉམ་པར་སེམས་ན། །སྐྱེས་ནས་ད་ལྟའི

ing them to some hierarchy of higher versus lower, outer versus inner."

To this I responded, "My guru, then to what decision should I come? To what level of experience should I hold? I ask you, sublime guru, show me."

The guru replied, "At no time throughout the beginningless succession of lifetimes has there ever been actual birth. There has been only the appearance of birth. There has never been actual death, only the transformation of sensory appearances, like the shift from the dream state to the waking state. All sensations—seen, heard, smelled, tasted, and felt as forms, sounds, odors, tastes, and tactile sensations by the eyes, ears, nose, tongue, and skin—are merely the mind being conscious of its own projections (*rang-nang*), without their ever having even a hair's tip of existence as something else.

"You may think that something other than this does exist in its own right (*rang-gyud*), since you can see it directly with your eyes, actually hold it in your hand, or experience it through your other senses. But in fact, although all the forms, sounds, odors, tastes, and tactile sensations in dreams seem to truly exist in their respective contexts, from the point of view of waking experience they have never existed, being nonexistent as objects (*yul-med*).

"Throughout the beginningless succession of lifetimes, there has never been any actual experience of transition or going from one state to another, or any actual experience of being located in some other place. This is analogous to the images in a dream.

"You may think that the relative validity of dream images

༈། བར་གྱི་རི་སྣང་དང་ཉིན་སྣང་གི་ལས་ཀ་སོ་ནམས་འབད་རྩོལ་གསོག
འཇོག་ཐམས་ཅད་མཉམ་མི་མཉམ་སློས་ཤིག །དེ་གཉིས་ལ་དུས་ཡུན་རིང་
ཐུང་དང་། གྲངས་མང་ཉུང་མེད་པའི་ཆུལ་ལ་ཞིབ་ཏུ་བརྟག་ན་མཆོངས་པར་
ཐག་ཆོད་པར་འགྱུར་རོ། །དེར་མ་ཟད་རྨི་སྣང་མི་བདེན་པ་དང་ཉིད་སྣང་བདེན་
པ་ཨིན་ན། རྨི་སྣང་འཁྲུལ་པ་དང་ཉིན་སྣང་མ་འཁྲུལ་པར་འགྱུར་བས། རྨི་
སྣང་དུ་སེམས་ཅན་དང་ཉིན་སྣང་དུ་སངས་རྒྱས་ཡིན་པར་འདོད་དགོས། །གཉིས་
ཀ་འཁྲུལ་སྣང་ཨིན་ན་ནི་བདེན་རྫུན་གྱི་ཁྱད་པར་ཡོད་དོན་མེད་དེ། མ་ཨིན་
པ་ལ་ཨིན་པར་སྣང་ཞིང་བཟུང་བ་ལ་འཁྲུལ་སྣང་ཞེས་བརྗོད་པ་ཨིན་པའི་ཕྱིར་རོ།།
སློན་ཆད་རི་རབ་ཟས་སུ་ཟོས་རྒྱ་མཚོ་སྐོམ་དུ་བཏུང་ཀྱང་ད་ལྟ་འགྲང་བ་མེད་པ་
དང་། སློང་གསུམ་གོས་སུ་གྱོན་ཡང་དྲོ་བ་མེད་པ་རྣམས་ནི་སྣང་ཚམ་ཉིད་ལས་
མ་གྲུབ་པའི་བརྟར་ཞེས་པར་བྱོ། །ལུས་སུ་སྣང་བ་འདི་སློང་པར་མ་ཤེས་ཤིང
དེ་ལ་བདེན་པར་ཞེན་པ་ནི་སློན་ཤིན་ཏུ་ཆེ་བ་ཨིན་ཏེ། ལུས་འདིའི་ཆེད་དུ་
འབད་རྩོལ་གྱི་དབང་གིས་རྣམ་མཁྱེན་གྱི་འབྲས་བུ་ལ་ཟ་བས་ན་ཟ་འཛི་དང་།

is not equal to that of waking appearances. But think of all the dream experiences and waking experiences from your birth until the present—the activities and occupations, the effort and striving, the saving and planning. Consider whether these are equal. If you examine them closely, without considering the short term versus the long term or more versus fewer occurrences of such experiences, you will arrive at the decision that they are equal.

"And that is not all, for if dream images were not true and waking appearances were, this would mean that dream images were states of confusion and waking experiences were not. You would have to hold that you are an ordinary being during dream experiences and a buddha during the waking state. But if both are cases of sensory appearances resulting from confusion, any distinction regarding their validity becomes pointless, because the expression 'sensory appearances resulting from confusion' implies fixation on that which does not exist but manifests as though it did.

"Up until now you have eaten an amount of food equivalent to Mount Sumeru and have drunk the equivalent of the oceans, but still you are not full. Although you have worn enough garments to clothe the three-thousand-fold universe, you still are not warm. You should understand these to be indications that things have never existed as anything but mere sensory appearances.

"It is an enormous flaw not to understand that what manifests as the body is empty, and instead to invest it with truth. This flaw is the consuming demon (*za-dre*), since the power of the efforts you make for the sake of the body eats away at the

༄༅། །འཁོར་བ་ནས་འཁོར་བར་ཁ་བརྒྱུད་དེ་སྐྱེ་འཆིའི་སྡུང་བ་སྟོན་པས་
ཤི་གཤིན། ལུས་ཀྱི་ཁེད་དུ་གོས་སོགས་བདེ་བ་དོན་དུ་གཉེར་ཞིང་རེ་དོགས་
ཏིར་ཡིན་ཆགས་སྡང་གི་ཞེན་པས་འཆིང་སྟེ་ཐར་པའི་སྒོག་རྩ་གཅོད་པས་སྒོག་
གཅོད། གཏན་དུ་བདེ་བའི་དབུགས་འབྱོག་པས་ན་དབུགས་ཨིན་ཀྱང་ཨིན།
དེས་ན་ཚོགས་དྲུག་གི་ཡུལ་སྣང་ལ་ཞེན་པ་ཐམས་ཅད་རེ་དགས་ཀྱིས་སྐྱིག་རྒྱུ་
ཀྱུ་རུ་མཐོང་ནས་རྒྱག་པ་ལྤུ་བུ་ལས་སྟེང་པོ་རྩལ་ཕུན་ཚམ་ཡང་མ་གྲུབ་པོ། །ཡང་
འདི་ལྟར་སྟོང་པར་ཤེས་ཀྱང་སྟར་བཞིན་བདེན་པའི་ཚུལ་དུ་གནས་པ་ལས་མེད་
དུ་ནི་མི་འགྲོ་བར་འདུག་པས་དེ་ལྟར་ཤེས་པ་ལ་དགོས་པ་ཅི་ཡོད་སྙམ་ན། བསྒོམ་
བྱའི་ཌོ་བོ་སྟོང་ཉིད་ཨིན་པར་མ་ཤེས་ན་སྒོམ་པ་ཐམས་ཅད་ལུང་མ་བསྟན་གྱི་ཕྱོགས་
སུ་ཆེས་པ་ཨིན། ལར་བསྐྱེད་སྒོམ་དམིགས་པ་གཞན་ཐམས་ཅད་ཀྱིས་ཀྱང་གོ་
ཚ་དོགས་ཚ་གྱིས་གྲོལ་བར་མི་འགྱུར་བས་ན་སྟོང་ཉིད་དོགས་ཚ་གྱིས་མེད་
པའི་གནས་ལུགས་མངོན་དུ་འགྱུར་དགོས་པའི་རྒྱ་མཚན་ཆེ་ཡོད། ཡང་གདོད་
ནས་སྟོང་ན་སྟོང་པར་ཤེས་དང་མ་ཤེས་འདྲོ་སྙམ་ན། རིག་དང་མ་རིག་
ཤེས་དང་མ་ཤེས་གཉིས་ཀྱི་ཁྱད་པར་ལས་འཁོར་འདས་དང་གྲོལ་འཁྲུལ་འབྱུང་

fruit of omniscience. It is the murderous executioner (*shi-shed*), since it provides the link from one cycle to the next in samsara, causing the appearances of birth and death to manifest. It is what cuts the life force (*srog-chod*), since for the sake of the body you are driven to seek happiness from clothing and so forth, and so you sever the lifeline of liberation with the fixation on attachment and aversion that perpetuates hope and fear. It is also what steals the breath (*ug-len*), since it robs you of the breath of lasting happiness. Therefore, all those who fixate on the apparent objects of the six modes of consciousness (*tsog-drug*) are like deer perceiving a mirage to be water and chasing after it, when not even an iota of an essence has ever existed.

"In addition, even though you know things to be empty in this way, they may remain as they were before, seemingly true without vanishing into nothingness. So you might wonder what purpose such knowledge serves. If you do not know that emptiness is the essence that must be cultivated in meditation, then all of your attempts at meditation will surely be ineffectual.

"Furthermore, you might think, 'Since mere understanding or intellectual comprehension in the context of all other approaches of visualization and meditation will not bring about freedom, why should the mere understanding of emptiness make evident the ineffable way of abiding (*nay-lug*)? Moreover, if things are primordially empty, surely it is immaterial whether I know that they are empty or not.' However, it is from this distinction of whether one is aware of this or not, of whether one knows this or not, that nirvana or samsara, free-

༄༅། བ་ཡིན་པས་ཤེས་ཞིང་རིག་པ་ནི་གནད་དུ་རྟོགས་པར་བྱའོ། །ཡང་
འགའ་ཞིག་གིས་རང་སྟོབས་ཀྱིས་མ་ཤེས་ན་ཐོས་བསམ་གྱིས་གོ་མི་ཆོད་ཟེར་
བར་འབྱུང་སྲིད་དེ། ཐོག་མ་མེད་པའི་དུས་ནས་རང་སྟོབས་ཀྱིས་མ་རྟོགས་
ནས་འཁོར་བར་འཁྱམས་པ་ཡིན། བསླབ་ཅིང་སྦྱངས་པས་རྒྱུད་ལུང་མན་ངག་
ཐམས་ཅད་དང་མཐུན་པའི་ལྟ་བ་སྟོང་ཉིད་རྟོགས་པར་འགྱུར་བ་ཡིན་པས་ཤེས་
པར་གྱིས་ཤིག །གཞན་ཡང་བསླབ་སྦྱང་སོགས་དགའ་བ་ཆེན་པོ་སྤྱད་ནས་
སྟོང་ཉིད་རྟོགས་ཀྱང་རུང་། དགའ་བ་སྤྱུ་ཚམ་མ་སྤྱད་པར་སྟོང་ཉིད་རྟོགས་
ཀྱང་རུང་། དཔེར་ན་དགའ་བ་ཆེན་པོ་སྤྱད་ནས་གསེར་རྙེད་པ་དང་། དགའ་
བ་སྤྱུ་ཚམ་མ་སྤྱད་པར་གསེར་མལ་ས་ནས་རྙེད་ཀྱང་གསེར་ལ་བཟང་ངན་མེད་
པ་ལྟ་བུའོ། །དེ་ལྟར་སྣང་བ་ཐམས་ཅད་སྟོང་ཉིད་དུ་གཏན་ལ་འབེབས་པའི་
དཔོད་བྱེད་ཀྱི་ཤེས་པ་ལ་སོ་སོར་རྟོག་པའི་ཤེས་རབ་ཅེས་བྱ་ཞིང་། འཁོར་
འདས་སྟོང་ཉིད་ཆེན་པོར་ངེས་པར་ཐག་ཆོད་པའི་རྟེས་ཤེས་རྒྱུན་ཆགས་པ་ལ་
བདག་མེད་རྟོགས་པའི་ཤེས་རབ་ཅེས་བྱའོ། །ཤེས་རབ་དེ་གཉིས་རྒྱུད་ལ་
བསྐྱེད་ནས་དང་པོ་རྟོགས། བར་དུ་སྒོམ། ཐ་མ་གདིང་ཐོབ་པར་བྱ་བ་
ནི་གནད་དོ། །ཡང་ལུས་སོགས་སྣང་ཚམ་ལས་མ་གྲུབ་པར་འདོད་པ་ནི་མི་

dom or confusion, comes about. Thus, you must understand that the key point is knowing this and remaining aware of it.

"Moreover, some might object that if you cannot understand this on the strength of your own abilities, then study and contemplation will not be effective. But from beginningless time you have not realized this on the strength of your own abilities, and so you have wandered in samsara. Be aware of the fact that it is by studying and training that you can come to realize emptiness—the view that is in accord with all tantras, explanatory commentaries, and pith instructions.

"Furthermore, you may realize emptiness by undergoing great difficulties in studying, training, and so forth, or you may realize emptiness without the slightest difficulty. This makes no more difference than, for example, finding gold by experiencing great hardship or without the slightest hardship, right in your own bed, makes a difference to the quality of the gold. Accordingly, the term 'discerning sublime knowing' (*sosor tog-pai shey-rab*) refers to knowledge gained through analysis which leads to the definitive conclusion that all sensory appearances are emptiness. The term 'sublime knowing which realizes that things have no identity' (*dag-med tog-pai shey-rab*) refers to the ongoing subsequent knowledge which follows the decisive experience of certainty that samsara and nirvana are supreme emptiness. The key point is that you cultivate these two aspects of sublime knowing in your mindstream initially as understanding, later on as personal experience, and finally as the attainment of indwelling confidence (*ding*).

"Still, you might protest that it is unreasonable to hold that

༄༅། འབད་དེ། སྟོང་པར་རྟོགས་པའི་གང་ཟག་ཞིག་གི་ལུས་ལ་
མི་ཆུས་རིག་ཅིང་མདའ་མདུང་དགྲུག་ལ་སོགས་ཀྱིས་བསྣུན་ན་རྗུག་ཏུ་འབྱུང་
བས་སོ་ཞེར་ན། ཆོས་ཉིད་ཟད་པའི་དབྱིངས་ལ་མ་སྐྱེལ་གྱི་བར་དུ་གཞིས་སྣང་
མི་རུབ། དེ་མ་རུབ་ཀྱི་བར་དུ་ཕན་གནོད་ཀྱི་སྣང་བ་རྒྱུན་མི་འཆད་པར་འབྱུང་
ཡང་དོན་ལ་ནི་དངུལ་བའི་མེས་ཀྱང་མ་ཚིག་པས་སྟོན་ཏོ། ཞེས་གསུངས་
ཤིང་མི་སྣང་བར་གྱུར་ཏོ།

the body and the rest of the world have never existed as anything other than mere sensory appearances, since those who understand the empty nature of their bodies still feel pain when touched by fire or water or when struck by arrows, spears, clubs, and so forth. The answer to this is the fact that as long as you have not arrived at the state of basic space in which phenomena resolve within their true nature (*chhö-nyid zad-pai ying*), dualistic appearances do not subside, and as long as they have not subsided, beneficial and harmful appearances occur without interruption. In actuality, though, even the fires of hell do not burn."

Saying this, he vanished.

Saraha

༄༅། །ཡང་རེ་ཞིག་གི་དུས་སུ་གྲུབ་ཆེན་ས་ར་ཧའི་ཞལ་མཇལ་བའི་ཚེ།
བདག་གིས་གྲུབ་པའི་དབང་ཕྱུག་ཆེན་པོ་ལགས། སྒྲིབ་པ་གང་གིས་སྦྱངས།
སྐུ་རྗེ་ལྷར་བསྒྱུབ། འདི་བགེགས་གང་གིས་སྐྲོལ། བདག་ལ་བཀའ་
སྩལ་དུ་གསོལ་ཞུས་པས། བགར་སྩལ་པ། ཀྱི་སྙིས་བུ་ཆེན་པོ་ཁྱོད་
ཀྱིས་ཕར་གཟོད་ཀྱི་མཚང་ལ་རྟོལ་དགོས་པས། སྒྲིབ་པ་ཞེས་བྱ་བ་དེ་གཞི་
སྟོང་ཉིད་ཀྱི་དོ་བོ་མ་རིག་པ་ལ་སྒྲིབ་པ་དང་མ་རིག་པ་དང་། དེ་བཅུན་པ་ལ་
བག་ཆགས་ཞེས་བྱའོ། །དེ་ནི་ལུས་ངག་གི་དགེ་སྒྱུར་ལ་འབད་པ་ལྟ་བུའི་ཙོལ་
བ་ཐལ་གྱིས་སྒྱོང་བར་མི་ནུས་ཏེ། འདི་ལྟར་སོ་སོར་རྟོག་པའི་ཤེས་རབ་
ཀྱིས་ཚོས་ཉིད་གཅུན་ལ་དབབ་པས་སྒྲིབ་པ་དེ་དང་གིས་འདག་པར་འགྱུར་བ་ཡིན།
ཕན་བྱེད་ལུས་ངག་གི་དགེ་བ་ཐམས་ཅད་གནས་གང་དུ་འདུག །བསགས་
པའི་བང་མཛོད་གང་དུ་མཆིས། བྱུང་བའི་ཁུངས། གནས་པའི་ས།

ON YET ANOTHER OCCASION, when I met the great siddha Saraha in a vision, I asked him, "Ah, great lord of siddhas, how can I purify obscurations? How can I prove that there are gods? How can I liberate demons and hindrances? I pray that you be so gracious as to tell me these things."

He bestowed the following reply: "Ah, great spiritual one, you must confront the hidden flaw of benefit and harm. As for what is called obscuration, the terms 'obscuration' (*drib-pa*) and 'nonrecognition of awareness' (*ma-rig-pa*) both refer to a lack of awareness of the ground of being as the essence of emptiness, and the term 'habitual pattern' (*bag-chhag*) refers to the entrenchment of that nonrecognition. These cannot be refined away by ordinary efforts such as striving through physical and verbal spiritual practices. Rather, these obscurations are purified as a matter of course when, through discerning sublime knowing, you come to a definitive conclusion concerning the true nature of phenomena.

"Where does all beneficial physical and verbal virtue abide? Where is the storehouse in which it is amassed? When you have examined and analyzed the source from which it comes, the location in which it abides, and the destination to which it

༄༅། འགྲོ་བའི་ཡུལ་ཐམས་ཅད་ལ་བརྟག་ཅིང་དཔྱད་པ་བཏང་བས་ཡུལ་

མེད་དུ་འདུག་ན་ཕན་གང་ལ་བཏགས། སེམས་ཉིད་སྟོང་པའི་ཕྱི་ནང་བར་

གསུམ་མགོ་མཇུག་གང་ལ་ཕན་ཐོགས་པ་ཡོང་ཅེས་བརྟག་ནས་ཡུལ་མེད་དུ་ཐག

ཆོད་ཚེ་འཁོར་བ་དུ་བསྡད་ནམས་བསགས་པ་ཚམ་དུ་ཟད་དོ། །དེ་བཞིན་

དུ་སྟིག་པ་བསགས་པའི་ཕུང་པོ་ཕྱོགས་མཆམས་གང་དུ་གདའ། དེའི་བང་

ཁང་གནས་ཡུལ་གང་དུ་མཆིས། སེམས་སྟོང་པའི་ཕྱི་ནང་མགོ་མཇུག

བར་གསུམ་གང་དུ་གནོད་བྱས་ཡོད་པའི་ཆུལ་ལ་བརྟག །ད་ལྟ་ཐག་ཏུ་ལུས་

ངག་དགེ་ལ་སྤྱོར་བའི་སྙིས་བུ་དང་། ཚེ་གཅིག་སྡིག་ལ་སྤྱོད་པའི་སྙིས་

བུ་གཉིས་ཀྱི་ཤེས་རྒྱུད་ལ་ཞིབ་ཏུ་བརྟག་ན་དེ་གཉིས་ཀའི་སེམས་ཀྱི་ཆགས་སྤང་

རེ་དོགས་སྟེར་ལེན་ཐམས་ཅད་ལ་ཁྱད་པར་རྡུལ་ཚམ་ཡང་མེད། གྲོལ་ན་ཡང་

ཤེས་རྒྱུད་གྲོལ་བས་གྲོལ། འཁྲུལ་ན་ཡང་ཤེས་རྒྱུད་འཁྲུལ་པས་འཁྲུལ།

གཉིས་ཀ་ཤེས་རྒྱུད་མ་གྲོལ་བར་འཁོར་བར་འཁྱམ་པ་ལ་ཁྱད་པར་སྒྱུ་ཚམ་མེད།

དེས་ན་དགེ་སྡིག་གཉིས་གནས་སྐབས་ཀྱི་བདེ་སྡུག་བསྐྱེད་པའི་ཁྱད་པར་ཚམ་

ལས་འཁོར་བའི་སྣོན་པ་ཁོ་ན་ལས་མ་འདས་སོ། །འདི་ལྟར་དགེ་བ་གཏན་

ལ་མ་ཕབ་ན་རྣམ་པར་གྲོལ་བའི་ལམ་དང་། གནས་སྐབས་བསོད་ནམས་

goes, consider how benefit accrues if it does not exist as some object.

"By examining how and where benefit could accrue to the empty nature of mind itself (*sem-nyid*)—whether outwardly, inwardly, or in between, whether high or low—you will decide that it does not exist as some object. At that point it amounts to nothing more than merit accumulated within samsara.

"Similarly, where are the amassed effects of harmful actions? Where is their storehouse located? Examine the manner in which any harm could be done to the emptiness of mind, outwardly or inwardly, above, below, or in between.

"If you examine minutely the mindstreams of people who continually devote this present life to physical and verbal acts of virtue and those who spend their whole lives engaging in harmful actions, you will find that there is not an iota of difference in the minds of both types of people with respect to the perpetuation of attachment and aversion, hope and fear. If they gain freedom, they gain freedom because their mindstreams are freed. If they are confused, they are confused because their mindstreams are confused. But since the mindstream of neither type of person has been freed, there is not a hair's tip of difference as far as their wandering in samsara. Hence, although there is a short-term distinction between virtuous and harmful actions—they give rise to temporary happiness and suffering, respectively—neither is more than something that prolongs samsara.

"If you have not come to such a definitive conclusion regarding virtuous actions, you will confuse two alternatives—

ༀ༔། བསགས་པའི་དགེ་བ་གཉིས་ནོར་ནས་རྣམ་མ་ཕྱིན་གྱི་འབྲས་བུ་
མི་འཐོབ། སྐྱིག་པ་གཏན་ལ་མ་དབབ་ན་རང་དོ་རང་གིས་མ་རིག་པ་ཉིད་
སྐྱིབ་པ་དང་འབྲལ་བ་ཞེ་ཡིན་པར་མི་ཤེས་ནས་འབྲལ་བའི་རྒྱུ་དོས་མི་ཟིན། དེས་
འཁོར་བ་མཐའ་མེད་དུ་འཁྱམ་པ་ལས་འོས་མེད་པས་གཏན་ལ་དབབ་པ་གནད་
དུ་ཤེས་པར་བྱའོ། །ཡང་ཕན་སྐྱོབས་ཀྱི་ལྷ་ཞེས་བྱ་བ་རྣམས་དང་པོ་བྱུང་ས་
བར་དུ་གནས་ས་ཐ་མ་འགྲོ་ས་གསུམ་ལ་བརྟག་པས་ཡུལ་མེད་པ་དང་། དབང་
པོའི་ཡུལ་དུ་སྣང་བའི་གཟུགས་སྐྱ་དེ་རོ་རིག་བྱ་གང་གི་ཡུལ་དུ་གྲུབ། སྟོང་
བཅུད་ཀྱི་འབྱུང་བའི་ཁམས་ཤིག་ཏུ་ཡོད་པར་སེམས་ན་ཇྭལ་དང་ཇྭལ་ཕྱན་ཆ་མེད་
ཀྱི་ཁོངས་སུ་བརྟག །འབྱུང་བ་རང་རང་གི་མིང་དང་དངོས་པོའི་རྒྱལ་ལ་འང་
བརྟག །ལྷ་དེས་ཕན་རྗེ་ལྷར་བཏགས་པའི་རྒྱལ་དང་། གཟོད་བྱེད་ཀྱི་
འདི་ཡང་དེ་ལྷར་ཞིག་ཏུ་བཏག་པས་ཡུལ་མེད་དུ་ཤེས་པར་འགྱུར་རོ། བདེ་
བ་དང་སྡུག་བསྔལ་ཐམས་ཅད་སེམས་ཀྱི་སྣང་རྣམས་རྟེ་ལས་ལྷ་བུ་ལས་ལྷ་འདྲེས་
ཕན་གཟོད་གདག་གཞིའི་སྟེང་ནས་ཅི་ཡང་མ་བྱུང་ངོ། །འདྲེས་གཟོད་པ་བྱེད་

the path to complete freedom versus the virtue of gathering temporary merit—and so you will not attain the goal of omniscience. If you have not come to a definitive conclusion regarding harmful actions, you will not understand that your very essence not recognizing itself is what constitutes obscuration and the ground of confusion, and so you will fail to identify the cause of confusion. Because this will only perpetuate your confusion endlessly in samsara, you must understand that the crucial point is to reach this definitive conclusion.

"Furthermore, when you examine what are called 'helpful and protective gods' as to their initial source, interim location, and final destination, you will see that they have no existence as sense objects. In which of the forms, sounds, odors, tastes, and tactile sensations—which manifest as objects of the sense faculties—have these gods ever existed? If you think that they exist in conjunction with one of the elements involved in the formation of the universe, examine these elements down to the level of molecules or subatomic particles. Also, examine the respective labels and seeming substantiality of the elements themselves.

"By examining closely how these gods could be of benefit, and similarly how demons could cause harm, you will come to understand that they do not exist as objects. All happiness and suffering are ephemeral experiences of sensory appearances manifesting to the mind like dreams. Nothing whatsoever occurs on any basis that could support the label of 'benefit' or 'harm' due to gods or demons.

"If you think that demons have caused you harm, examine how any harm could be caused by what amounts to the mere

པ་ཡིན་སྐྱམ་ན་གཟུགས་སྐུ་དེ་རོ་རིག་ཕྱིའི་ཡུལ་ལས་འདས་པས་འདི་ཞེས་མིང་
ཚམ་དུ་ཟད་པ་དེས་གཏོང་ཇེ་ལྟར་བྱས་བཏག་པས་ཡུལ་མེད་དུ་སྟོང་པ་ལས་ཡོད་
པར་མ་མཐོང་། མི་རྣམས་འཁྲུལ་པའི་དབང་གིས་རང་ལུས་སྟོང་སྐྱད་ལའང་
བཟང་ངན་དུ་བསླུས་ཏེ་ཁོག་སྟོད་གཅང་མར་སྐྱང་ནས་ལྟ་ལྟར་འཛིན། ཁོག་
སྐྱད་བཙོག་པར་སྐྱང་ནས་འདི་ལྟར་འཛིན་པའི་ཆུལ་གྱིས་རེ་དོགས་རྒྱུན་མི་ཆད་
པར་འབྱུང་བ་དང་། བདག་འཛིན་གྱི་འཆིང་བ་དམ་པོའི་སྟོབས་ཀྱིས་བདེ་
སྡུག་གི་ཉམས་རྒྱུན་མི་ཆད་པར་འབྱུང་བ་ཐམས་ཅད་འཁོར་བའི་སྡུག་རྣམས་ཁོ་
ན་ལས་གཞན་དུ་བདེན་པར་གྲུབ་པ་རྡུལ་ཙམ་མེད་པ་ནི་དཔེ་རྟེ་ལམ་ཁོ་ནས་སྟོན་
ཏོ། །འདིའི་གནད་དོན་ཡིན་ལུགས་ཤེས་པ་ནི་སྟོམ་པའི་གེགས་སེལ་ཡིན་
ཏེ། སྟོམ་པ་ལ་ཡིད་མི་ཆེས་ཤིང་རྒྱོ་མི་གཏོད་པའི་གེགས་ཐམས་ཅད་སེལ་
ནས་ཚོས་ཉིད་ཀྱི་དོན་ལ་ཡིད་ཆེས་ཤིང་བེ་མི་ཚོམ་པའི་གདིང་ཐོབ་པར་འགྱུར་
བ་དང་། མ་རིག་པའི་སྐྱིབ་པ་དང་བྲལ་ནས་རིག་པའི་ཡོ་ལངས་ཆེན་པོར་
དབང་བསྒྱུར་བར་བྱེད་དོ། །ཞི་བྱེད་བདུད་གཅོད་ཟབ་མོའི་རྩ་བའང་ཡིན་ཏེ།
རང་རིག་ལས་ལྷ་གཞན་དུ་མི་འཚོལ། རྣམ་རྟོག་ལས་འདྲེ་གཞན་ན་མེད་
པར་ཐག་ཆོད་པར་འགྱུར་བས། དེ་ནི་སྒྲུབ་པ་དང་གཏོ་ཡས་གཏོང་བ་

label 'demon,' since this label does not qualify as a sense object—a form, sound, odor, taste, or tactile sensation. You will not see anything that is existent, only what is empty and does not exist as an object.

"Human beings, under the influence of confusion, regard the upper and lower parts of their bodies as good and bad, respectively. Since the upper torso seems clean they regard it as they would a god, and since the lower torso seems unclean they regard it as they would a demon. Thus, hope and fear occur without interruption, and owing to the strength of the tight bonds of reifying identity, temporary experiences of happiness and suffering occur without interruption. All of these are nothing but ephemeral experiences of samsara, without ever having truly existed as something else in the slightest. This can be demonstrated by the simple metaphor of a dream.

"The key point here—understanding this mode of being—constitutes the means to dispel hindrances in meditation. All hindrances caused by a lack of conviction or trust in meditation will be dispelled. You will be convinced of the ultimate meaning, which is the true nature of phenomena, and will achieve an indwelling confidence that does not entertain doubt. Free of the obscuring nonrecognition of awareness, you will gain mastery over the great and ever-changing array of awareness.

"This is also the root of the profound approaches of Pacification and Cutting Through Maras. Do not seek any god, only self-knowing awareness. You will reach the decision that there is no demon other than conceptualization (*nam-tog*). In all sadhana practice and rituals undertaken to avert misfor-

༄༅། ཐམས་ཅད་ལའང་འདི་མེད་ཐབས་མེད་པ་ཡིན་ཏེ། དེ་ལྟར་
ཤེས་ན་ཆོས་ཐམས་ཅད་སྒྱུ་མ་ལྟ་བུར་རྟོགས་པའི་སྒྱུ་མའི་རྣལ་འབྱོར་ཆེན་པོར་
ངེས་པའོ། །ཀྱི་སེམས་མེད་རིག་པའི་ཐིག་ལེ་རྐྱང་ཁྱོད་ཀྱིས་འདི་གདུལ་བྱ་རྣམས་
ལ་སྟོན་དང་ངེས་གསང་ཐེག་པ་ཆེན་པོའི་རྣལ་འབྱོར་པ་ཤ་སྒྲུག་འབྱུང་སྲིད་དོ། །
ཞེས་གསུང་ཞིང་མི་སྣང་བར་གྱུར་ཏོ།

tune, this understanding is indispensable. If you have such understanding, you are definitely a great yogin of illusion who realizes all phenomena to be like illusions.

"Ah, little one with awareness, whose mind is no longer ordinary, teach this to those to be tamed and perhaps they, too, will become yogins of the great spiritual approach of the definitive secret."

Saying this, he vanished.

Vajrapani

༄༅། །ཡང་འོད་གསལ་དག་པའི་སྣང་ངོར་དཔལ་ཆེན་ཕྱག་ན་རྡོ་རྗེའི་ཞལ་མཇལ་བའི་ཚེ། བདག་གིས་འདི་སྐད་ཞུས། ཀྱེ་རྒྱལ་བ་རྡོ་རྗེ་འཆང་ཆེན་པོ་སངས་རྒྱས་ཞེས་བྱ་བ་རང་གཏོག་ཏུ་རང་སངས་རྒྱས་པ་ཡིན་ནམ། གཞན་ཞིག་གི་ཡུལ་དུ་འཚང་རྒྱ་བར་འགྲོ་རྒྱུ་ཡིན་ནམ། ཞུས་པས། བཀའ་སྩལ་པ། ཀྱི་ཏོ་སྐྱལ་སྤྲུལ་རིགས་ཀྱི་བུ། སངས་རྒྱས་ཞེས་བྱ་བ་ཡུལ་ཡངས་པ་ཆེན་པོ་ཞིག་ན་མི་རྗེ་གཞུགས་བཟང་བ་མཐོང་ན་མི་མཐུན་པ་མེད་པ་ཞི་བ་བསིལ་བ་དང་ས་པ་སྟོགས་པ་དང་བྱལ་བ་མཛེས་སྡུག་བསླུ་བས་ཚོག་མི་ཤེས་པ་ཞིག་གི་ཆུལ་དུ་ཡོད་པར་སེམས་ན་དེའི་ཕ་མ་གང་ལགས། མ་ལགས་སྐྱེ་ན་སྐྱེ་བའི་མཐའ་འཆེ། གནས་ན་གནས་པ་ཧྲག་པའི་མཐའ་འཆེ། འགག་ན་སྣང་མེད་ཆད་པའི་མཐའ་འཆེ་ཏེ། མདོར་ན་སྐྱེ་འགག་གནས་གསུམ་ཆུགས་ཐུབ་བདེན་གྱུབ་ཀྱི་དོ་བོར་ཡོད་ཕན་ཆད་མཐའ་གཉིས་དང་བྱལ་བའི་གནས་ལུགས་ཞིག་ཡོད་ཐབས་མེད་དེ། རྗེ་ལྟར་སྣང་བ་འདི་དག་སྐྱེ་འགག་ལྟར་སྣང་བ་

O N ANOTHER OCCASION I met the great and glorious Vajrapani in a pure vision (*dag-nang*) of utter lucidity (*od-sal*). On that occasion I asked him, "Ah, victorious one, great vajra holder, does buddhahood imply that awakening to enlightenment occurs right here in my own immediate situation or does it imply that there is some other place to go to become awakened?"

He bestowed the following reply: "Ah, fortunate son of spiritual heritage, you might think that the term 'buddha' implies existence as some majestic person, handsome and attractive to behold, peaceful and soothing, subtle and free of blemish, lovely, beautiful, someone you could never grow tired of looking at, living in some great, spacious country. If so, who are the parents of such buddhas? If they are born of mothers, they are subject to the limitation of origination. If they endure, they are subject to the limitation of permanence. If they cease to exist, they are subject to the limitation of annihilation.

"In brief, as long as there is an essence that truly exists in its own right with respect to the three phases of its origination, duration, and cessation, there cannot be a way of abiding that is free of dualistic extremes. The fact that sensory appearances, however they appear, manifest as though com-

༄༅། །རེ་བཏགས་པ་ཁོ་ནར་ཟད་དོ། །ཡང་དག་པ་རྣམ་གྲུང་གི་ཕྱོགས་
སུ་ཡང་བདེན་པར་བཟུང་ན་རང་གིས་རང་ཉིད་འཆིང་བར་འགྱུར་གྱི། འཁོར་
འདས་ཀྱི་ཆོས་ཉིད་ལ་མི་འདུ་བའི་ཁྱད་པར་ཞིག་ཡོད་ན་སྤྱོད་ཞི་མཉམ་ཉིད་ཀྱི་
གནས་ལུགས་ཟེར་བའང་ཁ་ཚམ་དུ་བས་ཕྱིན། མང་པོ་ཞིག་སྙུང་འདས་རང་
མཚན་པར་ཞེན་ནས་རེ་དོགས་ཀྱི་གཟེབ་ཏུ་འཆུག་མོད། དག་པའི་ཞིང་དུ་
ལོངས་སྤྱོད་རྣམ་པ་གྲངས་མང་ལ། བགོད་པ་རྒྱུ་ཆེ་བའི་ཁྱད་པར་དུ་བྱས་
ནས་དངོས་པོ་རང་མཚན་དུ་འཛིན་ན་དེའང་ཆོས་ཀྱི་བདག་འཛིན་དུ་འདུག་གོ། །དེ་
བཞིན་གཤེགས་པ་སྟེར་སྒྲག་དང་བདེན་གྲུབ་ཏུ་ལྟ་བ་དེ་མིང་རྗེ་ལྤར་བཏགས་གྱུང་
དོན་ལ་གང་ཟག་གི་བདག་ཏུ་ལྤ་བ་ལས་མ་འདས། མངས་རྒྱས་ལ་མིག་
ཡོད་པར་སེམས་ན་མིག་གི་རྣམ་པར་ཤེས་པ་ཡང་ཡོད། མིག་གི་རྣམ་པར་
ཤེས་པ་གྲུབ་ཚམ་ནས་གཟུགས་སུ་སྣང་བ་མི་མཆེད་པའི་ཐབས་མེད་པ་ཡིན།
དེ་དེ་མིག་གི་གཟུང་བ་ཡུལ་ཞེས་བྱ་སྟེ། དེ་ལྤར་གྲུབ་ཕན་ཆད་གཟུགས་ཉེར་
ལེན་གྱི་སེམས་རྟོག་ཕྲ་མོ་ཞིག་མི་འབྱུང་བའི་ཐབས་མེད། དེ་དེ་མིག་གི་
འཛིན་པ་སེམས་ཏེ། གཟུང་འཛིན་གཉིས་སུ་རྟོག་པ་ལ་སེམས་ཞེས་བྱ་
བས་སེམས་གང་ལ་ཡོད་པ་དེ་ལ་སེམས་ཅན་ཞེས་བྱའོ། །དེ་བཞིན་དུ་རྣ་

ing into being and ceasing amounts to nothing more than conceptual labeling.

"Furthermore, if you hold the authentic state of complete enlightenment to be something that truly exists, you will bind yourself. If there were a specific difference between the true nature of samsara and that of nirvana, then the reference to 'the way of abiding as the equalness of conditioned existence and the state of peace' would amount to mere lip service. Indeed, many people fall into the trap of hope and fear in fixating on nirvana as something with an independent existence (*rang-tsan-pa*). There are many descriptions of the experiences enjoyed in pure realms, but if you focus on the specific details of these vast arrays and so conceive of them as something with their own independent existence, you are still conceiving of phenomena as having identity.

"However we label it, the view that a tathagata is something constant that can be found to have true existence does not in fact go beyond the view that personal identity exists. If you think that a buddha has eyes, then there must also be a visual consciousness. Once a visual consciousness is established, the proliferation of sensory appearances as visual forms is inevitable—this context is the 'field for the perception of visual objects' (*mig gi zung-wa yul*). Once such a field is established, the subtle conceptualization of ordinary mind inevitably occurs, which contributes to perpetuating these forms. This is 'ordinary mind that reifies through vision' (*mig gi dzin-pa sem*). This dualistic framework of object and subject (*zung-dzin*) is called 'ordinary mind,' and whoever has ordinary mind is called an 'ordinary being.'

༄༅། །བ་ཡོད་པར་སེམས་ན་དེའི་རྣམ་པར་ཤེས་པ་སྐྱ་དང་བཙས་པ་དང་། སྐུ་ཡོད་པར་སེམས་ན་སྐུའི་རྣམ་པར་ཤེས་པ་རྟེ་དང་བཙས་པ་དང་། ལྷེ་ཡོད་པར་སེམས་ན་ལྷེའི་རྣམ་པར་ཤེས་པ་རོ་དང་བཙས་པ་དང་། ཕྱུས་ཡོད་པར་སེམས་ན་ཕྱུས་ཀྱི་རྣམ་པར་ཤེས་པ་རེག་བྱ་དང་བཙས་པ་ཐམས་ཅད་དེ་རྣམས་ཀྱི་གཟུང་ཡུལ་ཡིན་ཏེ། དེ་དག་ནི་བར་ལེན་པའི་རྟོག་ཚོགས་རྣམས་ནི་དེ་དག་གི་འཛིན་པ་སེམས་ཏེ། སྤྱ་མ་བཞིན་སེམས་གང་ལ་ཡོད་པ་དེ་ལ་སེམས་ཅན་ཞེས་བྱའོ། སངས་རྒྱས་ཞེས་གཟུང་འཛིན་ལས་མ་འདས་པའི་སངས་རྒྱས་ཞིག་ཡོད་པར་སྒྲིད་ན་དེའི་ཡིན་ཏན་སེམས་ཅན་ལ་འཇུག་པ་འང་མི་དང་མི་ལྟ་བུའོ། །སངས་རྒྱས་ཀྱིས་གཞན་ལ་ཚོས་སྟོན་པར་སེམས་ན་སྟོན་པ་པོ་བདག་དང་། བསྟན་བྱའི་ཚོས་དང་། སྟོན་ཡུལ་སེམས་ཅན་དུ་སྐྱང་ཞིང་འཛིན་པ་ཡོད་ན་དེ་ནི་སེམས་ཅན་ལས་ལ་ལ་ཕགས་པའི་ཁྱད་ཚོས་ཅི་ལ་འབྱུ་ཙམ་ཡང་མེད་པས་ཐམས་ཅད་སེམས་ཅན་ནོ། །ཕྱུལ་ཁམས་བདེ་བ། གཟུགས་མཛེས་པ། མཛའ་གྲོགས་ལེགས་པ། ལོངས་སྤྱོད་དང་བདེ་སྐྱིད་ཆེ་བ། ཁྲོ་བ་དང་ཆགས་པ་མེད་པ་རྣམས་ཁྱུད་ཚོས་ཡིན་པར་སེམས་ན་དེ་ཡང་གཟུགས་ཁམས་ཀྱི་ལྷ་ལས་མི་འཕགས་པས་སེམས་ཅན་ནོ། རིས་པའི་དོན་དུ་རང

"In the same way, if you think that a buddha has ears, there must also be an auditory consciousness with its attendant sensations of sounds. If you think that a buddha has a nose, there must also be an olfactory consciousness with its attendant sensations of odors. If you think that a buddha has a tongue, there must also be a gustatory consciousness with its attendant sensations of taste. If you think that a buddha has a body, there must also be a tactile consciousness with its attendant tactile sensations. All of these are fields for the perception of objects (*zung-yul*). The thought patterns that perpetuate them constitute ordinary mind that reifies (*dzin-pa sem*). As before, whoever has ordinary mind is called an 'ordinary being.'

"As for what is called 'buddha,' if it were possible for there to be a state of buddhahood that did not transcend dualistic perceptions of object and subject, then the enlightened qualities of that state could be passed to ordinary beings, just as ordinary qualities are passed from one person to another.

"You might think that buddhas give spiritual teachings to others, but if buddhas conceived of themselves as teachers, the spiritual teachings as something to be taught, and ordinary beings as recipients of the teachings, there would not be even a sesame seed's worth of difference between buddhas and ordinary beings. They would all be ordinary beings. If you think that the unique qualities of a buddha consist in having a blissful environment, physical beauty, excellent companions, great wealth and happiness, or an absence of anger and attachment, you are still describing an ordinary being, no more exalted than gods in the form realm.

"In the definitive sense, the wholly positive ground of your

༄༅། གི་གཞི་ཀུན་ཏུ་བཟང་པོའི་དུས་གསུམ་གྱི་བདེ་བར་གཤེགས་པ་
ཞེས་བྱ་བ་ཡིན་ནོ། །དོན་དམ་པར་སངས་རྒྱས་འཇིག་རྟེན་དུ་བྱོན་མ་མྱོང་
བ་དང༌། ཆོས་སྟོན་མ་མྱོང་བ་ནི་རྒྱུད་ལུང་མན་ངག་མང་པོར་གདུལ་བྱ་རང་
སྣང་གི་སྟོན་པ་རང་ལ་འཁར་བ་ཡིན་པའི་ཚུལ་གསལ་བར་གསུངས་པ་ལ་ལྟོས་
ཤིག །རྟོགས་ཤིག །ཡང་འཁོར་བའི་གནས་རིགས་གཞན་ཡོད་ཅིང་
གྲུབ་སྟེ་སེམས་ཅན་མང་པོ་ཡུལ་དེ་རུ་སོང་ཞིང་ཁ་བརྒྱུད་ནས་བདེ་སྡུག་མྱོང་བར་
སེམས་ན་དེ་ཡང་མི་རིགས་ཏེ། སྐྱ་མའི་ལུས་རྟེན་ཕུལ་དུ་བོར་བར་སྣང་བ་
བདེན་ན་བར་སྒྲིབ་ཀྱི་ལུས་དེ་གང་ནས་ལོན། དེང་སང་གི་སེམས་ཅན་རྣམས་
ལ་སྐྱ་དང་ཀྲང་ལག་ཆིག་པ་ཚམ་དང༌། དགུན་ཉེན་ཞག་རི་ཚམ་གྱི་གྲང་ལྔག་
གིས་འཆི་བར་འགྱུར་ན། དམྱལ་བ་ཚ་གྲང་སྨྱོང་བྱེད་ཀྱི་ལུས་གྲུབ་ནས་
བཙོ་བསྲེག་སོགས་ཡུན་རིང་བྱས་ཀྱང་མི་འཆི་བ་དེ་ཅིའི་ཕྱིར་ཡིན། དེ་
བཞིན་དུ་དེང་སང་རླུ་ཕས་ལྷག་ཕས་ཚམ་དུ་སྨུ་གི་བྱུང་བས་འཆི་སྲིད་ན། ཡི་
དྭགས་ཀྱི་སེམས་ཅན་བསྐལ་པར་སྨུ་གིས་ཚིམ་མི་འཚེ། དེས་ན་འགྲོ་བ་རིགས་
དྲུག་གི་སེམས་ཅན་བར་སྲིད་དང་བཅས་པ་ཐམས་ཅད་རྫི་ལམ་གྱི་སྣང་བ་མཆེད་
པ་ལྟ་བུར་སྣང་ཚམ་ལས་མ་གྲུབ་ཅིང་སྟོང་པ་ཡུལ་མེད་པ་ལ་བདེན་ཞེན་སྐྱེས་

own being—Kuntuzangpo—is what is meant by the phrase 'the one who has gone to bliss throughout the three times.' On the ultimate level, a buddha does not experience either coming into the world or giving spiritual teachings. Many tantras, explanatory commentaries, and pith instructions clearly set forth the way in which the manifestation of a teacher arises naturally in the perceptions of those to be tamed. Examine these and realize this point.

"Furthermore, it is illogical to think that other, separate states of being exist or have ever existed within samsara and that many beings go to those places in succession and experience pleasure or pain. If manifestation of the body—the mind's working basis in the preceding life that was discarded as residue—were the true experience, then where did one get a body in the bardo? If beings in their present circumstances can die merely from wounds or burns on their arms or legs, or merely from the cold wind on a single winter's day, how is it that once a body capable of experiencing the heat and cold of hell is formed, it does not die even though boiled or burned for a long time? Similarly, if beings in their present circumstances can die when famine occurs for a few months or even a few days, why do pretas not die from the starvation they experience for eons?

"Given this, all beings of the six classes, as well as those in the bardo, are confused because they become fixated, investing sensory appearances with truth even though they are in fact like the unfolding of dream images—never having existed as anything more than mere appearances, empty and not existent as objects.

"If you thus come to a definitive conclusion regarding the

༄༅། །པས་འཁྲུལ་པ་ཡིན། དེ་ལྟར་འཁྲུལ་སྣང་གཏན་ལ་ཕབ་ནས་

བདེན་མེད་སྟོང་པ་ཡུལ་མེད་དུ་རྟོགས་ན་འཁོར་བ་དོང་ནས་སྟུགས་པ་ཡིན།

སངས་རྒྱས་རང་གཞི་ལས་མེད་པར་ཐག་ཆོད་དེ་རང་ལ་རང་གདོང་ཐོབ་པར་བྱས་

ན་སངས་རྒྱས་དུ་མ་རང་གྲོལ་ཞེས་བྱ་བའི་མེང་དོན་གྱིས་ཐོབ་པ་ཡིན་ནོ། །གྱི

ནས་མཁའི་དབང་ཕྱུག་ཀུན་ཁྱབ་རྡོ་རྗེ་ཁྱོད་ཀྱིས་འཁོར་འདས་ཀྱི་ཆོས་ཐམས་ཅད་

ཅང་མེད་སྟོང་པ་རུ་གཏན་ལ་ཕབ་ནས་མེད་པའི་རང་བཞིན་རྟོགས་པར་གྱིས་ཤིག

ཅེས་གསུང་ཞིང་མི་སྣང་བར་གྱུར་ཏོ།

sensory appearances that arise from confusion, realizing that they lack true existence, are empty, and do not exist as objects, you will have dredged the pit of samsara from its depths. By arriving at the decision that buddhahood is none other than your own natural ground of being, and by gaining confidence within yourself, you will actually attain what is referred to as the 'natural freedom of myriad buddhas.'

"Ah, powerful lord of space, omnipresent vajra, you must come to the definitive conclusion that none of the phenomena of samsara and nirvana exist, but are all empty, and realize their nature to be that of ineffability (*med-pa*)."

Saying this, he vanished.

Dorje Drolod

༄༅། །དེ་ལྟར་བདག་གིས་ཡུན་རིང་པོར་གཏན་ལ་ཕབས་ནས་མེད་པར་ཐག་ཆོད་པ་བྱུང་ཞིང་སྲིད་བཅུད་ཀྱི་སྲུང་བ་ཐམས་ཅད་རང་དོས་ནས་སྲུང་པར་ཞིན་ཀྱང་སྲིང་པ་གྲངས་མང་བ་ལུང་མ་བསྟན་དུ་ཡོད་པའི་སྐབས་ཤིག་ན། ཚེ་མཆོག་རྡོ་རྗེ་གྲོ་ལོད་འཁོར་འདས་སྲིད་ཉིད་ཀྱི་རོལ་པར་སྟོན་པའི་ཧཱུྃ་བླ་གྱེར་བཞིག་གི་ཞལ་མཇལ་བའི་ཚེ་བདག་གིས། ཀྱི་སྤྲག་པའི་སྤྲ་མཆོག་ཆེན་པོ་ལགས། ངས་འཁོར་འདས་སྲིད་ཉིད་དུ་གོ་ཡང་སྟོང་པ་ཐར་མེད་གནོད་མེད་དུ་འདུག་པ་འདི་ཅིས་ལན་པ་ཡིན། ཅེས་ཞུས་པས། ཀྱི་སྨྲས་བུ་ནམ་མཁའི་དབང་པོ་ཁྲོད་ཀྱིས་འཁོར་འདས་ཐམས་ཅད་སྟོང་པ་ཉིད་དུ་འཁགས་སྟོམས་ཤིག །སྟོང་པ་ཉིད་དོ་བོ་ཉིད་དུ་འཁགས་བསྒྲམ་པར་གྱིས་ཤིག །དོ་བོ་ཉིད་གཞི་རུ་འཁགས་བསྒྲམ་པར་གྱིས་ཤིག །འཁོར་འདས་གཞིའི་རོལ་པར་འཁགས་སྟོམས་ཤིག །འཁོར་འདས་ཀྱི་སྤྲི་ཆེངས་གཞི་ཉིད་དུ་འཁགས་བསྒྲམ་པར་གྱིས་ཤིག །རྒྱ་མཚོའི་གཟབ་སྣར་རྒྱ་མཚོ། སྟོད་བཅུད་ནས

I N THIS WAY, after a long time I reached a definitive conclusion and came to a decisive experience concerning ineffability. However, although I understood that all sensory
appearances of the universe are empty in their own right,
there were still many implications of emptiness that seemed of
neutral consequence. At a certain point, I met in a vision the
supreme and sublime Dorje Drolod, chanting the song of
Hung that reveals samsara and nirvana to be the display of
emptiness.

On that occasion I said, "Ah, my special deity (*lha*), excellent and supreme. Although I intellectually comprehend that
samsara and nirvana are emptiness, this emptiness remains
neither beneficial nor harmful. What is the flaw in this?"

The deity replied, "Ah, spiritual one, lord of space, discern
the implication of all samsara and nirvana to be emptiness
(*tong-pa-nyid*). Discern emptiness to be the essence itself
(*ngo-wo-nyid*). Discern this same essence to be the ground of
being (*zhi*). Discern samsara and nirvana to be the display
(*rol-pa*) of that ground. Discern the common context of samsara and nirvana to be that very ground (*zhi-nyid*).

"The reflections of stars and planets in the ocean are the
display of the ocean. Space is the matrix of the universe. The

༄༅། མཁའ། འགྲོར་འདས་ཆོས་ཉིད་རྣམས་ཀྱི་རོལ་པ་དང་། ཆིངས་པ་དང་། ཆོས་ཉིད་ཁྱབ་ཆིང་བཙལ་བ་དག་དཔེ་དང་དཔེ་ཅན་ཡིན་ པའི་དང་ཚུལ་ཤེས་པར་གྱིས་ཤིག །དེས་འཁོར་འདས་ཐུབ་རྒྱུབ་ཀྱི་རྣལ་འབྱོར་ པར་འགྱུར་རོ། །ཞེས་གསུངས་ཤིང་མི་སླང་བར་གྱུར་ཏོ།

true nature of phenomena permeates and extends throughout samsara and nirvana. Understand the nature of these metaphors and what they exemplify. Thus, you will become a yogin who embraces the whole of samsara and nirvana."

With these words, he vanished.

Vajradhara

༄༅། །དེ་ནས་ཡང་ལོ་ཁྲིམ་བདུན་གྱི་རྗེས་སུ་རྐྱེ་ལམ་དག་པའི་སྤྱང་
ཏོར་ཆོས་སྐུའི་སྟོན་པ་རྡོ་རྗེ་འཆང་གི་ཞལ་མཐའ་བའི་ཚོ་བདག་གིས། གྱི་
སྟོན་པ་བཙོམ་ལྡན་འདས་ཐར་པ་དང་རྣམ་མཁྱེན་གྱི་ལམ་དུ་རྗེ་ལྟར་གྲོལ་བ་
དང་། མ་དག་པ་འཁོར་བའི་ལམ་དུ་རྗེ་ལྟར་འཁྲུལ་པ་ཡིན། སྟོན་པ་
ཉིད་ཀྱིས་བསྟན་དུ་གསོལ། ཅེས་ཞུས་པས་བཀའ་སྩལ་པ། གྱི་སྨྲེས་
བུ་ཆེན་པོ་ཁྱོད་ཉོན་ཅིག །སངས་རྒྱས་དང་སེམས་ཅན་གཉིས་ཀ་རིག་དང་
མ་རིག་གཉིས་ཀྱི་ཁྱད་པར་ལས་བྱུང་བ་ཡིན་ཏེ། གཞི་གདོད་མའི་མགོན་
པོ་ཀུན་ཏུ་བཟང་པོ་ཉིད་ནི་སྐུ་བཞི་ཡེ་ཤེས་ལྔའི་བདག་ཉིད་ཅན་ནོ། །ངོ་བོ་
སྟོང་པ་ཆོས་སྐུ། རང་བཞིན་གསལ་བ་ལོངས་སྐུ། ཐུགས་རྗེ་རང་གྲོལ་
བ་སྤྲུལ་སྐུ། འཁོར་འདས་ཀུན་ལ་ཁྱབ་ཅིང་བརྡལ་བ་ངོ་བོ་ཉིད་སྐུའོ། ཆོས་
ཐམས་ཅད་པོ་འབྱེད་པས་ཆོས་དབྱིངས། དངས་གསལ་རྟོག་མ་དང་བྲལ་
བས་མེ་ལོང་། འཁོར་འདས་དག་མཉམ་གྱི་རོལ་པ་མཉམ་ཉིད། མཐྱེན

S EVEN YEARS LATER, while having a pure vision in a dream, I met the dharmakaya teacher Vajradhara. On that occasion I asked, "Ah, teacher, transcendent and accomplished conqueror, how am I freed on the path of liberation and omniscience, and how am I confused on the path of samsara? Teacher, reveal this to me, I pray."

Upon my having made this request, he bestowed the following reply: "Ah, listen to me, great spiritual being. The two states—that of a buddha and that of an ordinary being—come about depending on whether there is recognition of awareness or not.

"The ground of being itself, the primordial guide Kuntuzangpo, is the epitome of the four kayas and the five aspects of timeless awareness (*ye-shey nga*). Its essence as emptiness is dharmakaya. Its nature as lucidity is sambhogakaya. Its responsiveness as natural freedom is nirmanakaya. Its pervasiveness (*khyab-pa*) and extension (*dal-wa*) throughout all samsara and nirvana are svabhavikakaya.

"As there is the limitless potential for all phenomena, there is the basic space of phenomena (*chhö-ying*). As there is pristine lucidity, free of sullying factors, there is a mirrorlike quality (*me-long*). As samsara and nirvana are the display of

89

༄༅། གཟིགས་ཨེ་ཤེས་ཀྱི་གོ་མ་འགགས་པས་སོར་རྟོག ཤ།དག
གྲོལ་གྱིས་བུ་བ་གྲུབ་པས་བུ་གྲུབ་བོ། དེ་ལྟར་རང་བྱུང་གི་སངས་རྒྱས་སུ་
གྲོལ་བའི་ལམ་རིག་པ་ཡང་སྐུ་བཞི་ཨེ་ཤེས་ལྔའི་བདག་ཉིད་ཅན་མངོན་དུ་བྱེད་
པ་སྟེ། རིག་པའི་ངོ་བོ་ཁྱབ་གདལ་རྣམ་མཁའི་ཁོར་ཡུག་ཡུལ་མེད་ཟང་ཐལ་
ཆེན་པོ་གཞི་མེད་རྩ་བྲལ་གྱི་རོལ་པ་དེ་ཉིད་སྤྲོས་པ་དང་བྲལ་བས་ཆོས་སྐུ། རང་
བཞིན་རང་གསལ་གྱི་ཆ་ནས་ལོངས་སྐུ། ཨེ་ཤེས་ཀྱི་གསལ་སྒོ་མ་འགག
པའི་ཆ་ནས་སྤྲུལ་སྐུ། འཁོར་འདས་ཀྱི་སྤྱི་གཞིར་གྱུར་པའི་ཆ་ནས་ངོ་བོ་ཉིད་
སྐུའོ། །གཞི་གཅན་ལ་ཐབ་ནས་འཁོར་འདས་ཆོས་ཉིད་ཀྱི་དབྱིངས་སུ་རོ་
གཅིག་པའི་དང་ཆུལ་རྟོགས་པ་ཆོས་དབྱིངས་ཨེ་ཤེས། སྟོང་པ་བེམ་སྟོང་
དུ་མ་སོང་བར་དྲངས་གསལ་རྟོག་མ་དང་བྲལ་ཞིང་ཅིར་ཡང་འཆར་དུ་རུང་བ་མེ་
ལོང་གཡའ་བྲལ་ལྟ་བུ་ལ་མེ་ལོང་ཨེ་ཤེས། འཁོར་འདས་སྟོང་ཉིད་ཆེན་པོར་
དག་མཉམ་དུ་ཡོད་པའི་དང་ཆུལ་ཤེས་པ་མཉམ་ཉིད་ཨེ་ཤེས། རིག་རྩལ་

equalness and purity, there is equalness (*nyam-nyid*). As there is the unimpeded avenue of omniscient timeless awareness, there is discernment (*sor-tog*). As all that is to be done is already ensured through freedom and purity, there is spontaneous fulfillment (*ja-drub*).

"In this way, the path of freedom within naturally occurring (*rang-jung*) buddhahood makes evident awareness—the epitome of the four kayas and five aspects of timeless awareness. The essence of awareness is pervasive and extensive, the panorama of space, not existent as any object, and supremely unobstructed. Given that its display, without underlying basis or foundation, is free of conceptual elaboration, it is dharmakaya. From the perspective of the nature of awareness being inherently lucid, it is sambhogakaya. From the perspective of awareness being an unimpeded avenue for the lucidity of timeless awareness, it is nirmanakaya. And from the perspective of awareness being the common ground of samsara and nirvana, it is svabhavikakaya.

"Once a definitive conclusion has been reached regarding the ground of being, there is realization of the context in which samsara and nirvana are of one taste in the basic space of the true nature of phenomena—this is timeless awareness as the basic space of phenomena (*chhö-ying ye-shey*). Emptiness is not an inert void but is pristinely lucid and free of sullying factors, like a polished mirror in which anything at all can arise—this is mirrorlike timeless awareness (*me-long ye-shey*). Knowing the way in which samsara and nirvana are equal and pure in supreme emptiness is timeless awareness as equalness (*nyam-nyid ye-shey*). The dynamic energy of aware-

༄༅། སོ་སོར་རྟོག་པའི་ཡེ་ཤེས་ཀྱི་གསལ་སྟོ་མ་འགགས་པ་སོར་རྟོག་ཡེ་
ཤེས། རིག་པ་ལ་རང་དབང་བསྒྱུར་བས་དག་གྲོལ་གཉིས་ལྡན་གྱི་བུ་རང་
གྲུབ་པས་བྱ་གྲུབ་ཡེ་ཤེས་སོ། །འདིའི་ཡིན་ལུགས་རྗེ་ལྭ་བ་བཞིན་དུ་མི་ཤེས་
ཤིང་སེམས་རིག་གི་དབྱེ་བ་མ་ཕྱེད་པའི་ཤེས་པ་བཟོ་མེད་ལམ་དུ་བྱེད་པ་མང་
ཡང་། དེ་རྣམས་ནི་ཕྱི་སྣང་བ་ལ་ལུང་མ་བསྟན་དངོས་པོ་མཚན་མ་ཅན་དུ་
བཟུང་། ནང་རང་ལུས་ལ་ལུང་མ་བསྟན་ཏག་པ་དངོས་འཛིན་གྱི་འཆིང་
བས་དམ་དུ་འབྱུང་། དེ་གཉིས་ཀྱི་བར་ལྭ་བུར་ཤེས་པ་གསལ་རིག་གོ་མ་འགག་
པ་ཅམ་ལ་བརྟན་པ་ཐོབ་ཀྱང་ཁམས་གོང་མ་གཉིས་སུ་འཕེན་བྱེད་ཀྱི་དགེ་བར་
འགྱུར་སྲིད་པ་ཅམ་ལས་ཐར་པ་དང་རྣམ་མཁྱེན་གྱི་གོ་འཕང་མི་འཐོབ་པས་སྨོན་
དང་བཅས་པ་ཡིན། འཁོར་འདས་ཀྱིས་བསྡུས་པའི་ཆོས་ཐམས་ཅད་ཆོས་
ཉིད་དེ་བཞིན་ཉིད་ཀྱི་དང་དུ་རོ་གཅིག་པའི་དང་ཚུལ་རྗེ་ལྭ་བ་བཞིན་དུ་ཤེས་པ་ལ་
རྗེ་ལྭ་བ་ཤེས་པའི་ཤེས་རབ། རིག་པའི་རོ་བོ་དེའི་དང་དུ་གནས་ཀྱང་ཀུན་
ཤེས་ཀུན་རིག་གི་ཤེས་པ་གོ་མ་འགགག་པར་རང་བྱུང་བ་ནི་རྗེ་སྟེད་པ་ཤེས་པའི་

ness, as the unimpeded avenue for the lucid expression of time-less awareness that understands each thing individually, is discerning timeless awareness (*sor-tog ye-shey*). Since the accomplishment of activities is naturally ensured in a state of purity and freedom through mastery of awareness, there is timeless awareness of spontaneous fulfillment (*ja-drub ye-shey*).

"Many do not understand this mode of being just as it is, and instead make their path a passive state of consciousness that does not differentiate between ordinary mind (*sem*) and awareness (*rig-pa*). Outwardly they perceive sensory appearances to have characteristics of substance (*ngö-po*) and karmic neutrality (*lung-ma-tan*). Inwardly they are rigidly bound by the concept that their bodies have substance and are karmically neutral and permanent. They may achieve a stable experience between these two poles, as it were, which is merely a state of unceasing consciousness, lucid and aware. There is the slight possibility that this will create virtue which propels them to the two higher realms. However, they will not attain a state of liberation and omniscience. This is, therefore, a flawed approach.

"The term 'sublime knowing that knows the nature of things just as it is' refers to knowing the fundamental nature just as it is—knowing that all phenomena subsumed within samsara and nirvana are of one taste within the context of suchness (*de-zhin nyid*), the true nature of phenomena. The term 'sublime knowing that knows things in their variety' refers to the fact that although one abides within the context of the essence of awareness, the unimpeded avenue of all-knowing, all-cognizing awareness occurs naturally. Although this avenue is

༄༅། །ཤེས་རབ་སྟེ། དེ་ལྟར་གོ་མ་འགགས་ཀྱང་ཡུལ་ལ་མི་འཇུག་
པ་ནི་དཔེར་ན་དངུལ་ཆུའི་ཐིག་པ་ས་ལ་ལྷུང་བ་ལྟ་བུའོ། །སེམས་ནི་འཁོར་
འདས་རང་རྐྱང་པར་བལུ་ཞིང་སྣང་བ་ལ་དངོས་པོར་འཛིན་པ་གཉིའི་གནས་ལུགས་
མ་རིག་པའོ། །དེ་ལས་སེམས་བྱུང་གི་རྟོག་པ་སྐྱེ་འགགག་ཅན་ཡུལ་དང་འཛིན་
པར་བྱུང་བ་ནི་ས་སྐྱ་དུ་ཆུ་ཐིག་བབས་པ་ལྟ་བུའོ། །གཞི་ལ་རང་དབང་
བསྒྱུར་བ་དགའ་པ་གཞིའི་སངས་རྒྱས་ཀྱི་རང་ཞལ་མ་རིག་པས་བསྒྲིབ་པ་ལས་གཞིའི་
དང་མདངས་ཀྱི་སྐྱ་དང་ཡེ་ཤེས་ཐམས་ཅད་རང་མདངས་སུ་རྣབ་སྟེ་ཕྱི་གདངས་
ཕྱི་རུ་འཁོས་ཏེ་འོད་ལྔའི་རྣམ་པས་འབྱུང་ལྔའི་རོལ་པར་མཆེད་པའི་ཆུལ་ནི། ཆོས་
དབྱིངས་ཡེ་ཤེས་མ་རིག་པས་བསྒྲིབ་པས་ཕྱི་གདངས་འོད་མཐིང་དུ་སྣང་བ་ནང་
འབྱུང་དང་ནམ་མཁའི་དངས་མ་འབྱུང་ཆེན་ཞེས་བྱ་བ་ཡིན། འོད་ལ་བདེན་
འཛིན་དངོས་ཞེན་སྐྱེས་པས་ནམ་མཁར་སྲང་སྟེ་དེ་ལ་ཕྱི་འབྱུང་དང་འབྱུང་ཕྲན་
སྐྱིགས་མའི་སྲང་བ་ཞེས་བྱུའོ། །མེ་ལོང་ཡེ་ཤེས་མ་རིག་པས་བསྒྲིབ་སྟེ་ནང་
མདངས་སུ་རྣབ་པས་ཕྱི་གདངས་འོད་དཀར་པོའི་ཁ་དོག་ཏུ་སྲང་བ་ཆུའི་དངས་
མ་དང་འབྱུང་ཆེན་ནང་འབྱུང་། དེ་ལ་དངོས་འཛིན་བདེན་ཞེན་སྐྱེས་པས་ཆུ

unimpeded, it does not become caught up with sense objects. This is likened to a drop of quicksilver falling on the ground.

"Ordinary mind views samsara and nirvana as existing in their own right (*rang-gyud*) and perceives sensory appearances as having substance. This constitutes nonrecognition of the way in which the ground of being abides. From this, mental events originate and cease, being caught up with sense objects. This is likened to a drop of water falling onto dry earth.

"When the true face of the ground aspect of buddhahood—a state of purity and mastery of the ground of being—is obscured by the nonrecognition of awareness (*ma-rig-pa*), the kayas and timeless awareness—the innate glow of the ground of being—subside into an inner glow whose radiance (*dang*) is directed outwardly, unfolding as the display of the five elements through light of five colors. This takes place in the following way.

"When timeless awareness as the basic space of phenomena is obscured by the nonrecognition of awareness, the outwardly directed radiance manifests as dark blue light. This is termed the 'inner element,' 'major element,' or 'subtle essence of space.' When this radiance is fixated on as having substance and conceived of as truly existing, it manifests as space. This is termed the 'outer element,' 'minor element,' or 'manifestation that constitutes the dregs.'

"When mirrorlike timeless awareness is obscured by the nonrecognition of awareness, it subsides into an inner glow whose outwardly directed radiance manifests as white light. This is the subtle essence of water, or the major or inner element. When this radiance is conceived of as having substance

༄༅། རུ་སྡུང་བ་སྟེགས་མ་དང་འབྱུང་ཕུན་ཕྱི་འབྱུང་། མཚམས་ཉིད་
ཨེ་ཤེས་མ་རིག་པས་བསྒྲིབ་སྟེ་ནང་མདངས་སུ་རུབ་པས་ཕྱི་གདངས་འོད་སེར་
པོའི་ཁ་དོག་ཏུ་སྡུང་བ་པའི་དྭངས་མ་དང་རང་འབྱུང་འབྱུང་ཆེན། དེ་ལ་དངོས་
འཛིན་བདེན་ཞེན་སྐྱེས་པས་ས་རུ་སྡུང་བ་སྟེགས་མ་འབྱུང་ཕུན་ཕྱི་འབྱུང་། སོར་
རྟོག་ཡེ་ཤེས་མ་རིག་པས་བསྒྲིབ་སྟེ་ནང་མདངས་སུ་རུབ་པས་ཕྱི་གདངས་འོད་
དམར་པོའི་ཁ་དོག་ཏུ་སྡུང་བ་མེའི་དྭངས་མ་དང་རང་འབྱུང་འབྱུང་ཆེན། དེ་
ལ་དངོས་འཛིན་བདེན་ཞེན་སྐྱེས་པས་མེ་རུ་སྡུང་བ་སྟེགས་མ་འབྱུང་ཕུན་ཕྱི་
འབྱུང་། བྱ་གྲུབ་ཡེ་ཤེས་མ་རིག་པས་བསྒྲིབ་སྟེ་ནང་མདངས་སུ་རུབ་པས་
ཕྱི་གདངས་འོད་ལྗང་གུའི་ཁ་དོག་ཏུ་སྡུང་བ་རླུང་གི་དྭངས་མ་དང་རང་འབྱུང་འབྱུང་
ཆེན། དེ་ལ་དངོས་འཛིན་བདེན་ཞེན་སྐྱེས་པས་རླུང་དུ་སྡུང་བ་སྟེགས་མ་འབྱུང་
ཕུན་ཕྱི་འབྱུང་ཞེས་བྱོ། །འོད་གདངས་དེ་དག་རང་ན་གནས་པའི་རྐྱེན་ལས་
ཁ་དོག་སྣ་ཚོགས་དང་འབྱུང་བ་ལྔའི་སྣང་བ་རྒྱུན་མི་ཆད་པར་སྡུང་བ་ཡིན་ནོ།།
འབྲུལ་པའི་གཞི་ལྔ་དེ་དག་གི་རྩ་ལ་དུ་ཕར་བ་ནི་འདི་ལྟ་སྟེ། གཞི་མ་རིག་པས་

and is fixated on as truly existing, it manifests as water. This is the dregs, or the minor or outer element.

"When timeless awareness as equalness is obscured by the nonrecognition of awareness, it subsides into an inner glow whose outwardly directed radiance manifests as yellow light. This is the subtle essence of earth, or the inner or major element. When this radiance is conceived of as having substance and is fixated on as truly existing, it manifests as earth. This is the dregs, or the minor or outer element.

"When discerning timeless awareness is obscured by the nonrecognition of awareness, it subsides into an inner glow whose outwardly directed radiance manifests as red light. This is the subtle essence of fire, or the inner or major element. When this radiance is conceived of as having substance and is fixated on as truly existing, it manifests as fire. This is the dregs, or the minor or outer element.

"When timeless awareness as spontaneous fulfillment is obscured by the nonrecognition of awareness, it subsides into an inner glow whose outwardly directed radiance manifests as green light. This is the subtle essence of air, or the inner or major element. When this radiance is conceived of as having substance and is fixated on as truly existing, it manifests as air. This is the dregs, or the minor or outer element.

"The fact that these luminous radiances are indwelling ensures that sensory appearances of various colors and the five elements manifest uninterruptedly.

"The following is a discussion of what arises as the dynamic energy of this fivefold basis of confusion. The obscuring of the ground of being by the nonrecognition of awareness

༄༅། །བསྐྱབ་པ་ལས་ཀུན་གཞི་མཚན་ཉིད་པ་ཝེམ་སྟོང་རྣམ་མཁའ་ལྟ་
བུ་ཅི་ཡང་མི་སེམས་ཤིང་མི་སྐྱང་བ་སྟེ། དཔེར་ན་གཉིད་འཐུག་པོ་དང་བརྒྱལ་
བའི་གནས་སྐབས་ལྟ་བུའོ། །དེའི་དང་དུ་འབྱམས་ཀྱས་པ་ནི་གཏི་མུག་གི་
རོ་བོ་སྟེ་མ་རིག་པའི་ཡོ་ལངས་ཆེན་པོའོ། །དེ་ལས་བསྐལ་པ་ལས་ཀྱི་རླུང་
འགུལ་བ་ནི་ཕྱག་དོག་གི་རོ་བོ་ཡིན། །དེའི་བྱེད་ལས་ཀྱིས་སྟོང་པ་ལས་གསལ་བ
ཆ་ཐོན་པ་ཀུན་གཞིའི་རྣམ་ཤེས་ཏེ་ཞེ་སྡང་གི་རོ་བོར་གནས་པ་ཡིན། །དེ་ལས་
བདག་སྲུང་ཚམ་ལ་ངར་འཛིན་སྐྱེས་པ་ཉོན་ཡིད་དེ་ང་རྒྱལ་གྱི་རོ་བོར་གནས། །དེ་
ལས་ཡིད་ལངས་ཏེ་གཉི་ཝེམ་སྟོང་ལ་སྐྱང་བ་མཆེད་དྲང་གི་ཉུས་པ་བཞག་ཅིང་
གསལ་ཆ་བཏོན་པ་འདོད་ཆགས་ཀྱི་རོ་བོར་གནས་པ་ཡིན། །དེ་དག་ཐམས་
ཅད་ནང་མདངས་ལས་རོ་བོ་ལྔ་ཕྱི་རྣལ་དུ་ཕྱར་བ་ཡིན། དུག་ལྔའི་རོ་བོ་མི་
ལྟ་བུ་ལས་ཉོན་མོངས་པའི་རྟོག་ཚོགས་མི་སྲུག་མཆེད་པ་ལྟ་བུའོ། །དེ་ལྟར་
ཀུན་གཞི་དང་ཡིད་མཉམ་པར་བཏལ་བའི་སྟོང་གསལ་གྱི་ཆ་ལ་སྐྱང་བ་མཆེད་
པའི་ཡུལ་གོ་མ་འགགག་པར་ཡོད་པ་ལས། ལས་རླུང་གཡོ་བའི་རྐྱེན་དང

is indisputably the ground of all ordinary experience (*kun-zhi*), an inert void, like empty space, in which no thought at all takes place and no sensory appearances manifest. It is like deep sleep or a loss of consciousness. To be thoroughly absorbed in this state is the essence of ignorance—the great shifting array of the nonrecognition of awareness. From this state, one's own share of the subtle energy of karma (*lay kyi lung*) is aroused, being the essence of envy. Its functioning causes an aspect of lucidity—consciousness stirring from the ground of all ordinary experience (*kun-zhii nam-shey*)—to be elicited from emptiness; this constitutes abiding in the essence of aversion. From this comes emotionally afflicted consciousness (*nyon-yid*), the onset of the concept of an 'I' where there is merely the appearance of a self; this constitutes abiding in the essence of pride. From this arises conceptual mind (*yid*), which constitutes the potential for sensory appearances to proliferate within the ground of this inert void. An aspect of lucidity is thus elicited, which constitutes abiding in the essence of desire and attachment. All of these five essences arise as outward dynamic energy from the inner glow. These essences of the five emotional poisons are like a fire from which emotionally afflicted thought patterns fly like sparks.

"Furthermore, this voidness with a lucid aspect—the congruence of the ground of all ordinary experience and conceptual mind—provides a field for objectification, which is an unimpeded avenue for the proliferation of sensory appearances. With the synchronicity of the two factors of cause and condition—where the cause is the ground of being, endowed with the potential for things to arise, and the condition is the

༄༅། །རྒྱ་གཞི་འཆར་རྡུང་གི་རྣམ་པ་ཅན་གཉིས་ཀ་རྒྱུ་ཀྱེན་དུས་འཛོམ་
པ་ལས་གཞི་ལ་བརྟེན་ཅིང་གཞི་རང་ལས་མི་གཞན་པར་འབྱེལ་བའི་ཆུལ་གྱིས་
གཟུགས་སུ་སྣང་བ་སྤྲུ་ཚོགས་མཆེད་པ་སྟེ། གཟུགས་སྣང་མཆེད་པའི་ཡུལ་
གང་ཡིན་པ་དེ་ལ་མིག་གི་རྣམ་པར་ཤེས་པ་ཞེས་ཐ་སྙད་ཚམ་དུ་བཏོད་པའོ། །དེས་
ན་སྣང་ཡུལ་རྒྱུ་མཚོ་ལྟ་བུ་ཡུལ་དང་། གཟུགས་སྣང་གཟན་སྣར་ལྷ་བུ་ལ་
གཟུང་བ་ཞེས་བྱའོ། དེ་ལས་འཛིན་པ་ཡིད་ཀྱི་རྣམ་ཤེས་སུ་མོས་གཟུགས་
དེ་ལ་མིང་བཏགས་དོན་བཟུང་དངོས་པོར་བལྟས་ཏེ་བདེ་སྡུག་བར་མ་གསུམ་དེ
བར་ཨེན་པའི་རྣམ་པར་རྟོག་པ་འར་བ་དེ་མིག་གི་འཛིན་པ་སེམས་ཞེས་བྱའོ། །དེ
བཞིན་དུ་སྒྲ་མཆེད་པའི་ཡུལ་གོ་མ་འགག་པ་ལ་ཡུལ་དང་། སྒྲ་དུ་སྣང་
བ་མཆེད་པ་ལ་གཟུང་བ་དང་། ཉེར་ཨེན་ཡིད་ཤེས་ལ་འཛིན་པ་སེམས་ཞེས་
བྱ་སྟེ། གོང་ལྟར་རྒྱུ་ཀྱེན་ཚོགས་པའི་རྟེན་འབྱེལ་ལོ། །དེ་བཞིན་དུ་དེ
དུ་སྣང་བ་མཆེད་པ་ལ་སྣའི་རྣམ་པར་ཤེས་པ་དང་། རོ་དུ་སྣང་བ་མཆེད་པ་
ལ་ལྩེའི་རྣམ་པར་ཤེས་པ་དང་། རེག་བྱའི་སྣང་བ་མཆེད་པ་ལ་ལུས་ཀྱི་རྣམ

stirring of the subtle energy of karma—myriad manifestations of visual forms proliferate such that they are dependent on that ground and connected to it, being nothing other than the ground itself. The context within which sensory appearances proliferate as visual forms is conventionally described as 'visual consciousness.'

In this regard, the term 'field for objectification' (*yul*) refers to the field in which sensory appearances manifest; this can be likened to an ocean. The 'perception of objects' (*zung wa*) refers to the manifestation of sensory appearances as visual forms; this can be likened to the reflection of stars and planets. Furthermore, as the subtle reifying function of consciousness based on conceptual mind (*yid kyi nam-shey*) labels these forms, invests them with meaning, and regards them as having substance, there arises conceptualization that perpetuates three types of experience—pleasant, painful, and neutral. This is termed 'ordinary mind that reifies through vision' (*mig gi dzin-pa sem*).

"Similarly, the field that is the unimpeded avenue for the proliferation of sounds is the 'field for objectification.' The proliferation of sensory appearances that manifest as sounds is the 'perception of objects.' Consciousness based on conceptual mind, which perpetuates these perceptions, is the 'ordinary mind that reifies.' As before, there is an interdependent connection, with cause and condition coming together.

"And this can be applied in a similar way to 'olfactory consciousness,' within which there is the proliferation of sensory appearances that manifest as odors; to 'gustatory consciousness,' within which there is the proliferation of sensory appearances

༄༅། །པར་ཞེས་པ་རྣམས་མིང་ཙ་སྒྲུད་ཚམ་དུ་བརྗོད་པ་ལས་བུག་སློ་བ་

དད་པར་སྣང་བ་མ་ཡིན་པར་རྟེ་ལམ་དང་བར་སྒྲིད་ཀྱི་སྣང་བས་སྟོན་ཏོ། །འགའ་

ཞིག་གིས་སྣང་བ་སེམས་སུ་འདོད་ཅིང་ཕྱི་རོལ་གྱི་སྣང་བ་ཐམས་ཅད་རྣམ་རྟོག་

དང་རང་སེམས་དངོས་ཡིན་ནམ་སྣམ་དུ་སེམས་ཀྱང་དེ་ལྟར་མ་ཡིན་ཏེ། སྣང་

བ་རྣམས་སྣང་ཙམ་ཉིད་ནས་གནས་འགྱུར་ཏེ་སྐྱ་ཅིག་ལྟ་ཕྱིའི་རིམ་པས་འགག

ནས་འགྲོ་བ་ལ། སེམས་ནི་དེ་དང་དེའི་རོ་བོར་འཕོས་ཏེ་རང་ཉིད་སེམས་

མེད་དུ་མ་སོང་བ་དེས་སྟོན་ཏོ། །དེ་ལྟར་ཚོགས་བརྒྱད་ཀྱི་སྣང་བ་ལུགས་

སུ་འབྱུང་བས་འཁོར་བ་ཡོངས་སུ་མ་ཆད། ཡང་ཀུན་གཞིའི་རྣམ་ཤེས་ཀྱི་

བར་ལུགས་སུ་ལྡོག་པས་སྲིད་པའི་རྒྱུ་དུ་དུབ་པ་ཡིན་ནོ། །དེ་ལྟར་སྣང་སྲིད་

འཁོར་འདས་ཐམས་ཅད་གཞི་རང་ལས་མི་གཞན་པར་གཞི་ཉིད་དུ་རོ་གཅིག་པ་

དཔེར་ན་རྒྱ་མཚོར་གཟབ་དང་རྒྱ་སྐར་གྱི་གཟུགས་བརྙན་སྣ་ཚོགས་སྣང་ཡང་དོན་

ལ་རྒྱ་ཉིད་དུ་རོ་གཅིག་པ་ལྟ་བུར་ཞེས་པར་གྱིས་ཤིག །སྣང་བ་ཐམས་ཅད་

རང་སྣང་དུ་སྟོན་པ་རྡོ་རྗེ་འཆང་གི་མན་ངག་གོ། །ཞེས་གསུངས་ཞིང་མི་སྣང་

བར་ཡལ་ལོ།

that manifest as tastes; and to 'tactile consciousness,' within which there is the proliferation of sensory appearances that manifest as tactile sensations. Though we describe these in conventional terms, consciousness does not actually manifest through distinct orifices, as is demonstrated by the manifestation of sensory appearances in dreams and the bardo.

"Some people hold sensory appearances to be mind. They might wonder whether all outer sensory appearances are actually conceptualization and, therefore, their own minds, but that is not the case. This is demonstrated by the fact that while sensory appearances change from the very moment they manifest, ceasing and passing away in a succession of later moments following former ones, ordinary mind does not take on the essence of every passing phenomenon and thereby become itself nonexistent as mind.

"And so, in the usual way that things manifest to the eight avenues of consciousness, samsara proliferates in its entirety. However, even by tracing this process back to consciousness that stirs from the ground of all ordinary experience, one is still left stranded at the very pinnacle of conditioned existence.

"In summary, the world of all appearances and possibilities, whether of samsara or nirvana, is none other than the ground of being itself and is of one taste with that very ground. To use a metaphor, although myriad reflections of the planets and stars appear in the ocean, in actuality they are of one taste with the water itself. Understand that things are like this. Revealing all sensory appearances to be awareness's own manifestations (*rang-nang*) is the heart advice of Vajradhara."

Saying this, he faded away.

Hungchhenkara

༄༅། །ཡང་དུས་རེ་ཞིག་གི་ཚེ་རིག་འཛིན་ཆེན་པོ་ཊཱུ་ཆེན་ཀུ་རའི་ཞལ་ནས་མཇལ་བའི་ཚེ། བདག་གིས་སྐྱང་བའི་བཀོད་པ་འདི་ཇི་ལྟ་བུ་ལགས་ཞེས་ཞུས་པས། བཀའ་སྩལ་པ། ཀྱི་སྙིས་བུ་ཆེན་པོ་སྲོ་ལུའི་རྣམ་ཤེས་ནམ་མཁའ་ལྟ་བུ་ཅེར་ཡང་མཆེད་དུ་རུང་བ་དང་། རྣམ་པར་རྟོག་པ་སྒྱུ་མའི་རྫས་སྤྲུགས་ལྟ་བུ་གཉིས་དུས་འཛོམ་པ་ལས་སྐྱང་བའི་བཀོད་པ་སྒྱུ་འཕྲུལ་ལྟ་བུར་འབྱུང་བ་ཡིན་ལ། ཉེར་ལེན་གྱི་ཞེས་པ་ནི་སྐྱད་མོ་མཁན་ལྟ་བུའོ། །དེས་ན་མཆོད་རྟེས་དང་སྙིན་པའི་རྟས་ཐམས་ཅད་སྒྱུ་མའི་རྟས་ལྟ་བུ་དང་། སྒྱང་སྤྲུལ་གྱིས་སྟོང་ཉིད་དུ་སྒྱངས་ནས་སྒྱེལ་སྤྲུལ་གྱིས་མཆོད་སྙིན་གྱི་ཡུལ་གང་ཡིན་པ་འདིའི་དབང་པོ་དྲུག་གི་ཡུལ་དུ་འདོད་ཡོན་གྱི་སྒྱང་བ་དཔག་ཏུ་མེད་པ་མཆེད་པར་བྱས་ཏེ་མཉེས་པར་བྱེད་པ་སྒྱུ་མ་ལྟ་བུའི་རྣལ་འབྱོར་གྱི་སྐོ་དང་། ཡང་སྒྱུ་མ་ལྟ་བུའི་རྣལ་འབྱོར་གྱིས་སྒྱལ་པ་ལྟ་བུའི་སེམས་ཅན་ལ་ཊེ་ཟཝའི་གྲོང་ཁྱེར་ལྟ་བུའི་སྲུང་ཡུལ་བཀོད་དེ་སྨྲི་ལམ་ལྟ་བུའི་དམིགས་བཟུང་གྱིས་བསྐུལ་འདེན་སོ་གས་བྱེད་པས་སྒྱུ་མའི་རྣལ་འབྱོར་ཆེན་པོར་དབང་བསྒྱུར་བའོ། མཆོ་ལ

O N YET ANOTHER OCCASION, when I met the great rigdzin Hungchhenkara in a vision, I asked, "What is this array of sensory appearances like?"

He bestowed the following reply: "Ah, great spiritual being, the five sense consciousnesses are like space, in which anything can happen, while conceptualization is like the substances and incantations used in magic. The array that appears from the synchronicity of these two occurs like a magical illusion. Consciousness that perpetuates this is like a spectator.

"This being the case, all substances offered or given are like substances used in magic. The yogic approach to the illusion-like nature of things uses mantras of purification, which refine these substances into emptiness, and mantras of increase, which cause immeasurable appearances of sense pleasures to proliferate and so become objects of the six senses, delighting all who are recipients of these offerings and gifts. Furthermore, for the sake of beings, who are like phantom emanations, through the yoga of the illusion-like nature, one arranges the apparent environment like a city of the gandharvas. One carries out the activities of liberating and guiding beings as though changing the contents of a dream, thus gaining mastery of the supreme yoga of illusion.

༄༅། །གཟབ་སྐར་རྗེ་ལྟར་མང་ཡང་རྒྱུ་ཉིད་ཀྱིས་ཆེངས་པ་དང་། སྡོད་
བཅུད་རྗེ་ལྟར་མང་ཡང་ནམ་མཁའ་གཅིག་གིས་ཆེངས་པ་དང་། འཁོར་འདས་
ཀྱི་སྣང་བ་རྗེ་ལྟར་རྒྱ་ཆེ་ལ་གྲངས་མང་ཡང་སེམས་ཉིད་གཅིག་གིས་ཆེངས་པའི་
ཆུལ་ལ་སློས་ཤིག །སེམས་ཉིད་བདེ་གཤེགས་སྙིང་པོ་ཞེས་བྱ་བ་ནི་ཕྱལ་
བ་སྐྱོན་གྱིས་མ་གོས་པ། དཔེར་ན་སངས་རྒྱས་ནམ་མཁའ་གང་བཞིག་ཡོད་
སྲིད་ནའང་དེའི་ཡེ་ཤེས་ཡོན་ཏན་གྱིས་ཕན་བདགས་པའི་ཡུལ་མེད་པས་ཕྱལ་
བ་དང་། སེམས་ཅན་རང་རྒྱུད་པ་ནམ་མཁའི་མཐའ་དང་མཉམ་པ་ཚམ་ཡོད་
སྲིད་ནའང་གནོད་པ་བྱེད་པའི་ཡུལ་མེད་པས་ཕྱལ་བའོ། །གཞིའི་ཚོས་སྐུ་
བདེ་བར་གཤེགས་པའི་སྙིང་པོ་དེ་སྐྱེ་བའི་གནས་ཡུལ་བདག་པོ་ཐམས་ཅད་དང་
བྲལ་བས་སྐྱེ་བའི་མཐའ་དང་བྲལ་བ། འགག་པའི་དུས་དང་བདག་པོ་ལས་
འདས་པས་འགག་པའི་མཐའ་དང་བྲལ་བ། ཡོད་པ་དངོས་པོའི་ཕྱོགས་སུ
མ་ལྷུང་བར་རྒྱལ་བའི་སྲུན་གྱིས་ཀྱང་མི་གཟིགས་པའི་ཕྱིར་རྟག་པའི་མཐའ་དང་
བྲལ་བ། མེད་པ་ཅང་མེད་དུ་མ་སོང་བར་འཁོར་འདས་ཀྱི་སྣྲི་གཞིར་གྱུར
པས་ཆད་པའི་མཐའ་དང་བྲལ་བ། འགྲོ་བའི་གནས་ཡུལ་བདག་པོ་ཐམས
ཅད་ལས་འདས་པས་འགྲོ་བའི་མཐའ་དང་བྲལ་བ། ཞིང་བའི་གནས་ཡུལ

"Consider the fact that no matter how many planets and stars are reflected in a lake, these reflections are encompassed within the water itself; that no matter how many universes there are, they are encompassed within a single space; and that no matter how vast and how numerous the sensory appearances of samsara and nirvana may be, they are encompassed within the single nature of mind (*sem-nyid*).

"The nature of mind, referred to as 'buddha nature' (*desheg nying-po*), is openness (*khyal-wa*) unsullied by flaws. For example, even though buddhas might fill space, there is openness in that there is no one or no thing to be benefited by their timeless awareness and enlightened qualities. Although there may be ordinary beings equal to the limits of space, each with an individual mindstream, there is openness in that there is no one or no thing that can be harmed.

"The ground aspect of dharmakaya, buddha nature, is free of everything related to origination—any location, object, or creator—and so is free of the limitation (*t'ha*) of origination. It is beyond there being any time at which it ceases or anything that causes it to cease, and so it is free of the limitation of cessation. Because it does not fall into the extreme of existence as something having substance—since even the eyes of a victorious one cannot see it—it is free of the limitation of permanence. Since it is nonexistent without being nothing whatsoever and constitutes the common ground of samsara and nirvana, it is free of the limitation of absolute nonexistence. Since it is beyond everything related to going—any location, object, or agent—it is free of the limitation of going. Because nothing related to coming—no location, object, or agent—

༄༅། བདག་པོ་མ་གྲུབ་པའི་ཕྱིར་འོང་བའི་མཐའ་དང་བྲལ་བ། གཞི་
བདེ་གཤེགས་སྙིང་པོའི་ཀློང་དུ་འཁོར་འདས་ཀྱི་ཆོས་ཐམས་ཅད་རྒྱ་མཚོའི་ནང་
གི་གཟའ་སྐར་ལྟར་མ་འདྲེས་སོ་སོར་ཤར་བའི་ཕྱིར་དོན་གཅིག་པའི་མཐའ་དང་
བྲལ་བ། འཁོར་འདས་ཀྱི་རྣམ་པ་རྗེ་ལྟར་འཁར་ཡང་རྒྱ་མཚོའི་གཟའ་སྐར་རྒྱ་
མཚོ་ལས་མི་གཞན་པ་ལྟར་གཞི་བདེ་གཤེགས་སྙིང་པོ་ཉིད་དུ་རོ་གཅིག་པའི་ཕྱིར་
ཐ་དད་པའི་མཐའ་དང་བྲལ་བ་སྟེ། སྤྲོས་པའི་མཐའ་བཞི་པོ་གང་དུ་འང་མ་
ལྷུང་བའི་ཕྱིར་ཕྱལ་བ་སྐྱོན་གྱིས་མ་གོས་པའོ། །ཡང་སྟེང་འོག་ཕྱོགས་མཆམས་
བར་དང་དུས་ལས་འདས་པས་སྟོང་པ་དང་། ཡོངས་ལ་ཁྱབ་ཅིང་ཡོངས་
སུ་བརྟལ་བས་སྟོང་པ་དང་། ཕྱི་སྣང་བ་ཐམས་ཅད་དངོས་མཚན་བདེན་གྲུབ་
ཏུ་མ་མཆིས་པས་ཕྱི་སྟོང་པ་དང་། ནང་རང་སེམས་གཞི་རྩ་ཐམས་ཅད་ལས་
འདས་པས་ནང་སྟོང་པ་ཉིད་དང་། བར་གཟུང་འཛིན་གཉིས་སུ་མི་ཕྱེད་པས་
བཙལ་ཁྱབ་ཆེན་པོ་དོར་བ་མེད་པའི་སྟོང་པ་ཉིད་དེ་རྣམ་པར་ཐར་པའི་སྒོ་སྟོང་པ་
ཉིད་དང་། གཞིའི་ཆོས་སྐུ་བདེ་གཤེགས་སྙིང་པོ་ཆེན་ཏུ་བཟོད་བྱའི་མཚན་
མ་དང་བྲལ་བ། དཔེའི་མཚུངས་ཀླ་ལས་འདས་པ། དོན་གྱིས་སྟོན་བྱའི་
དངོས་པོས་སྟོང་པ་སྟེ་རྣམ་པར་ཐར་བའི་སྒོ་མཚན་མ་མེད་པ་དང་། ཆོས་

has ever existed, it is free of the limitation of coming. Because all phenomena of samsara and nirvana arise distinctly and individually within the expanse of the ground of being, or buddha nature, like the planets and stars reflected in a lake, it is free of the limitation of being identical to them. Because the modes of samsara and nirvana, however they arise, are of one taste with this same ground of being, or buddha nature—just as the planets and stars reflected in the ocean are none other than the ocean—it is free of the limitation of being separate from them. Because it does not fall into any of these eight limitations of conceptual elaboration (*trö-pa*), it is openness unsullied by flaws.

"Furthermore, it is empty in that it is beyond upper or lower, cardinal or intermediate direction, interval or time frame. It is empty in that it is totally pervasive and totally extensive. There is outer emptiness, in that outwardly all sensory appearances are such that they have never truly existed as something that can be characterized as having substance. There is inner emptiness, in that inwardly one's mind is beyond all basis or foundation. There is intermediate, nonexclusive emptiness—supremely extensive and pervasive—in that there is no differentiation due to dualistic perception. This is emptiness (*tong-pa-nyid*), which is a doorway to complete liberation.

"The ground aspect of dharmakaya, buddha nature, is free of being characterized in ways that can be expressed in words, beyond metaphorical approximation, and devoid of being anything that could actually be demonstrated. This is the absence of characteristics (*tsan-ma med-pa*), which is another doorway to complete liberation.

༄༅། ཉིད་བདེ་གཤེགས་སྙིང་པོ་དུས་གསུམ་དུ་བདེ་བར་གཤེགས་པ་དེ་
ལ་ལུས་དང་ངག་གི་དགེ་སྟོར་ཚམ་གྱིས་འབྲས་བུ་ཡུལ་ཞིང་ཁམས་གཞན་དུ་
འགྲོ་ཞིང་གྲོལ་བར་སེམས་ན་ཁྱབ་བརྟལ་རྣམ་མཁའི་ཁོར་ཡུག་འགྲོ་ཞིང་གི་ཡུལ་
དང་བདག་པོར་སེམས་པ་ནི་ཅིན་ཏུ་མགོ་འབོར་ཞིང་སྟྲྲྩོང་པར་གྱུར་ཏོ། །ལས་
གང་ཡིན་ན་རང་ཐོག་ཏུ་རང་ས་བཟུང་བ་ཉིད་དང་། རྟོགས་པ་གང་ལགས་
ན་རང་ངོ་གནས་ལུགས་ཆུལ་བཞིན་ཤེས་པ་ཉིད་དང་། གྲོལ་བ་གང་ལགས་
ན་རང་ངོར་རང་སངས་རྒྱས་པ་ཉིད་ལས། གྲོལ་ས་དང་གྲོལ་ཡུལ་གཞན་
དུ་འཛིན་ཅིང་འབད་རྩོལ་བྱེད་པ་ནི་ཕིན་ཏུ་འཁྲུལ་པ་ཡིན་པས། དོན་དམ་
པར་འབྲས་བུ་ལ་ཡིད་སྟོན་ཚམ་ཡང་འཆའ་བའི་གནས་མེད་པས་ན་རྣམ་པར་བར་
པའི་སྒོ་སྟོན་པ་མེད་པོ། །ཀྱི་ཐིའུ་རྒྱང་རིག་པའི་དབང་པོ་ཁྱོད་ཀྱིས་འདི་
ལྟར་བཞད་པ་དང་ཐོས་པ་ཚམ་གྱིས་གྲོལ་བར་མི་འགྱུར་ཏེ། བཤད་ཐིན་པ་
དེ་དག་གི་དང་ཆུལ་ལ་བཤག་ཅིང་དཔྱོད་ལ་སྐྱོང་བ་གཏིང་ནས་ཐོན་ཞིང་ཤེས་རིག་
རྒྱུད་བཅུན་པ་ཞིག་མཆོང་ལ་སྐྱོང་དང་ཕུན་པའི་སྐལ་ལྡན་རྣམས་ལ་སྐྱོན་ཆིག །རྩེ
གཅིག་རྣམས་སུ་ཡིན་པའི་སྐྱེས་བུ་རྣམས་ལ་འདའི་དགོངས་རྒྱུད་འཕོས་ཏེ་རིང་
པོར་མི་ཐོགས་པར་གྲོལ་བ་འཐོབ་པར་གདོན་མི་ཟའོ། །ཞེས་གསུངས་ཤིང་
མི་སྲུང་བར་ཡལ་ལོ།

"Regarding this nature of phenomena, or buddha nature—this 'reaching a state of bliss throughout the three times'—to think of the goal as gaining freedom in some other place or realm, going there by merely applying oneself to virtue physically or verbally, is to think that the pervasive and extensive panorama of space is an object or agent that comes or goes. What an extremely bewildered and deluded state of mind!

"What, then, constitutes the path (*lam*)? It is simply holding to one's own place in the immediacy of one's own situation. What constitutes realization (*tog-pa*)? It is simply understanding correctly one's true nature as the way of abiding. What constitutes freedom (*drol-wa*)? It is the naturally awakened state of buddhahood as one's very essence (*rang-ngo*). One who exerts oneself, conceiving of this level of freedom and its context as something else, is extremely confused. Since there is no context in ultimate reality on which to base the slightest speculation concerning the goal, there is the absence of speculation (*mon-pa med-pa*), which is another doorway to liberation.

"Ah, my young lad, powerful lord of awareness, you will not be freed merely by my explaining and your hearing such things. Examine and analyze the fundamental nature (*ngang-tsul*) of what I have set forth, so that direct experience is elicited from the depths of your being, and stabilize your ongoing understanding and awareness. Teach this to those fortunate ones who are worthy recipients. My enlightened mindstream will be transferred to those spiritual individuals who put this into practice one-pointedly, and they will attain freedom before long. Have no doubt about this."

Saying this, he faded away.

Manjushri, Lion of Speech

༄༅། །ཡང་འོད་གསལ་ཐམས་ཅད་ཀྱི་སྣང་ངོར་འཇམ་དཔལ་སྒྱུ་བའི་མིང་
གིའི་ཞལ་མཐའ་བའི་ཚེ། བདག་གིས་འདི་སྐད་ཉུས། ཀྱི་སྤྲིན་པ་འཇིག་
ཏེན་མགོན་པོ་ལགས། །སྤྱོད་བཅུད་ཀྱི་སྒྱང་བ་ཐམས་ཅད་རང་སྒྱང་ལས།
མི་གཞན་པའི་དང་ཆུལ་ཇེ་སྤྲ་བ་བཞིན་དུ་ཐག་ཆོད་ཀྱང་། །སངས་རྒྱས་ཐམས་
ཅད་ཀྱི་མིང་དང་ཞིང་ཁམས་ཐ་དད་དུ་ཡོད་པ་རྣམས་ཡུལ་རང་རྒྱུད་པར་གྱུབ་དང་
མ་གྲུབ་པའི་ཆུལ་བདག་ལ་བསྟན་དུ་གསོལ། ཅེས་ཞུས་པས་སྟོན་པ་དེ་ཉིད་
ཀྱིས་བཀའ་སྩལ་པ། ཀྱི་སྨྲེས་བུ་ཆེན་པོ་ཁྱོད་ཉོན་ཅིག །གཞིའི་ཚོས་
སྐུ་བདེ་གཞིགས་སྙིང་པོའི་རང་མདངས་སྤྲུན་གྲུབ་རིན་པོ་ཆེའི་ཡོན་ཏན་ལ་གཞི་
བྱས་ཏེ་སངས་རྒྱས་ཀྱི་ཞིང་དང་ལྷ་ཡབ་ཡུམ་གཞལ་ཡས་ཁང་དང་བཅས་པར་
བསྟན་པ་རྣམས་གཞི་རང་ལ་རང་ཚས་སུ་རྫོགས་པ་དེ་ཤེས་རབ་དང་། ཡུལ་
གཞན་དུ་གྲུབ་པར་བསྟན་པ་དེ་ཐབས་སོ། །གཞི་རང་ལ་ཡོན་ཏན་རྫོགས

O N YET ANOTHER OCCASION, during a meditative experience of utter lucidity, I met Manjushri, the Lion of Speech, and asked the following question: "Ah, teacher, guide of the world, I have come to a decision about the fundamental nature, just as it is—that all sensory appearances of the universe are nothing other than awareness's own manifestations (*rang-nang*). But I pray that you show me whether or not the distinct names and pure realms of all buddhas can be found to exist as objects in their own right."

Upon my having made this request, the teacher bestowed the following reply: "Ah, listen, great spiritual one. The qualities of precious spontaneous presence (*lhun-drub*) constitute the inner glow of the ground aspect of dharmakaya, buddha nature. With this as a basis, the pure realms of buddhas, the masculine and feminine deities, and the immeasurable mansions about which you have been taught are perfect as natural attributes of the ground of being itself. This is the principle of sublime knowing (*shey-rab*). To teach that these are objects that can be found to exist as something other than ground is the principle of skillful means (*t'hab*).

"The perfection of qualities within the ground of being itself is ultimate reality (*don-dam*). The explanation that these

117

༄༅། པ་ནི་དོན་དམ་པ། གཞན་དུ་ཡུལ་སྣང་བཅུད་ཅན་ཡོད་པར་

འཆད་པ་ཀུན་རྫོབ་བོ། །ཡང་གཞི་རང་གི་སྣུན་གྲུབ་སྐུ་དང་ཡེ་ཤེས་ཀྱི་རོལ་

པ་ནི་རིས་དོན་དང་། ཡུལ་གཞན་དུ་སངས་རྒྱས་ཀྱི་ཞིང་དང་ལྷ་པོ་མོའི་མིང་

སོགས་དངོས་པོ་མཚན་མ་ཅན་དུ་འཆད་པ་ཐམས་ཅད་དང་དོན་ཨེན་ནོ། །འགོར་

བའི་སྐོར་བསྐྱེན་ནས་དོན་དམ་ཀུན་རྫོབ་ཏུ་བསྐྱེན་པ་ནི་འདི་ལྟ་སྟེ། རྒྱལ་

བ་ཐམས་ཅད་སྐུ་ལྷའི་ཆེངས་ཀྱིས་བཅིང་ཆུལ་ནི། སྣང་སྲིད་འཁོར་འདས་

ཀྱིས་བསྐྱས་པའི་ཆོས་ཐམས་ཅད་གཞི་དབྱིངས་སྤོང་ཉིད་ཆེན་པོར་མ་བཅོས་རང་

ཆས་སུ་ཡོད་པའི་ཆོས་ཉིད་ཆེན་པོ་ལ་ཆོས། །ཁམས་དང་དབང་པོའི་བྱེ་བྲག

བསམ་གྱིས་མི་ཁྱབ་པ་ལས་ལམ་གྱི་འཇུག་སྒོ་དང་ཉམས་ཀྱི་སྐྱོང་བ་དང་། འབྲས་

བུའི་ཐོབ་ཏུ་བསམ་གྱིས་མི་ཁྱབ་པ་རང་ཆས་སུ་ཡོད་པ་ལ་སྐུ་ཞེས་བྱའོ། །ལྷུན་

གྲུབ་སྐུ་དང་ཡེ་ཤེས་ཀྱི་རོལ་པ་ལོངས་སྤྱོད་དུ་རང་ཆས་སུ་རྫོགས་པ་ལ་ལོངས་

སྐུ། དང་ལས་སྤྲུལ་པ་འགྱེད་སྐྱམ་གྱི་ཁྲོ་ཨེད་མ་གཡོས་ཞིང་། གཞི་

exist as something else—as the objects comprising the universe—is relative reality (*kun-dzob*).

"Again, the definitive meaning (*ngey-don*) is the display of the kayas and timeless awareness as the spontaneous presence of the ground of being itself. The provisional meaning (*drang-don*) includes all the explanations of the pure realms of buddhas, the names of masculine and feminine deities, and so forth as objects other than that ground—that is, as things that can be characterized as having substance.

"The following is a demonstration of ultimate reality on the relative level, in accord with modes of samsaric experience. Let us consider the way in which all victorious ones are encompassed within the model of the five kayas. All phenomena subsumed within the world of appearances and possibilities, whether of samsara or nirvana, are present as uncontrived natural attributes within the supreme emptiness of the ground of being as basic space. This supreme nature of phenomena is 'dharma' (*chhö*). Due to the inconceivable range of diverse temperaments and capacities, there is an inconceivable range of approaches to the spiritual path, of meditative experiences, and of goals to be attained. The presence of these as natural attributes is 'kaya' (*ku*).

"The spontaneously present display of the kayas and timeless awareness is perfect as natural attributes to be enjoyed. This is sambhogakaya (*long-ku*).

"Without any conscious intention to send forth emanations stirring from the fundamental nature, the nirmanakaya (*trul-ku*) of enlightened teachers, artisans, reincarnate masters, and inanimate matter manifests such that it is none other than the

༄༅། རང་ལས་མི་གཞན་པའི་ཆུལ་དུ་སྟོན་པ་སྤྲུལ་སྐུ་དང་། བཟོ་
སྤྲུལ་སྐུ་དང་། སྐྱེ་བ་སྤྲུལ་སྐུ་དང་། ཞིམ་པོ་སྤྲུལ་སྐུ་རྣམས་ངར་འཛིན་
གྱི་ཤེས་པ་རྒྱུ་སྟོད་ལྷུ་བུ་དང་བདེ་གཤེགས་སྙིང་པོའི་དབྱིངས་ཀྱི་ཡོན་ཏན་ནས་
མཁའི་གཟའ་སྐར་ལྷུ་བུ་དུས་འཛོམ་པའི་ཚེ་རྟེན་འབྲེལ་སྤྲུལ་པ་རྣམ་བཞིར་སྣང་
བ་ཡིན་ནོ། །དོན་ལ་སྤྲོད་བཅུད་སྐུ་གསུམ་གྱི་རོལ་པ་ལས་མ་འདས་པ་སྟེ།
ཏིང་བོ་སྟོང་པའི་ཆ་ལ་ཆོས་སྐུ། རང་བཞིན་གསལ་གྲུབ་ཀྱི་ཆ་ལ་ལོངས་སྐུ། སོ་
སོར་སྣང་བའི་ཆ་ལ་སྤྲུལ་སྐུ་ཞེས་བྱའོ། ཡང་གཞི་རིད་འཁོར་འདས་ཐམས་
ཅད་ཀྱི་དོ་བོར་གྱུར་ཅིང་དོ་བོ་རྡེད་དུ་ཐམས་ཅད་རོ་གཅིག་པས་དོ་བོ་རྡེད་ཅེས་བྱའོ། །
ཡེ་ཤེས་ཡོན་ཏན་ཐམས་ཅད་བསགས་ནས་སྐྱངས་པ་ལྷུ་བུ་ལ་སྐུ་ཞེས་བྱའོ། །
དུས་གསུམ་འཕོ་བ་མེད་ཅིང་དོ་བོ་གཞན་དུ་མི་འགྱུར་བས་མི་འགྱུར། གཞན་
གང་གིས་རྒྱུ་མི་འབྱུང་བས་མི་ཚོད་པ། རང་དང་གཞན་གྱིས་མི་ཤིགས་པ།
འཁོར་འདས་ཀྱི་སྤྱི་གཞིར་གནས་པས་བདེན་པ། བཟང་ངན་གྱི་བསྒྱུད་མི་
འཇུག་པས་སྲ་བ། གཡོ་འགུལ་དང་བྲལ་བས་བརྟན་པ། ཤེས་སྒྲིབ་
ཕྲ་བ་ཡན་ཆད་འབིག་ནུས་པས་ཐམས་ཅད་དུ་ཐོགས་པ་མེད་པ། ཡུལ་རྐྱེན་
གང་གིས་མི་ཐུབ་པས་ཐམས་ཅད་དུ་མ་ཐམ་པའོ། །དེ་ལྟར་དོན་དམ་མི་ཤིགས་

ground of being itself. These four distinct modes of emanation manifest through interdependent connection when there
is the synchronicity of a consciousness that conceives of an 'I,'
which is like a vessel filled with water, and the qualities of the
basic space of buddha nature, which are like the planets and
stars in the heavens.

"In actuality, the universe does not go beyond the display
of the three kayas. The term 'dharmakaya' refers to the aspect
of its essence as emptiness, 'sambhogakaya' to the aspect of its
nature as spontaneous presence, and 'nirmanakaya' to the aspect of its distinct manifestations.

"Furthermore, 'svabhavika' (*ngo-wo-nyid*) implies that the
ground of being itself is the essence of all samsara and nirvana,
and that everything is of one taste within that same essence.
'Kaya' (*ku*) denotes the gathering and amassing, as it were, of all
aspects of timeless awareness and enlightened qualities.

"Without any transition throughout the three times, the
essence of being is 'unchanging' (*mi-gyur*), since it does not
change into anything else. It is invulnerable, since it cannot be
damaged by anything. It is indestructible, since it is not destroyed by itself or anything else. It is authentic, since it abides
as the common ground of all samsara and nirvana. It is incorruptible, since it is not affected by good or bad qualities. It is
stable, since it is free of fluctuation. It is in all ways unobstructed, since it is capable of penetrating even subtle cognitive obscuration. It is in all ways invincible, since no object or
condition is equal to it.

"Thus, the way in which things abide—the ultimate and
indestructible vajra (*dor-je*) way of abiding—entails four

༄༅། །པའི་རྗེ་རྗེའི་གནས་ལུགས་ལས་དང་རྐྱལ་བར་ལྡན་པའི་སྙེས་བུ་མ་
གཏོགས་སེམས་ཅན་གང་རུང་གིས་རྟོགས་མི་སྲིད་པ། རྟོགས་ནས་ནམས་
སུ་བླངས་པས་གདེང་མི་ཐོབ་མི་སྲིད་པ། གདེང་ཐོབ་ཚེ་མི་གྲོལ་མི་སྲིད་པ།
གྲོལ་ཆད་འཆང་མི་རྒྱ་མི་སྲིད་པས་ན་དམ་བཅའ་བཞི་དང་ལྡན་པའོ། །སྐྱུ་ལྟ་
པོ་དེ་དག་གཞི་རང་ལ་རང་ཆས་སུ་ཡོད་པ་དོན་དམ་པ་ཨིན་ཏེ། དེ་ལས་ཐ་
དད་པར་འཆད་པ་དེ་ཀུན་རྟོག་ཐབས་ཀྱི་ལམ་ཞེས་བུའོ། །འགྲོ་བ་རྣམས་
རིགས་ལ་མཛོན་པར་ཞེན་པ་དེ་དང་བསྟུན་ཏེ་ལྷ་ལ་རིགས་བརྟོད་པའི་གཞི་ནི།
གཞི་སྲིད་བག་ཆགས་ཀྱི་དྲི་མ་དབྱིངས་སུ་སངས་པས་སངས། ཨེ་ཤེས་དང་
ཡོན་ཏན་གྱི་དང་རྒྱས་པས་རྒྱས་ཞེས་བུའོ། མི་ཤེགས་པ་རྗེ་རྗེའི་ཚོས་བདུན་
དང་ལྡན་པས་རྗེ་རྗེ། སྐུ་དང་ཨེ་ཤེས་ཐམས་ཅད་ཀྱི་འབྱུང་ཁུངས་སུ་གྱུར་
བས་རིན་པོ་ཆེ། སྤྲོན་དང་དྲི་མས་མ་གོས་པས་པདྨ། ཐྱིན་ལས་ཡོངས་

assurances.[1] Except for spiritual people with the appropriate karma and good fortune, it is impossible for just any ordinary being to realize it; once it is realized and put into practice, it is impossible not to gain an indwelling confidence in it; once confidence is gained, it is impossible for freedom not to come about; and it is impossible for all those who have found freedom not to awaken to buddhahood.

"The presence of these five kayas as natural attributes of the ground of being itself is ultimate reality. The explanation of them as distinct from that ground is termed 'relative reality' and the 'path of skillful means.'

"The following is the basis on which deities are described in terms of families, corresponding to the identification of beings with their species. Since the ground of being itself is such that the distortions of habitual patterns are cleared away in basic space, the term 'cleared away' (*sang*) is used. Since this context of timeless awareness and enlightened qualities unfolds, the term 'unfolding' (*gyay*) is used.[2] Since the ground is endowed with the seven indestructible vajra attributes, there is the 'vajra' (*dor-je*) family. Because it functions as the source of all kayas and aspects of timeless awareness, there is the 'ratna,' or 'jewel' (*rin-chhen*), family. Because it is not sullied by any flaw or distortion, there is the 'lotus' (*pad-ma*) family.

---

[1] Not as clearly highlighted in the text as the other four, the fifth kaya for which the etymology is explained here is the "unchanging vajrakaya (*mi-gyur dor-je ku*)."

[2] The Tibetan term for buddha is *sang-gyay,* which is explained etymologically as the clearing away (*sang*) of negative factors and the unfolding (*gyay*) of positive ones.

༄༅། །སུ་གྲུབ་པས་ལས་ཀྱི་རིགས་སོ། །རིགས་ཞེས་བྱ་བ་དེ་ཅིངས་
དེས་བཅིངས་པའི་རང་རང་གི་ཁྱབ་པ་ལ་བརྗོད་པའོ། །མི་རྣམས་ཡུལ་ལ་
མཆོན་པར་ཞེན་པའི་ཡུལ་དང་བསྟུན་པའི་ཞིང་ཁམས་སྤྲུ་རུ་བསྒྱུན་པ་ནི། གཞི་
དབྱིངས་ཡོན་ཏན་ལྷུན་སྒྲུབ་པའི་ཆ་ལ་སྒྲུག་པོ་བཀོད་པ། ཡུལ་ཀྱེན་བདག
པོས་མ་བསྐྱེད་པའི་དགའ་བ་ཆེན་པོ་དང་ལྡན་པས་མཆོན་པར་དགའ་བ། ཡེ་
ཤེས་ཡོན་ཏན་གྱི་དཔལ་ཕུན་སུམ་ཚོགས་པ་དང་ལྡན་པས་དཔལ་ལྡན། བདེ་
སྟོང་ཟག་པ་མེད་པའི་ཡེ་ཤེས་དང་ལྡན་པས་བདེ་བ་ཅན། དག་པ་དང་གྲོལ་
བའི་ལས་ཐམས་ཅད་རབ་ཏུ་རྫོགས་པས་ལས་རབ་རྫོགས་པའོ། །ཞིང་ཞེས་
བྱ་བ་དབྱིངས་ལ་བརྗོད་པ་དང་། །ཁམས་ཞེས་བྱ་བ་ཁམས་དེ་ལས་མི་གཞན་
པ་ལ་བྱའོ། །གཞིའི་ཡོན་ཏན་གཟལ་དུ་མེད་པས་གཟལ་ཡས། འཕོར་

Because enlightened activities are completely accomplished, there is the 'karma,' or 'activity' (*lay*), family. The term 'family' (*rig*) describes the respective associations embraced by this model.

"The following is a demonstration of pure realms as fivefold, which corresponds to the identification of human beings with their territory: From the perspective of the density of enlightened qualities (*yon-tan*) that are spontaneously present within the ground of being as basic space, there is the realm of Dense Array (Ghanavyuha). Since the ground of being is endowed with supreme joy that has not been brought into being by any object, condition, or agent, there is the realm of Manifest Joy (Abhirati). Since it is endowed with the abundant glory of timeless awareness and enlightened qualities, there is the realm of Endowed with Glory (Shrimat). Since it is endowed with the timeless awareness of inexhaustible bliss and emptiness, there is the realm of Endowed with Bliss (Sukhavati). And since there is the utter perfection of all activities of purification and freedom, there is the realm of Utterly Perfect Activity (Sukarmapurna). The term 'field' (*zhing*) denotes basic space; the term 'realm' (*kham*) denotes that which is none other than the fundamental nature of being.[3] Since the enlightened qualities of the ground of being cannot be measured, the term 'immeasurable' (*zhal-yay*) is used. Since they completely fill the whole of samsara and nirvana, the term 'mansion' (*khang*) is used.

[3] The Tibetan term that is translated in this work as "pure realm" is *zhing-kham*, the etymology of which is explained here according to its components of "field" (*zhing*) and "realm" (*kham*).

༄༅། །འདས་ཡོངས་སུ་གང་བས་ཁང་བའོ། །གཞི་དབྱིངས་ཁྱབ
བརྡལ་གྱི་རང་མདངས་ཁྱབ་བྱེད་ཀྱི་ཤེས་རབ་ཆེན་པོས་མངོན་དུ་གྱུར་པའི་ཚོ་གཞི
བདེ་གཤེགས་སྙིང་པོའི་ཁམས་ཀྱི་ཡེ་ཤེས་ཡོན་ཏན་ཐམས་ཅད་རྣམ་པར་སྣང
བར་མཛད་པ་དང་། མི་ཤིགས་པ་རྡོ་རྗེའི་ཚོས་བདུན་དང་ལྡན་ཅིང་དུས་གསུམ
གཡོ་འགུལ་བྲལ་བས་མི་བསྐྱོད་རྡོ་རྗེ། །ལམ་དང་འབྲས་བུའི་ཚོས་ཐམས
ཅད་ཀྱི་འབྱུང་གནས་དང་ཡོན་ཏན་ཕུན་སུམ་ཚོགས་པ་དང་ལྡན་པས་རིན་ཆེན
འབྱུང་ལྡན། གཞི་སྣང་མཐའ་ཡས་པ་ལ་སྣང་བ་མཐའ་ཡས། ཡང་དག
པའི་དོན་ཐམས་ཅད་རང་བྱུང་དུ་ཡོད་པ་ལས་དོན་ཡོད་གྲུབ་པ་ཞེས་བྱའོ།།
དོན་གྱི་རྡོ་རྗེ་སློང་པ་ཉིད་ཀྱི་མཁའ་ལ་འཁོར་འདས་ཀྱི་ཚོས་ཐམས་ཅད་འགྲོ་འོང
གི་རྣམ་པར་སྣང་བས་རྡོ་རྗེ་མཁའ་འགྲོ། རིན་པོ་ཆེའི་མཛོད་ཁང་ལྟ་བུར་ཡེ
ཤེས་ཡོན་ཏན་ཐམས་ཅད་རང་བྱུང་བའི་ཆ་ལ་རིན་ཆེན་མཁའ་འགྲོ། ཆགས
པ་ཐམས་ཅད་དང་བྲལ་བའི་ཆ་ལ་པདྨ་མཁའ་འགྲོ། ལྷུན་གྲུབ་སྐུ་དང་ཡེ
ཤེས་ཀྱི་ལས་ཐམས་ཅད་བྱ་བས་མ་བྱས་རྩོལ་བས་མ་བསྒྲུབ་པར་རང་བྱུང་བའི
ཆ་ལ་ལས་ཀྱི་མཁའ་འགྲོ། དོན་ཤེས་ཀྱི་དེ་མ་དབྱིངས་སུ་སངས་ཤིང་ཡེ
ཤེས་ཡོན་ཏན་གྱི་དངོས་རྒྱས་པས་སངས་རྒྱས། སྟོང་ཉིད་ཆེན་པོའི་མཁའ་ཀློང

126

"When the natural glow of the pervasive and extensive ground of being as basic space has been made evident by sublime knowing that is supreme and pervasive, there is Distinct Manifestation (Vairochana) of all aspects of timeless awareness and enlightened qualities of the ground of being—that is, of buddha nature as the fundamental nature of being (*kham*). Since the ground is endowed with the seven indestructible vajra attributes and is free of fluctuation throughout the three times, there is Unshakable Vajra (Akshobhyavajra). Since it is the source of all elements of the path and its fruition and is endowed with an abundance of enlightened qualities, there is Source of Preciousness (Ratnasambhava). Limitless Illumination (Amitabha) refers to the unlimited manifestation of the ground. Since all that has authentic meaning occurs naturally, there is Accomplishment of Meaning (Amoghasiddhi).

"Ultimate vajra emptiness is the space in which all phenomena of samsara and nirvana manifest in specific forms that come and go, so there is Vajradakini. Ratnadakini refers to all aspects of timeless awareness and enlightened qualities occurring naturally, similar to a treasure house of precious jewels. Padmadakini refers to the aspect of freedom from all attachment. Karmadakini refers to the aspect of all activities of the spontaneously present kayas and timeless awareness occurring naturally, not created or accomplished through effort. Since emotional and cognitive distortions (*dri-ma*) are cleared away in basic space and the scope of timeless awareness and enlightened qualities unfolds, there is 'Buddha.' And 'dakini' refers to the way in which all sensory appearances of samsara and nirvana manifest as specific forms that come and

༉། དུ་འཁོར་འདས་ཀྱི་སྣང་བ་ཐམས་ཅད་འགྲོ་འོང་གི་རྣམ་པར་སྣང་
བས་མཁའ་འགྲོ་ཞིས་བྱའོ། །དེ་ལྟར་གཞིའི་ཆོས་སྐུ་བདེ་གཤེགས་སྙིང་པོ་
འཁོར་འདས་ཀུན་ཁྱབ་ཀྱི་བདག་ཉིད་ཆེན་པོའི་རང་མདངས་དུ་བྱེད་པ་ཉིད་ནི་གཞིའི་
རིག་པ་མཐའ་གྲོལ་ཆེན་པོ་ཡིན་ལ། དོན་དམ་པའི་སྐུབ་པ་ཐམས་ཅད་འདིར་
འདུས་པ་ནི། གཞིའི་རིག་པ་དགོན་མཆོག་ཀུན་འདུས་ཀྱི་རོ་བོར་རང་དམ་
བཅས་ནས་རང་དབང་བསྒྱུར་པ་ནི་གནས་ལུགས་དོན་གྱི་སྐྱབས་འགྲོ་བླ་ན་མེད་
པ་ཡིན། ཚ་རབས་ཐོག་མ་མེད་པའི་དུས་ནས་རང་ཉིད་བདེན་པར་བཟུང་ཞིང་
ཡུལ་ལ་མཛེན་པར་ཞེན་པས་སྟོ་རྒྱུ་ཉིད་དུ་ཆུང་བ་ལ། དེ་ནི་འཁོར་འདས་
རིག་པ་གཅིག་གི་ཡོ་ལང་དུ་ཐག་བཅད་ནས་སེམས་ཀྱི་རྒྱ་བསྐྱེད་པ་ནི་སེམས་
བསྐྱེད་ཐམས་ཅད་ཀྱི་དམ་པར་གྱུར་པའོ། །གཟུང་འཛིན་གྱི་སེམས་ནི་ཁམས་
གསུམ་འཁོར་བར་འཁྱམས་པའི་སྱིད་པའི་འདྲེ་བོ་ཆ་ཡིན་ལ། དེ་སོ་སོར་
རྟོག་པའི་ཤེས་རབ་ཀྱིས་ཡུལ་མེད་སྟོང་པ་ཉིད་དུ་བསྐྲད་ཅིང་། བདག་མེད་

go (*dro*) within the expanse of the space (*kha*) of supreme emptiness.[4]

"The ground aspect of dharmakaya, buddha nature, becomes evident as the supreme principle that pervades all of samsara and nirvana. This is the ground aspect of awareness as supreme freedom from limitations. All sadhana practice concerned with ultimate reality is subsumed within it as follows.

"To gain true independence (*rang-wang gyur-wa*)—through the natural premise that the ground aspect of awareness is the essence in which all of the highest spiritual principles unite— is to take the way of abiding as the unsurpassable, ultimate refuge (*kyab-dro*).

"Throughout a beginningless series of lifetimes, the scope of your intellect has been severely limited by conceiving of yourself as truly existing and by fixating on sense objects. Now that you have reached the decision that samsara and nirvana are the phantasmagoria of a single awareness, the scope of your ordinary mind has grown. This is the most sacred of all means of arousing awakening mind (*sem-kyed*).

"The ordinary mind of dualistic perception is the great demon of conditioned existence that causes one to wander in the three realms of samsara. The discerning quality of sublime knowing (*so-sor tog-pai shey-rab*) banishes this demon (*geg-trad*) into emptiness, in which nothing exists as some object. Making evident sublime knowing which realizes that things have

---

[4] The Tibetan term for the Sanskrit "dakini" is *kha-dro,* the etymology of which is explained here according to its components of "space" (*kha*) and "go(er)" (*dro*).

༄༅། །ཚིགས་པའི་ཤེས་རབ་མཛོད་དུ་བྱེད་པ་གྲུང་རྒྱབ་སེམས་ཀྱི་སྒྲུང་

འཁོར་གཞིམ་གཞིག་དང་བྲལ་བ་ཡིན། མ་རིག་པའི་མུན་ཁམས་སུ་རིག་

པ་ཨེ་ཤེས་ཀྱི་བྱིན་ཆེན་དབབ་པ་བྱིན་འབེབས་ཉིད་དང་། སྒང་བ་རིག་པའི་

རྒྱན་དུ་ཕར་བའི་རང་རྩལ་ཚིགས་པས་རང་བྱུང་འདོད་ཡོན་ཀྱི་བཀོད་པ་མཆོད་

པ་ཉིད་ཀྱང་ཡིན། ཀུན་གཞི་ཚོས་སྐྱར་འཕོ་བ་གཏོད་མ་གཞིའི་སངས་རྒྱས་

ཏེ། དེའི་གནས་ལུགས་རྗེ་སྤྲུ་བ་བཞིན་དུ་མ་ཁྱིན་པའི་ཤེས་རབ་དང་། ཀུན་

ཤེས་ཀུན་གསལ་ཀྱི་བདག་ཉིད་རྗེ་སྟེད་པ་གཟིགས་པའི་ཤེས་རབ་མཛོན་དུ་གྱུར་

པའི་རྒྱལ་དང་རྒྱལ་སྲས་ཐམས་ཅད་ཀྱི་གསང་བ་འདུས་པ་ཉིད་ཡིན་ལ། དང་

པོ་ཚིགས་པའི་ཆ་ལ་བགར་སྒྲུང་དྲེགས་ཚོགས། ས་བརྒྱད་ཡན་ཆད་དུ་དབང་

བསྒྱར་བ་ལ་བྱུང་རྒྱབ་སེམས་དཔའ། མཛོན་སངས་རྒྱས་པའི་ཆ་ལ་སངས་

རྒྱས་དང་སངས་རྒྱས་ཀྱི་ཞིང་ཁམས་བཀོད་པ་ཐབས་ཀྱི་ལམ་ཡིན་ནོ། །ཀུན་

གཞི་མ་རིག་པ་དབང་ཕྱུག་ཆེན་པོ། དེ་ལས་ལྱང་བའི་ཚིག་ཚོགས་ཐམས་

ཅད་བགའ་སྒྲུང་ཚོས་སྒོང་སྟེ་བརྒྱད་ལྱ་འཛིར་བཞད་པ་ཐབས་ཀྱི་སློ་སྟེ། གཏོད

no identity (*dag-med tog-pai shey-rab*) constitutes the protection circle (*srung-khor*) of awakened mind (*jang-chhub sem*), not subject to defeat or destruction.

"Infusing the supreme blessing of the recognition of timeless awareness into the darkness of nonrecognition constitutes the actual stage of bringing down blessings (*jin-beb*).

"With the realization of the way in which sensory appearances arise as the adornment of awareness, the naturally occurring array of sense experiences is the offering (*chhod-pa*) itself.

"The shift from the perspective of the ground of all ordinary experience to that of dharmakaya brings one to buddhahood as the primordial ground of being. There is sublime knowing that understands the way in which this abides, just as it is, and sublime knowing that perceives things in their variety and is the epitome of omniscience and total lucidity. These two aspects of sublime knowing becoming evident is the union of the secrets of all victorious ones and their heirs.

"The path of skillful means constitutes the array of the hosts of arrogant guardians of the teachings, analogous to the first glimpses of realization; that of bodhisattvas, analogous to mastery of the eighth and higher levels of realization; and that of buddhas and pure realms, analogous to actual buddhahood. This avenue of skillful means explains the ground of all ordinary experience—the nonrecognition of awareness—as Maheshvara, and all thought patterns that arise from it as the guardians of the teachings—the dharmapalas who are the eight classes of gods and demons. These expressions of naturally occurring and supreme timeless awareness—which arise

༉། མ་གཞིའི་ཆོས་སྐུ་མངོན་དུ་གྱུར་པ་ལས་རང་བྱུང་གི་ཡེ་ཤེས་ཆེན་
པོ་རྩལ་དུ་ཤར་བ་རྣམས་དུམ་བུར་བཅད་དེ་ཐབས་ཀྱི་ལམ་དུ་བཙལ་བ་ཡིན་ནོ།།
དོན་དམ་པའི་སངས་རྒྱས་མངོན་དུ་བྱེད་པ་སྒྲུབ་པ་ཡིན་ཏེ། སྒྲུབ་དང་དཀྱིལ་
འཁོར་ཐམས་ཅད་འདིར་འདུས་ཤིང་རྫོགས་པའོ། །ཁམས་གསུམ་འཁོར་
བའི་ཆོས་ཐམས་ཅད་ཆོས་ཉིད་ཆེན་པོ་གཅིག་གི་རོལ་པར་འཕོས་ཏེ་རང་མངོན་
དུ་བྱེད་པ་སྐྱེ་འཆེན། དུས་གསུམ་འཕོ་འགྱུར་དང་བྲལ་བར་རང་ཐོག་ཏུ་
རང་ས་འཛིན་པ་བཞགས་གསོལ། ལྷ་བའི་རྒྱལ་པོ་གདོད་མ་གཞིའི་ཆོས་སྐུའི་
རང་ཞལ་མཇལ་བའི་ཆེ་དོ་མཚར་ཆེན་པོ་ཐོབ་པ་ལྷ་བ་མཇལ་བའི་ཡུག །ཆོས་
ཅན་ཆོས་ཉིད་དུ་རོལ་པའི་མཆོད་པ་ཆེན་པོ། འཁོར་འདས་རྫོགས་པ་ཆེན་པོའི་
གནས་ལུགས་ཇེ་བཞིན་མཐོང་ནས་དོ་མཚར་ཞིང་ཡིད་ཆེས་པ་དོན་གྱི་བསྟོད་པ་
ཉིད་དོ། །སྐུ་ཆོགས་སྤྲུང་བ་མ་འདྲེས་སོ་སོར་སྟུང་བ་སྐུའི་བཀོད་པ། སྤྲུན་
གྱིས་རྟོགས་ཤིང་གྲུབ་པ་གསུང་གི་རོལ་པ། །ཀ་དག་སྟོང་མཐའ་བྲལ་བའི་
དབྱིངས་ཉིད་ཐུགས་ཀྱི་རོལ་པ་སྟེ། སྐུ་དང་ཡེ་ཤེས་ཀྱི་རོལ་པ་མ་བཙལ་བྱུན་

132

as its dynamic energy, due to the primordial ground aspect of dharmakaya becoming evident—are categorized and structured into the path of skillful means. Sadhana practice makes the ultimate awakened state fully evident. All sadhanas and mandalas are subsumed and perfect within this.

"The shift in perspective from all phenomena of the three realms of samsara to the display of the single supreme nature of phenomena makes the fundamental nature fully evident. This constitutes the stage of invitation (*kyan-dren*).

"Holding to the natural state (*rang-sa*) in all its immediacy, free of transition or change throughout the three times, constitutes the request to remain (*zhug-sol*).

"To experience a great sense of wonder upon encountering your own true face—the primordial ground aspect of dharmakaya, the most majestic of views—is to pay homage (*khyag-tsal*) by encountering the view.

"The display of phenomena within the context of their true nature constitutes the supreme offering (*chhod-pa*).

"To feel a sense of wonder and conviction when you perceive, just as it is, the way in which samsara and nirvana abide as great perfection is the ultimate praise (*tod-pa*).

"The array of enlightened form (*ku*) is that of things manifesting distinctly and individually in all their variety. The display of enlightened speech (*sung*) is their spontaneous presence (*lhun-drub*) and perfection. The display of enlightened mind (*t'hug*) is basic space itself as original purity (*ka-dag*), free of the limitations of conceptual elaboration. What distinguishes awareness as great perfection are these enlightened qualities, which are due to realization of the fundamental nature, the

༄༅། །གྲུབ་པའི་དང་ཚུལ་རྟོགས་པའི་ཡོན་ཏན་རྣམ་བཞིའི་ཕྱིན་ལས་

ལ་དབང་བསྒྱུར་བ་རྣམས་རྟོགས་ཆེན་རིག་པའི་མཚན་ཉིད་ཡིན་ནོ། །དབང་

བཞི་ཡང་དེ་བཞིན་དུ་སྐུ་གསུང་ཐུགས་ཡོན་ཏན་ཕྲིན་ལས་རང་བྱུང་ཉིད་ལ་གཅིག་

ཆར་དུ་རྟོགས་པ་ཡིན་པར་ཤེས་པར་གྱིས་ཤིག །དེ་ལྟར་རྟོགས་པའི་དང་

ཆུལ་ཇི་ལྟ་བ་བཞིན་དུ་ཤེས་ཤིང་རྟོགས་པ་ནི་རྟོགས་པ་ཆེན་པོར་ངེས་པའོ། །དེ

མ་ཤེས་པའི་དབང་གིས་སྟོན་ཡང་འཁོར་བར་འཁྱམས་པ་ཡིན། །གཏོད་ནས་

རྟོགས་ཀྱང་མ་རིག་པས་བསྐྱིབས་ཏེ་ཆུ་རང་གྲོལ་དུ་ཡོད་པ་འཁྱག་པས་བསྐུམ་

པ་དང་། །གསེར་དང་ནོར་བུ་ངོ་མ་ཤེས་པས་རྐྱུད་པ་མི་སེལ་བ་ལྟ་བུར་གྱུར་

པའོ། །དོན་དམ་པར་གཞི་བདེ་གཤེགས་སྙིང་པོའི་ཡེ་ཤེས་རང་ཡོན་ཏན་

རྩལ་དུ་རྟོགས་པ་རྟེན་དང་བརྟེན་པའི་འཁོར་ལོ་སོ་སོར་འཕད་པ་རྣམས་ནི་གདུལ་

བྱ་ཐག་འཛིན་ཅན་རྣམས་ཀུན་རྟོབ་རྩོལ་བཅས་ཀྱི་ལམ་ལ་བརྟེན་ནས་དོན་དམ་

རྩོལ་མེད་ཀྱི་དབྱིངས་སུ་ཁ་དྲང་བའི་ཐབས་སུ་བསྟན་པ་ཡིན། །དེས་ན་གསལ་

དག་སྟོང་པ་གསུམ་གྱི་གནད་དང་ལྡན་པས་འཕགས་བུ་རྒྱན་མེད་པའི་དབྱིངས་

སུ་ཁ་དྲང་བ་ཡིན་ནོ། །ཞེས་གསུངས་ཤིང་མི་སྣང་བར་ཡལ་ལོ།

display of the kayas and timeless awareness that is unsought yet spontaneously present—qualities that constitute mastery of the four kinds of enlightened activity (*lay*). In a similar way, understand that, with the natural occurrence of enlightened form, speech, mind, qualities, and activities, the four empowerments are simultaneously complete.

"To understand and realize the fundamental nature of such perfection, just as it is, is certainly great perfection. Before this, you have wandered in samsara due to a lack of such understanding. Although there is primordial perfection, it has been obscured by the nonrecognition of awareness. It is like water, which is naturally free-flowing, being confined—frozen into ice—or like gold and gems not being recognized for what they are and so not alleviating poverty.

"Ultimately, the timeless awareness and qualities of the ground of being—buddha nature—are perfect as the dynamic energy of that ground. The explanations of these as distinct mandalas of supporting and supported factors constitute skillful means, which are demonstrated to lead those to be tamed—those who invest things with permanence—along the relative path of effort to ultimate basic space, which entails no effort. Therefore, with three key factors—clarity, purity, and emptiness—one is led to the basic space of the unsurpassable goal."

Saying this, he faded away.

Orgyan Tsokyey Dorje

༄༅། །སྐྱར་ཡང་བར་སྐབས་ཤིག་ཏུ་དཔལ་ཡོ་རྒྱུན་མཚོ་སྐྱེས་རྡོ་རྗེའི་ཞལ་མཇལ་བའི་དུས་སུ་བདག་གིས། ཀྱི་ཁྱབ་བདག་གདོད་མའི་མགོན་པོ་ཞིང་ཁམས་དང་གཞལ་ཡས་ཁང་དང་ལྷར་བསྐྱེད་ཅིང་བསྒྲུབ་པ་རྣམས་ཅིའི་ཕྱིར་བསྐྱེན་པ་ཡིན་ལགས། ཞེས་ཞུས་པས་བཀའ་སྩལ་པ། རྣམ་མཁས་གར་ཁྱབ་ཀྱི་འཛིག་རྟེན་འདིའི་དག་ཕྱི་བདག་ལྷའི་དུ་དུ་སྟེ། དེའི་གནས་པོར་སྒྲུལ་པའི་འོད་ལས་གྲུབ་པའི་ཞིང་ཁམས་སྨོང་བ་དང་། ནང་གནས་ཁང་འོངས་སྨྱོད་ལུས་དང་བཅས་པར་འཛིན་པ་ནང་བདག་ལྷའི་དུ་དུ་སྟེ། དེའི་གནས་པོར་གཞལ་ཡས་ཁང་དང་ལྷ་བསྒོམ་པ་དང་། དུས་དང་རྣམ་པ་ཀུན་ཏུ་ང་ཞེས་བདག་ཏུ་སྣང་བའི་ཤེས་པ་བག་ལ་ཉལ་བ་རྒྱུ་དང་རྒྱུན་མ་ཆད་པ་ནི་གསང་བ་བདག་ལྷའི་དུ་དུ་སྟེ་འཁོར་བའི་སྣང་སེམས་ཐམས་ཅད་ཀྱི་སྒྱུན་ཐག་གོ །དེའི་གཉེན་པོར་ལྷའི་ང་རྒྱལ་བརྟན་པོ་བཟུང་བ་ཡིན་ནོ། །འདིའི་གནད་མ་ཤེས་ན་ལ་ལས་ནི་བསྐྱེད་གསལ་ང་རྒྱལ་བཟུང་བ་དང་བཅས་པ་དོར

O N YET ANOTHER OCCASION, I met the glorious Or-gyan Tsokyey Dorje in a vision and asked the following question: "Ah, sovereign lord, primordial guide, why are visualizations and sadhana practices concerning pure realms, immeasurable mansions, and deities taught?"

He bestowed the following reply: "The universes that extend throughout space constitute the outer rudra of viewing things in terms of identity. The antidote to this is to refine them into emanated pure realms formed of light.

"On the inner level, the perception of dwellings and wealth to be enjoyed, as well as one's body, constitutes the inner rudra of viewing things in terms of identity. The antidote to this is to meditate on immeasurable mansions and deities.

"At all times and in all ways, there is the cohesive and un-interrupted latent consciousness that perceives a self—an 'I'—which constitutes the secret rudra of viewing things in terms of identity, that is, the common thread running through all sensory appearances and states of mind in samsara. The antidote to this is to hold firmly to the pride of the deity.

"If these key points are not understood, some people will neglect clear visualization and the holding of vajra pride, and concentrate solely on the repetition of mantra. Some will hold

༄༅། །རྣས་དག་གི་བརྒྱས་པ་ཁོན་ལ་འབད། ལ་ལས་ནི་སྤྱ་དང་

ཞིང་ཁམས་རང་རྒྱུད་པར་བཟུང་ནས་བསྒྲུབ་ཀྱང་འཆང་མི་རྒྱ་བས་ན་གནད་འདི་

ཤེས་པར་གྱིས་ཤིག ཅེས་གསུངས་ཤིང་མི་སྡུང་བར་ཡལ་ལོ།

that the deities and pure realms exist in their own right, and so even though they engage in sadhana practice they will not awaken to buddhahood. Thus, you must understand these key points!"

Saying this, he vanished.

Ekajati

༄༅། །ཡང་རེ་ཞིག་གི་ཚེ་དབྱིངས་ཀྱི་རྗེ་མོ་ཨེ་ཀ་ཛ་ཊིའི་ཞལ་མཐའ་དག་བའི་ཚེ། བདག་གིས། ཀྱི་འཁོར་འདས་ཀུན་གྱི་ཨ་ཕྱི་གཅིག་མ་ལགས། འཁོར་འདས་སྟོང་ཆེན་དབྱིངས་ཀྱི་རྗེ་མོའི་མཁའ་གསང་དུ་རོལ་པའི་ཐིག་ལེ་འདི་ལ་མིང་གང་ཞེས་བྱ། ཞེས་ཞུས་པས་བཀའ་སྩལ་པ། ཀྱི་ཨ་མའི་བུ་ཆུང་ཁྱོད་ལ་དགོངས་བརྒྱུད་ལུས་ཀྱི་ཆུལ་དུ་རྟོགས་པར་བྱས། བཀའ་བརྒྱུད་དུ་ཞིའི་ཆུལ་དུ་བསྟན་ནས་ནར་སོན་པར་བྱས། སྙན་བརྒྱུད་སྙིང་གཏམ་ལྟ་བུར་གདམས་ནས་བློ་དང་ལྡན་པར་བྱས་ཡོད། གདུལ་བྱ་ལས་སྣོན་གྱིས་འབྲེལ་བའི་སྐལ་ལྡན་རྣམས་ལ་སྟོན་དང་འབྲེལ་ཆད་དོན་དང་ལྡན་པ་ཡིན་ནོ།། ཐེག་པ་ཐམས་ཅད་ཀྱི་རྒྱལ་པོ་འདའི་མིང་ནི་སྔ་བྱགས་ཆད་ཐམས་ཅད་དའི་མིང་ཡིན་ཅིང་ངས་གསང་བླ་ན་མེད་པ་མཁའ་སྤྱོད་ཨ་མའི་མཁའ་དུ་ཐུབ་རྒྱབ་པའི་རོལ་པ་འདི་ལ་མིང་གི་རྣམ་གྲངས་དུ་མ་ཡོད་ཀྱང་མིང་བདུན་དུ་ངས་སྦྱོར། །ཅེས་འདི་གསང་ཆེན་གཉིས་དང་ལྡན་པས་གསང་། བདག་ཏོག་མཚན་མ་ཡིན

O N YET ANOTHER OCCASION, when I met the queen
of basic space, Ekajati, in a vision, I made the following
request: "Ah, sole grandmother of all samsara and nirvana,
what do you call the spiritual approach of delighting in the
secret sky of the queen of basic space, in the supreme emptiness of samsara and nirvana?"

She bestowed the following reply: "Ah, mother's little child,
I have given you in its entirety the lineage of the mind-to-mind
transmission of enlightened intent (*gong-gyud*), as though providing you with a body. I have reared you, nursing you with the
lineage of transmission through symbols (*da-gyud*) as though
suckling you with mother's milk. I have fostered your intelligence, imparting the lineage of oral transmission (*nyan-gyud*)
to you as heartfelt advice. Teach those fortunate ones to be
tamed who are connected to you by karma and by aspiration.
All connected to you will find meaning in this.

"My name is given to this most majestic of all spiritual approaches. All audible sounds are my name, and so this all-
embracing display of the sky of the mother who enjoys space,
the unsurpassable and definitive secret, is referred to by many
names, but here I shall speak of only seven.

"Since this teaching involves two great kinds of secrecy, it is

༄༄། བྱེད་ཀྱི་འཇིགས་པ་ལས་སྐྱོབས་པར་བྱེད་པས་སྐྱགས། དོན་
དམ་མི་ཤིགས་པའི་རྡོ་རྗེ། ལས་ཐམས་ཅད་ཀྱི་ཡིན་ཏན་བཅུད་དུ་འདུས་པས་
ཐིག་པའོ། ཚོས་ཐམས་ཅད་ཀྱི་ཡིན་ལུགས་མཐར་ཕྱག་ཏུ་གནས་པས་དོན།
རྟོགས་བྱུ་རྣམས་ཀྱི་གཙོ་བོར་གྱུར་པས་དམ་པ། སྐྱོན་དང་དྲི་མ་ཐམས་ཅད་
བྱུང་བ། སྐུ་དང་ཡེ་ཤེས་ལས་དང་འབྲས་བུའི་ཚོས་ཐམས་ཅད་ཁོང་དུ་
ཆུབ་རྒྱབ་པ། ཐམས་ཅད་དག་མཉམ་གྱི་རྫོལ་པ་སྐུ་ཚོགས་པའི་འཁར་གཞི་
རྡོ་རྗེ་གསུམ་གྱི་སྒོག་གཅིག་པུར་བཤུགས་པས་ཙེ་ཧྲུའམ་སྙིང་སྤྱི་མེམས་སོ།།
འཁོར་འདས་ལས་གསུམ་རྟོགས་པ། ཐིག་པ་ཐམས་ཅད་དོན་གཅིག་ཏུ་དྲིལ་
མདོ་གཅིག་ཏུ་བསྡུས་པས་ཐིག་པ་ཐམས་ཅད་ཀྱི་སྤྱི་གཞིར་གྱུར་པས་ཆེན་པོའོ།།
རྟོག་པའི་གྲུ་བྱར་ཐམས་ཅད་ལས་འདས་པས་ཐིག་ལེ། འཁོར་འདས་བྱུང་
རྒྱབ་ཀྱི་མེམས་སུ་རོ་གཅིག་པས་རྡ་གཅིག་གོ། རིག་པ་བདེ་གཤེགས་སྙིང་
པོའི་དང་དྲངས་གསལ་ལ་རྟོགས་མ་དང་བྲལ་བས་འོད་གསལ། མི་ཤིགས་
པ་རྡོ་རྗེའི་ཚོས་བདུན་དང་ལྡན་པས་རྡོ་རྗེ། འཁོར་འདས་ཀྱི་ཚོས་ཐམས་ཅད་
ཀྱི་བཅུད་དུ་གནས་པས་སྙིང་པོའོ། འཁོར་འདས་ཀྱི་ཚོས་ཐམས་ཅད་བདེ་

'secret' (*sang*). Since it protects one from the fearful conse-
quences of conceiving of a self and imagining it to have characteristics, it is 'mantra' (*ngag*). It is the indestructible 'vajra'
(*dor-je*) of ultimate reality. In that the qualities of all paths are
distilled to their vital essence, it is 'yana,' or 'spiritual approach' (*t'heg-pa*).

"Since it abides as the consummate mode of all phenomena, it has ultimate 'meaning' (*don*). In that it is the foremost
of what is to be realized, it is 'sacred' (*dam*). It is the 'refine-
ment' (*jang*) of all flaws and distortions. It is the all-embracing and consummate state (*chhub*) of all qualities of the kayas, timeless awareness, the path, and the goal. And it is
'chitta,' or 'heart'—that is to say, 'mind' (*sem*)—abiding as the
single life force of the three vajras, the ground for the arising
of the display of myriad things in their equalness and purity.

"It is the 'perfection' (*dzog-pa*) of three modes—samsara,
nirvana, and the path. It is 'great' (*chhen-po*), since it functions as the common ground of all spiritual approaches, sub-
suming all of them within a single purpose and bringing them
to a single point of convergence.

"Since it is beyond all the sharp edges of concepts, it is
'sphere' (*t'hig-le*). Since samsara and nirvana are of one taste
in awakened mind, it is 'unique' (*nyag-chig*).

"Since the fundamental nature of awareness, buddha nature, is pristine and lucid, free of sullying factors, it is 'utter
lucidity' (*od-sal*). Since it is endowed with the seven indestructible vajra attributes, it is 'vajra' (*dor-je*). And since it abides
as the vital essence of all phenomena of samsara and nirvana,
it is 'heart essence' (*nying-po*).

༄༅། གཞིགས་སྐྱིང་པོའི་རང་དུ་ཐུབ་ཀྱིས་འདུས་ཤིང་ཡོངས་སུ་རྒྱབ་པས་
འཁོར་འདས་ཐུབ་རྒྱབ་བོ། སྐྱེ་འཆི་བསྐྱེས་རྒྱུད་ཐམས་ཅད་དང་བྲལ་བས་
གཞན་དུ། སྤྲུན་གྲུབ་ཀྱི་ཕྱི་རྒྱུ་མ་རལ་བས་བུམ་པ། ཨེ་ཤེས་ཡོན་ཏན་
ཐམས་ཅད་བསགས་ནས་སྒྲུངས་པ་ལྟ་བུས་སྐུ་ཞེས་བྱའོ། ཞེས་གསུངས་
ཤིང་མི་སྲུང་བར་ཡལ་ལོ། །དེ་ལྟར་སྒྱིར་བཞད་ནས་བྲི་བྲག་རིས་དགུའི་
ཐེག་པའི་ལམ་གྱི་ཡོན་ཏན་ཐམས་ཅད་རྫོགས་ཚུལ་གྱིས་མཚོན་ནས་བཤད་ན།
ང་དང་བདག་ཏུ་འཛིན་པའི་གཞི་གནང་ཟག་ཏུ་སྤྱོང་བ་ཐམས་ཅད་རང་བཞིན་མེད་
པར་མཐོང་བས་ཉན་ཐོས། ཕྱི་ནང་གི་དངོས་པོ་རྟེན་འབྲེལ་སྒྲུ་མའི་སྤྱང་བ་ལྟག
གཅིག་ཏུ་རྟོགས་པ་རང་བྱུང་རྒྱབ། སྟོང་ཉིད་རྟོགས་པའི་རྩལ་སྐྱེང་རྗེའི་ཏོ་
བོར་འབར་ནས་ཐབས་དང་ཤེས་རབ་ཀྱི་ཕྱོགས་ཐམས་ཅད་འབད་རྩོལ་མེད་པར་དང་
གིས་འདུ་བས་ན་བྱང་སེམས་ཏེ། ཀུན་འབྱུང་འཛིན་པའི་ཐེག་པ་གསུམ་གྱི་
ཡོན་ཏན་ཡར་སྤྲུན་དུ་རྟོགས་ཤིང་། བྱ་བའི་རྒྱུད་ཀྱི་དཀའ་ཐུབ་དང་གཙང་
སྤྲས་ལྟ་མཉེས་པར་བྱ་བ་དང་། ཨུ་པ་ཡའི་རྒྱུད་ཀྱི་བརྒྱས་བཟོད་དང་ཏེང

"Since all phenomena of samsara and nirvana (*khor-day*) are subsumed within the embrace (*ub*) of buddha nature and are totally consummated (*chhub*) therein, it is the 'all-embracing consummation of samsara and nirvana.'

"Since it is free of all birth, death, decay, and decrepitude, it is 'youthful' (*zhon-nu*). Since there is no violation of its encompassing spontaneous presence, it is 'vase' (*bum-pa*). And since it is, as it were, an amassing, or gathering, of all enlightened qualities and aspects of timeless awareness, it is 'body' (*ku*).

Saying this, she vanished.

I will elaborate on her general explanation by illustrating the way in which all qualities of the paths of the nine developmental spiritual approaches (*t'heg-pa rim-pa gu*) are complete.

In the shravaka approach, one perceives that none of the manifestations of personal identity—that is, none of the bases for the conception of an 'I' or self—have any independent nature (*rang-zhin med-pa*). The pratyekabuddha approach is the realization that all things, whether external or internal, are solely the illusory appearances of interdependent connection (*ten-drel*). In the bodhisattva approach, the dynamic energy of the realization of emptiness arises as the essence that is compassion (*nying-je*), and so all aspects of skillful means and sublime knowing are effortlessly subsumed as a matter of course. The qualities of these three approaches, which lead one away from the origin of suffering, are complete in that each higher approach incorporates the lower ones.

The kriyatantra approach is one of delighting the deity through ascetic practices and ritual purification. In the upaya-

༈། དེ་འཛིན་གྱིས་དངོས་གྲུབ་སྒྲུབ་པ་དང་། རྣལ་འབྱོར་གྱི་རྒྱུད་
དུ་མཚན་མ་མེད་པ་དབྱིངས་ཀྱི་ཕྱིན་རྣབས་རྡོ་རྗེ་དབྱིངས་ཀྱི་དཀྱིལ་འཁོར་ཆེན་
པོར་ལྷ་བའི་ཞི་གནས་དང་ལྷག་མཐོང་གི་རྣལ་འབྱོར་ཏེ། དགའ་སྦུབ་རིག་
བྱེད་ཀྱི་ཐིག་པའི་ཡོན་ཏན་དང་བྱེད་ལས་ཐམས་ཅད་ཀྱང་དངོས་གྲུབ་ཀྱི་སྙིང་པོ་
བཟོད་དུ་མེད་པའི་རང་སེམས་ལྷུན་ཅིག་སྐྱེས་པའི་དབྱིངས་གཅིག་པུ་འདིར་རྫོགས་
ཤིང་། ཕ་རྒྱུད་མ་རྡུ་ཡོ་གའི་ཚོས་ཐམས་ཅད་གཏོད་མ་ཉིད་ནས་དོན་དམ་
དགོར་བདུན་ནས་ལྷག་པའི་བདེན་གཉིས་དབྱེར་མེད་ཀྱི་ཚོས་སྐུ་ཆེན་པོར་དག
པ་དང་། ལྱང་ཨ་ནུ་ཡོ་གའི་ཡེ་རྗེ་བཞིན་པ་དང་ཡེ་ཞེས་ལྷུན་གྱིས་གྲུབ་པའི་
དགྱིལ་འཁོར་གཉིས་རྣང་དུ་འཛུག་པའི་སྲས་བདེ་བ་ཆེན་པོ་བྱང་ཆུབ་སེམས་ཀྱི་
དགྱིལ་འཁོར་དུ་སྲང་སྲིད་དགའ་མཉམ་ཆེན་པོར་རྫོགས་པའི་དོན་རྣམས་ཀྱང་། རང་
བཞིན་རྫོགས་པ་ཆེན་པོ་འོད་གསལ་མཐའ་དབུས་ལས་འདས་པའི་དབྱིངས་
གཅིག་ཏུ་གཞི་སྲང་ལྷུན་གྲུབ་རིན་པོ་ཆེའི་སྲང་བ་རྒྱ་ཆད་ཕྱོགས་ལྷུང་དང་བྲལ་
བར་རང་འཕར་བ་ཐམས་ཅད་གསེར་དང་དེའི་མདངས་བཞིན་དུ་སོ་སོ་མ་ཡིན་པའི་

tantra approach, spiritual attainment (siddhi) is accomplished through mantra repetition and meditative absorption (*ting-nge-dzin*). The yogatantra approach is the yoga of calm abiding (*zhi-nay*) and profound insight (*lhag-t'hong*)—the view of the blessing of basic space, which cannot be characterized, within the supreme mandala of vajra basic space. All of the qualities and functions of these three approaches, which evoke awareness through ascetic practices, are complete within the single basic space that is coemergent with indescribable natural mind (*rang-sem*), the very essence of spiritual attainment.

In the approach of mahayoga, or father tantra, all phenomena are pure from the very beginning in supreme dharmakaya as ultimate reality endowed with the seven attributes, or as the inseparability of the two levels of profound truth. In the approach of anuyoga, based on explanatory commentaries, the supremely blissful mandala of awakened mind is the child born of the union of two mandalas—timeless reality just as it is and the spontaneous presence of timeless awareness. Within this mandala of awakened mind, the world of appearances and possibilities is perfect as a supreme state of purity and equalness. In the approach of natural great perfection—utter lucidity, a single basic space transcending center or circumference—the ground of being manifesting as sensory appearances is the manifestation of precious spontaneous presence, with everything arising naturally such that it is not subject to restrictions or extremes, and with no separation, just as there is none between gold and its luster. So the very meaning of buddha nature—dharmakaya without transition or change,

༄༅། ཆོས་སྐུ་འཕོ་འགྱུར་མེད་པ་རིག་པ་མཐའ་གྲོལ་ཆེན་པོ་གཞི་དབྱིངས་

བདེ་གཤེགས་སྙིང་པོའི་དོན་ཉིད་ལ་གཅིག་ཆར་དུ་འདུས་པ་སྟེ། སོ་སོར་བསྟན་

པ་རྣམས་ནི། གདུལ་བྱ་རིམ་གྱིས་དགྲི་བའི་ཆེད་དུ་བསྟན་པར་ཟད་དོ།

awareness supremely free of limitation, the ground of being as basic space—is subsumed simultaneously.

The presentation of these approaches individually is simply a teaching so that those to be tamed can be led in progressive stages.

Shri Simha

༄༅། །སྐྱར་ཡང་རིག་འཛིན་གྱི་རྒྱལ་པོ་ཕྲི་མེང་ཏའི་ཞལ་མངལ་
བའི་ཚོ། གྱི་སྤྲོན་པ་ལགས། རྫོགས་པ་ཆེན་པོའི་ལམ་གང་ལགས་
བདག་ལ་བསྟན་དུ་གསོལ། ཞེས་པས་བཀའ་སྩལ་པ། རྫོགས་པ་ཆེན་པོ་ནི་
འཁོར་འདས་ཀྱི་སྤྱི་གཞི་ཆེན་པོ་འཁོར་འདས་ལམ་གསུམ་རྫོགས་པའི་དབྱིངས་
ཆེན་པོ་ཡིན་ཏེ། དེའི་ངང་ཚུལ་ཡིན་ལུགས་ཤེས་པ་ནི་ལྟ་བ་ཡིན་ནོ། །གཏོང་
མའི་ཡེ་གཞི་ཆེན་པོར་རང་དབང་བསྒྱུར་ཏེ་རང་ཐོག་ཏུ་རང་སད་ཅིང་བཙལ་བ་ནི་
བསྒོམ་པ་དམིགས་གཏད་དང་བྲལ་བ་ཉིད་ཡིན་ནོ། །དེ་ནི་དཔེར་ན་རྒྱ་ཐེག་
རྒྱ་མཚོ་དང་འདྲེས་ཚེ་རྒྱ་མཚོ་བཙོས་སུ་མེད་པར་རྒྱ་མཚོར་འགྱུར་བ་འམ།
བུམ་ནང་གི་ནམ་མཁའ་ཕྱིའི་ནམ་མཁའ་དང་འདྲེས་ཚེ་ནམ་མཁའ་བཙོས་སུ་མེད་
པར་ནམ་མཁར་འབྱམས་ཀློས་པ་ལྟ་བུའོ། །གཞི་དང་སེམས་ལ་ཕྱེ་ནང་མེད་
གྱང་བདག་འཛིན་གྱིས་ཕྱེ་ནང་དུ་བཅད་པ་ཙམ་དུ་ཟད་དེ། རྒྱ་རང་གྲོལ་དུ་
ཡོད་པ་གྲང་ལྷག་གི་སྟུན་ཐག་གིས་འཁྱག་པར་བསྒུམས་པ་ལྟར་གཞི་རང་གྲོལ་

LATER, WHEN IN A VISION I met Shri Simha, king of rigdzins, I asked the following question: "Ah, respected teacher, I pray, please reveal to me the path of the Great Perfection!"

Upon my having made this request, he bestowed the following reply: "The great perfection is the supreme common ground of samsara and nirvana, the supreme basic space in which the three modes of samsara, nirvana, and the path are perfect.

"Knowing this fundamental nature as it actually is, is the view.

"Gaining mastery within this supreme and timeless primordial ground—by awakening to it, and opening up to it, in all its immediacy—is meditation free of any fixed frame of reference. It is like a drop of water blending with the ocean and becoming the ocean without altering it, or space within a vase blending with the space outside, extending freely throughout that space without altering it. Although there is no distinction between inner and outer with respect to ordinary mind versus the ground of being, what amounts to such a division is caused by perceiving in terms of identity (*dag-dzin*). Just as water, which exists in a naturally free-flowing state, freezes

༄༅། །དུ་ཡོད་པ་ལ་བདག་འཛིན་གྱི་སྒྲུབ་ཐག་གཅིག་པུས་འཕོར་བ་ཡོངས་

སུ་གྲུབ་པའོ། །དིའི་ངང་ཚུལ་ཤེས་ཏེ་ལུས་ཀྱི་སྟོ་ནས་བཟང་ངན་བར་གསུམ་

གྱི་བུ་བ་བཏང་སྟེ་བྱར་མེད་དུ་དུར་ཁྲོད་ཀྱི་མེ་རོ་ལྟར་སྡོད་པ་དང་། ངག་གི་བུ་

བ་གསུམ་པོ་ཡང་དེ་བཞིན་དུ་བཏང་སྟེ་ལྐུགས་པ་ལྟར་སྡོད་པ་དང་། སེམས་

ཀྱི་བུ་བ་གསུམ་པོ་ཡང་བཏང་ནས་སྟོན་ནམ་བསྐྱེད་བྱེད་ཀྱི་རྐྱེན་གསུམ་དང་

བྲལ་བ་ལྷུ་བུ་མི་འཚོས་པར་བཞག་པ་ནི་མཉམ་པར་བཞག་པ་ཞེས་བྱའོ། །བྱ་

བ་དགུ་ཕྱུགས་སུ་བཏང་བས་བྱ་བཏང་དང་བྱར་མེད་སློས་མ་བཅོས་པས་ཀྲོ་འཛིན་

ཞེས་ཀྱང་བྱའོ། །གནད་དེ་ཉིད་ཀྱི་དང་དུ་རང་གདིང་ཆེན་པོ་འཐོབ་པར་འགྱུར་

རོ། །གཞན་ཡང་འགྲོ་འདུག་འགྱལ་བསྡོད་བརྐྱབས་བརྫོང་བསམ་སྤྱོད་ཐམས་

ཅད་ཀྱི་དུས་ཀུན་ཏུ་ལྷ་བའི་སྣང་ས་མ་ཕོར་བར་སྲུང་སྲིད་སྒྱུ་མ་ལྟ་བུ། སློམ་

པའི་གདིང་མ་ཕོར་བར་དང་མཛིན་གྱུར་དུ་རིག་པ། སྡོད་པ་བག་མེད་དུ་མ་

སོང་བར་སྡོད་ལམ་རྣམ་བཞི་ཆུལ་བཞིན་བསྟེན་པའོ། །གནད་དེ་ནི་ཕི་བའི་

མཐར་མ་ཕྱག་བར་དུ་བརྟེན་དགོས་པ་ཡིན། དེ་ནི་བསློམ་པ་རང་གྲོལ་ཀྲོ

into ice under the influence of a cold wind, so the ground of being exists in a naturally free state, with the entire spectrum of samsara established solely by the influence of perceiving in terms of identity.

"Understanding this fundamental nature, you give up the three kinds of physical activity—good, bad, and neutral—and sit like a corpse in a charnel ground, with nothing needing to be done. You likewise give up the three kinds of verbal activity, remaining like a mute, as well as the three kinds of mental activity, resting without contrivance like the autumn sky free of the three polluting conditions.[5] This is termed 'formal meditative equipoise' (*nyam-par zhag-pa*). It is also termed 'letting go of anything to be done' or 'nothing needing to be done' (*jar-med*), since all manner of activities have been given up, and 'beyond ordinary consciousness' (*lo-day*), since there is no contrivance by ordinary consciousness. In the context of this key point, you will discover a great indwelling confidence.

"Furthermore, at all times while going about, sitting, shifting, moving, repeating mantras, speaking aloud, thinking, or otherwise conducting yourself, without losing the perspective of view (*ta-wa*) you are aware that the world of appearances and possibilities is like an illusion. Without losing the indwelling confidence of your meditation (*gom-pa*), you are aware of your fundamental nature (*ngang*) becoming evident. And without your conduct (*kyod-pa*) becoming careless, you rely correctly on the four kinds of authentic conduct. These are the key points to rely on until the end of your days. This is

---

[5] Clouds, fog, and haze.

༄༅། །འདས་སོ། །སྒྱུད་པའི་གནད་ནི་ཐམས་ཅད་སྟོང་པ་ཉིད་ཡིན་

པས་རྗེ་ལྱར་སྒྱུད་ཀྱང་ཉེས་པས་མི་གོས་སྐྱམ་དུ་ལྱ་བའི་ཕྱོགས་སུ་སྒྱུད་པ་མི་འཚལ་

བར་ལུས་ངག་གི་མི་དགེ་བ་དུག་བཞིན་སྤངས་ཏེ་ཞེ་དུལ་བག་ཡོད་དང་ལྡན་པ་

ཁྲིམས་བདག་རྒྱལ་པོའི་མདུན་སར་སྐྱིབ་པ་ལྱ་བུ་ཞིག་དགོས། ཡང་ལུས་

ངག་ཡིད་གསུམ་གྱི་དགེ་བ་གཞན་ཐབ་ཐབ་འདྲ་བའི་ཡུལ་དུ་ཞིན་ནས་ཡང་དག་

པའི་ལྱ་སྒོམ་ཟིལ་གྱིས་མནན་ཏེ་འཁོར་བར་བསོད་ནམས་བསགས་པ་ཚམ་ལ་

མི་ཚེ་འདས་ན་གསེར་གྱི་སྒོག་གིས་བཅིངས་པ་ལྱ་བུ་སྒྱུད་པའི་ཕྱོགས་སུ་ལྱ་

བ་མི་འཚལ་བར་དཔེར་ན་སྟེར་ཆགས་གང་གིས་ཀྱང་ཟིལ་གྱིས་མི་ནོན་པ་མེང་

གི་གངས་ལ་འགྱིང་བ་ལྱ་བུ་ཞིག་དགོས་པ་ཡིན་ནོ། །ཁྱད་པར་ལྱ་བ་སྟོང་

ཉིད་རྟོགས་ཀྱང་སྙིང་རྗེ་གཞན་ནས་བསྒོམ་དགོས་ཟེར་བ་དག་ཡོད་པའི་རྗེས་སུ་

འབྲངས་ན་རྒྱ་རང་ལ་ཡོད་ཀྱང་རྙེན་གཞན་ནས་ཚོལ་དགོས་པར་སྐྱད་པ་དང༌།།

མི་རང་ལ་ཡོད་ཀྱང་ཚོ་ཏོད་གཞན་ནས་ཚོལ་བ་དང༌། རྣང་རང་ཉིད་ཡིན་ཀྱང་

བསིལ་གཞན་ནས་འབྱུང་དགོས་ཟེར་བ་ལྱ་བུའི་ཕྱོགས་སུ་ཟེས་ཏེ། འཁོར་

འདས་སྟོང་ཉིད་ཆེན་པོ་ཉིད་དུ་ངེས་པར་ཐག་ཆོད་པ་ནི་འཁོར་འདས་དག་མཉམ་

དུ་རོལ་པའི་སྙིང་རྗེ་བྱང་ཆུབ་ཀྱི་སེམས་རླ་ན་མེད་པའོ། །ལྱ་སྒོམ་གྱི་གནད་

meditation that is naturally free and beyond ordinary consciousness.

"The key point of conduct is to renounce nonvirtuous physical and verbal activities as if they were poison, not overemphasizing view at the expense of conduct by thinking that since everything is emptiness you will not be sullied by flaws no matter how you behave. You must be calm, restrained, and careful, like someone who has been brought before the highest judge.

"On the other hand, by clinging to three kinds of incidental virtuous acts—physical, verbal, and mental—as though they were profound, you override correct view and meditation. If you spend this human life merely accumulating merit within samsara, it is as though you were bound by chains of gold. Without overemphasizing conduct at the expense of view, you must be like a snow lion roaming majestically across glaciers, whom no other beast of prey can overwhelm.

"In particular, if you follow those who say that although one realizes emptiness one must cultivate compassion elsewhere, you are similar to someone who claims that although one has water one must seek wetness elsewhere, that although one has fire one must seek warmth elsewhere, or that although one is fanned by the wind one must seek coolness elsewhere. The decisive experience of certainty that samsara and nirvana are supreme emptiness itself is unsurpassable awakened mind—compassion as the display of samsara and nirvana in their equalness and purity.

"There are those who, once they have been directly introduced to and are aware of the key points and fundamental

༄༅། །དང་རང་ཆུལ་ཇེ་ལྟ་བ་བཞིན་དུ་རོ་འཕོད་ནས་ཤེས་ནའང་དེས་ཆོག
པ་ཚམ་དུ་ཐག་བཅད་དེ་འཁོར་བའི་བྱ་བ་ལ་ཞིན་ནས་ཆགས་སྲང་གི་སྐྱོང་པ་སྲ་
ཚོགས་པས་མི་ཚེ་སྲུག་ཟད་དུ་གཏོང་བ་དག་ནི་ལྟ་སྒོམ་ཐམས་ཅད་འཁྱལ་པ་
འཁོར་བའི་བུ་བྱེད་ཀྱིས་ཟིལ་གྱིས་མནན་པ་ཡིན། ཉམས་ཀྱི་སྲུང་བ་ནི་སེམས་
དང་ཤེས་རྒྱུད་སྤར་ལྤར་མ་ཡིན་པར་འདོད་ལྤར་འཐེན་པའི་བདེ་སྲུང་འབོལ་ལེ་
བ་དང་། གཟུགས་ཁམས་སུ་འཐེན་པའི་གསལ་ཉམས་གསལ་ཇིག་གེ་
བ་དང་། གཟུགས་མེད་སུ་བཞིར་འཐེན་པའི་སྟོང་ཉམས་མི་རྟོག་པ་ཁ་ནང་
ལྟ་ཐོམ་ཡོ་རེ་བ་དྲན་མེད་ཤེས་མེད་གཏིང་འཐུག་ལྤ་བུ་དང་། ལྤ་བ་སྟོང་ཉིད་
ལ་རྒྱས་མེད་ཅིང་སེམས་སྟོང་པ་དངོས་པོར་མ་གྲུབ་པ་ཚམ་ལ་རློ་ཐག་བཅད་དེ
སྟོང་པའི་དང་དུ་ཇེ་གཅིག་ཏུ་འཛིག་པ་ནི་སྟིད་པའི་ཇེ་དང་། འདུ་ཤེས་མེད
པའི་ལྤར་འཐེན་པའི་ལྤ་བ་ཡིན་ནོ། །གཞན་ཡང་ཕྱི་སྟོང་ལྤ་འདྲེའི་ཚོ་འཕུལ་
ཐན་དང་ལྤས་དན་ལ་སོགས་པ་དབང་པོའི་ཡུལ་ལ་ཚོ་འཕུལ་སྣ་ཚོགས་འབྱུང་
བ་དང་། རང་སྟོང་ལུས་ལ་ན་ཚ་རྒྱག་ཏུ་སྣ་ཚོགས་པ་འབྱུང་བ་དང་། གསང་
སྟོང་སེམས་ཀྱི་བདེ་སྲུག་མ་རེས་པར་འབྱུང་བ་ཐམས་ཅད་ཉམས་རྟེན་པོ་ཆེའི་
མཚང་དུ་རེག་ཅིང་ཐག་བཅད་ན་རང་ཡལ་དུ་འགྲོ་བ་ཡིན། བདེན་ཞེན་རོ་དོགས་

nature of view and meditation just as they are, arrive at the decision that this introduction alone is sufficient. Still fixated on the need to do things in samsara, they squander their human lives engaging in various kinds of behavior based on attachment and aversion. All of their view and meditation is overwhelmed by the plans and actions of samsara.

"Meditative experiences (*nyam*) occur in which your ordinary mind—the continuum of your consciousness—is different from what it was before. Pleasurable experiences of bliss will propel you toward rebirth as a god of the desire realm. Vivid experiences of lucidity will propel you toward rebirth in the form realm. Experiences of voidness—blank, imploded nonconceptual states like that of deep sleep, without recollection or consciousness—will propel you toward rebirth in one of the four states of the formless realm. Without the slightest inkling of the view of emptiness, you may decide intellectually that mind is empty merely in that it has never existed as anything substantial, and so rest one-pointedly in that context of emptiness. This view will propel you toward the pinnacle of conditioned existence, that is, rebirth as a god in a state devoid of perception.

"As well, you may encounter upheavals (*long*). External upheavals consist of various phantasmagoria that affect one's senses, such as negative portents and omens that are the machinations of gods and demons. Internal upheavals include various diseases and bodily pains. Secret upheavals are random mood swings. If you are aware of their hidden flaw, that they are all enormously false experiences, and arrive at a decision about this, they will vanish naturally. If you reinforce them

༄༅། །ཀྱི་ངང་བཟུན་པར་གྱུར་ན་སྐྱོ་འབོག་བརྒྱལ་བ་ལ་སོགས་པས་འཆེ་བ་སྟོག་ལ་འབབ་པའི་རྒྱུ་རྐྱེན་དུ་འགྱུར་བ་དང་། །ལྱར་སྐྱང་འདིར་སྐྱང་ལ་མཆོན་པར་ཞེན་པའི་དབང་དུ་གྱུར་ན་བསྒོམ་ཆེན་ཐ་མལ་དུ་འཆོལ་བའི་རྒྱུར་འགྱུར་པ་ཡིན་ནོ། །ཞེས་གསུངས་ཤིང་མི་སྣང་བར་ཡལ་ལོ།

within the context of hope and fear, investing them with true existence, they can become potentially life-threatening circumstances, such as psychotic episodes, fits, and seizures. Being obsessed with what manifests as gods or demons will cause a great meditator to degenerate into someone very ordinary."

Saying this, he vanished.

Zurchhung Sheyrab Dragpa

༄༅། །ཡང་རེ་ཞིག་གི་ཚེ་རང་སྐྱོང་དོན་གྱི་འོག་མིན་དུར་ཁྲོད་མེ་རི་
འབར་བའི་གནས་ནས་རྩུར་ཆུང་ཤེས་རབ་གྲགས་པ་དང་མཇལ་ཚེ། བདག་
གིས། ཀྱི་བླ་མ་ལགས། གདམས་ངག་ཕྱོགས་ཀྱི་ཡང་བཅུད་ཚིག་ཆུང་
ལ་དོན་འདུས་པ་ཞིག་བདག་ལ་གནང་བར་མཛད་དུ་གསོལ། ཅེས་ཞུས་པས་
བཀའ་སྩལ་པ། ཀྱི་བསྐལ་པ་དཔག་ཏུ་མེད་པའི་གོང་རོལ་ནས་ཚོགས་སྟོན་
ལས་འཕྲོ་དུས་འཛོམ་པའི་སྐྱེས་བུ་ཁྱོད་ཉིད་ཅིག །རྣམ་པ་ཐམས་ཅད་མཁྱེན་
པ་སངས་རྒྱས་ཀྱི་གོ་འཕང་ལ་བགྲོད་པར་འདོད་ན། བླ་མ་ལ་མོས་གུས་
ཐང་ལྷོད་མེད་པའི་སྒོ་ནས་སྒོང་ལམ་ཀུན་ཏུ་བསྙེན་པ་དང་། མཆེད་གྲོགས་
ལ་བརྩེ་གདུང་དང་དག་སྣང་སྒོང་བ་རྒྱུན་མི་ཆད་པ་དང་། སེམས་ཅན་ལ་
སྙིང་རྗེ་དྲག་པོའི་སྒོ་ནས་ཐར་པ་དང་ཐམས་ཅད་མཁྱེན་པའི་གོ་འཕང་དོན་དུ་གཉེར་
བ་དང་། འདུས་བྱས་ཐམས་ཅད་མི་རྟག་པའི་ངང་རྒྱལ་ལ་རྟག་ཏུ་བསམ་
ནས་འཁོར་བའི་བྱ་བ་བཏང་སྟེ་བྱར་མེད་ཀྱི་ངང་དུ་གནས་པར་བྱ་བ་རྣམས་ནི་དམ་
པའི་ཆོས་ཐམས་ཅད་ཀྱི་ཡང་སྙིང་རྣ་ན་མེད་པ་ཡིན་ནོ། །གདམས་ངག་ཆུང་

O N YET ANOTHER OCCASION, in a naturally manifesting vision of the ultimate pure realm of Akanishtha (Ogmin) as the charnel ground of Meri Barwa (Erupting Volcano), I met Zurchhung Sheyrab Dragpa. I said, "Ah, respected guru, grant me, I pray, the innermost essence of your enlightened mind, an instruction of condensed meaning in a few words."

Upon my having made this request, he bestowed the following reply: "Ah, listen, spiritual one. The accumulations, aspirations, and positive karmic tendencies reinforced for immeasurable eons have come together simultaneously in you. If you wish to reach the omniscient state of buddhahood, do the following: Please your guru with unflagging devotion in all your conduct. Train without interruption in affectionate love and pure view toward your spiritual companions. Strive for the state of liberation and omniscience through intense compassion for beings. And abide in the state in which nothing need be done, always thinking of the impermanent nature of everything composite and so letting go of the need to do anything in samsara. This is the unsurpassable innermost essence of all the sacred teachings of the Buddha.

"The following are three key points: Not to waste your

༄༅། ཆོས་སུ་མི་གཏོང་བ་བླ་མ་དམ་པའི་ཞབས་ཏོག ཁྱད་ཆོག་
ལ་རོ་ལྗོག་མེད་པ་ལྷ་དང་སྲུང་མའི་ལྷ་རོ། མི་ཆོ་ཆོས་ལ་དྲིལ་བ་འཆི་དུས་
རྡོ་ལྷག་མེད་པའི་གནད་གསུམ་ཡིན་ནོ། ཁྱད་ཆོག་དང་སྦྱོམས་པ་སྦྱོག་ལྕར་
བསྲུང་བ་སྦྱོམ་ཆེན་ཐ་མལ་དུ་མི་འཆོལ་བའི་གནད་དང་། འདོད་ཡོན་ལ་
ཆོག་ཤེས་བསྟེན་པ་ཡུལ་ངན་དུ་མགོ་མི་འཁོར་བའི་གདམས་པ་དང་། འཁོར་
བ་ལ་སྙིང་པོ་མེད་པར་ཤེས་པ་ཆགས་སྲང་གི་ཞེན་པ་གཏོད་པའི་གདམས་པ་
ཡིན་ནོ། །འཇིག་རྟེན་གྱི་བྱ་བ་ལ་ཞེན་དུས་མེད་པ་སྣོས་རྒྱའི་རི་མོ་ལྟ་བུར་
ཤེས་པ་བྱ་བའི་མཐའ་སྲུད་པའི་མན་ངག་ཡིན་ནོ། །དང་པོ་བསྐྱབ་པ་ལ་
བརྟེན་ནས་ཤེས་པ་དང་། བར་དུ་བཅུག་ཅིང་དཔྱད་པས་རང་རྒྱུད་ལ་སྐྱོང་
བཐོན་ནས་རྟོགས་པ་དང་། དེ་ལྟར་ཤེས་པ་དང་རྟོགས་པ་ཚམ་གྱིས་གྲོལ་
བ་མི་འཐོབ་པའི་ཆུལ། དཔེར་ན་ཟས་ཡོད་ཀྱང་མ་ཟོས་ན་མི་འགྲང་བ་ལྟ་
བུ་ཡིན་པས། བྱ་བ་དགུ་ཕྱུགས་སུ་བཏང་ནས་བསྒོམ་པའི་སྐྱོབས་ཀྱིས་རང་
ཐོག་ཏུ་བརྟན་པ་ཐོབ་པ་ནས་ལངས་ཆོ་མུན་པ་མི་འབྱུང་བ་ལྟ་བུར་རིག་པའི་
ཁོར་ཡུག་ཏུ་རྒྱས་ཆད་པའི་དུས་ཉེ་རིག་པ་རང་ཐོག་ཏུ་རང་གནོང་ཐོབ་པ་ཡིན།

spiritual instructions is service to the holy guru; to honor your samaya without hypocrisy is the 'spirit stone' of the deities and guardians; and to blend this human life with the Buddha's teachings is to know that there will be nothing unfinished at the time of your death.

"Guard your samaya and precepts as you would your life—this is another crucial point, one which ensures that a great meditator will not degenerate into someone very ordinary. Maintain contentment with respect to sense pleasures—this is advice on not being fooled by ignoble sense objects. Understand that samsara has no true essence—this is advice on cutting through the fixations of attachment and aversion. Know that just as in the case of incense clocks that burn continuously, there is no end to things that could be done in samsara—this is the heart advice (*man-ngag*) that brings them to an end.

"At first, you develop comprehension by relying on training. Later, you develop deeper understanding by eliciting personal experience through examination and investigation. But the situation is such that mere comprehension and understanding of this kind will not bring freedom. By analogy, even though you have food, you will not be satiated if you do not eat it.

"Just as darkness cannot occur once dawn has broken, when you have given up every kind of activity, you will gain stability in your immediate situation through the strength of your meditation. At the point where there is no restriction of the panoramic sweep of awareness, you will discover a natural indwelling confidence in your immediate situation.

༄༅། དྡུདྡེ་ཙམ་གྱིས་འཆད་རྒྱ་བར་མི་འགྱུར་བས་ཚོས་ཅན་གྱི་སྣང་
བ་ཚོས་ཉིད་དུ་ཟད་ནས་འཕོར་བའི་སྣང་སེམས་ཀྱི་དེ་ཙམ་ཡང་མེད་པའི་ཚོས་
དབྱིངས་ཀུན་ནས་རྒྱལ་བ་ཆེན་པོའི་དང་དུ་འཕྱམས་གྲུས་པ་ནེ་གྲོལ་བའི་ས་རུ་
ཕེབས་པ་ཡིན། སྣང་བ་དེར་ཡང་ཤེས་སྒྲིབ་པྲ་བའི་ཕྲ་བ་ཡུལ་མེད་དུ་སངས་
ནས་ཇེ་ལྷ་ཇེ་སྒྲེད་ཀྱི་ཡེ་ཤེས་ཆེན་པོར་དབང་བསྒྱུར་ནས་ཚོས་སྐུ་རྣམ་མཁའ་ལྟ་
བུ་སྐུ་གསུམ་མཉམ་བརྗལ་གྱི་རོལ་པར་སངས་རྒྱས་པ་ཡིན་ནོ། །རིགས་
ཀྱི་བུ་གཞི་མ་རིག་པ་རྩལ་རྣམ་པར་རྟོག་པ་སྐྱེ་འགག་ཅན་ནེ་སེམས་ཀྱི་མཚན་
ཉིད་ཡིན་ནོ། །གཞིའི་གནས་ལུགས་ཤེས་པ་ནེ་གཞིའི་རིག་པ་ཡིན། ཚོས་
ཉིད་མངོན་བྱེད་ཀྱི་ཤེས་པ་དངས་གསལ་རྟོགས་མ་དང་བྲལ་བ་ནེ་ལམ་རིག་པ་
སྟེ། གཉིས་ཀ་དུས་འཛོམ་པ་ལ་ཁྱབ་བརྗལ་རིག་པ་རྟོགས་པ་ཆེན་པོ་ཡིན
ནོ། །རྣམ་པར་རྟོག་པའི་ཚོ་འཕུལ་མཆེད་པའི་སྣང་བ་ཐམས་ཅད་མཛོན་དུ་
བྱེད་པའི་ཤེས་པ་ལ་ཡིན་ཅེས་བྱ་བ་དང་། སྣང་བ་མཆེད་པའི་ཡུལ་དྲུག་གོ

But even at this point, you still will not have awakened to buddhahood.

"When phenomena resolve within their true nature, you will experience infinite expansiveness within the context of the basic space of phenomena, supreme and all-inclusive, beyond the slightest distortion of ordinary mind and the phenomena it perceives in samsara. Then you will have reached the level of freedom. Within that state of experience, moreover, even the most subtle cognitive obscurations (*shey-drib*) are cleared away, leaving no trace, and mastery is gained through supreme timeless awareness, both of the real nature of things just as it is and of things in their multiplicity. So you awaken to buddhahood in dharmakaya, which is like space— the display of the congruence of the three kayas.

"Ah, son of spiritual heritage, ordinary mind (*sem*) can be characterized as the nonrecognition of awareness (*ma-rig-pa*)—that is, of the ground of being—with conceptualization that is subject to origination and cessation being the dynamic energy of that nonrecognition. Awareness (*rig-pa*) can be characterized as the ground of being becoming evident as supreme dynamic energy, timelessly present.

"The ground aspect of awareness is knowing the way in which the ground of being abides. The path aspect of awareness is pristine and lucid knowing, free of sullying factors, making the nature of phenomena fully evident. When these two aspects occur simultaneously, this is the great perfection—awareness that is pervasive and extensive.

"The term 'conceptual mind' (*yid*) refers to consciousness that makes evident all sensory appearances, which proliferate

༄༅། །མ་འགགས་པ་ལ་ཡིད་ཀྱི་རྣམ་པར་ཤེས་པ་ཞེས་ཚིག་ཏུ་བཏོད་པའོ།།

འཁོར་འདས་སྟོང་ཉིད་ཆེན་པོའི་ངང་ཚུལ་རྗེ་བླ་བ་བཞིན་དུ་ཤེས་པ་གཞིའི་

ཤེས་རབ། ཤེས་པ་ཟང་ཀ་རྒྱུན་གོ་མ་འགགས་པ་ཉིད་རོ་འཕོང་པ་ལམ་གྱི་

ཤེས་རབ། དེ་གཉིས་ཀ་དུས་འཙོམ་པ་ལ་ཁྱབ་བྱེད་ཀྱི་ཤེས་རབ་ཞེས་བྱའོ།།

འདོད་ཡོན་གྱི་སྣང་བ་མཆེད་པའི་སྣང་ཡུལ་གོ་མ་འགགས་པ་ལ་རྣམ་པར་ཤེས་པ་

དང་། སྣང་བ་ལ་དངོས་པོར་འཛིན་པའི་རྣམ་པར་རྟོག་པ་ལ་ལས་རླུང་ཞེས་

བྱའོ། །ཡིད་ཀྱི་ཤེས་པ་ཕྲ་རགས་དུས་འཛོམ་པས་འཁོར་བ་ཡོངས་སུ་

གྲུབ་པའོ། །ཚོས་ཉིད་བདེ་གཤེགས་སྙིང་པོའི་དང་ཚུལ་རྗེ་བླ་བ་བཞིན་དུ་

ཤེས་པ་རྗེ་བླ་བ་མཁྱེན་པའི་ཡེ་ཤེས། ཚོས་ཉིད་དེ་བཞིན་ཉིད་ཀྱི་གནས་ལུགས་

མངོན་དུ་བྱེད་པའི་དུས་སུ་ཀུན་ཤེས་ཀུན་རིག་གི་གོ་མ་འགགས་པ་ལ་རྗེ་སྙིང་པ་

གཟིགས་པའི་ཡེ་ཤེས། དེ་མཉམ་དུ་བརྫལ་བ་ལ་ཀ་དག་མཉམ་པ་ཉིད་ཀྱི་

ཡེ་ཤེས་ཞེས་བྱའོ། །གཞི་མ་རིག་པའི་དབང་གིས་ལྱུང་མ་བསྱན་དུ་སོང་

བ་དཔེར་ན་གཉིད་ཀྱི་དང་དུ་རྨི་ལམ་སྣ་ཚོགས་སྣང་བ་ལྱར་ཀུན་གཞིའི་མཁའ

through the intricate workings of conceptualization. The term 'consciousness based on conceptual mind' (*yid kyi nam-shey*) refers to the unimpeded avenue through which appearances proliferate as the six kinds of sense objects.

"The ground aspect of sublime knowing (*shey-rab*) is knowing the fundamental nature of samsara and nirvana, just as it is, to be supreme emptiness. The path aspect of sublime knowing is direct introduction to the unimpeded avenue of bare, unrestricted awareness. These two aspects occurring simultaneously is termed 'pervasive sublime knowing.'

"The term 'consciousness' (*nam-par shey-pa*) refers to the unimpeded avenue for apparent sense objects to proliferate in one's perceptions. The term 'subtle energy of karma' (*lay kyi lung*) refers to conceptualization that invests these sensory appearances with reality. The entire spectrum of samsara is thoroughly established from the synchronicity of these subtler and coarser aspects of consciousness based on conceptual mind.

"Timeless awareness (*ye-shey*) that knows the real nature of things, just as it is (*ji-ta-wa khyen-pai ye-shey*), knows the fundamental nature of phenomena—buddha nature—just as it is. Timeless awareness that discerns things in their multiplicity (*ji-nyed-pa zig-pai ye-shey*) is the unimpeded avenue of all-knowing, all-cognizing awareness that functions when the way in which suchness abides—the true nature of phenomena—is actually made evident. The congruence of these is termed 'originally pure timeless awareness as equalness.'

"Due to the nonrecognition of awareness—that is, of the ground of being—a karmically neutral state results. Myriad aspects of the subtle energy of karma move within the space

༄༅། ལ་ལས་རྐྱང་སྒྲུ་ཚོགས་གཡོས་པ་འཕོར་བ་ཀུན་གྱི་གཞི་དང་རྩ་
བའོ། །ཆོས་ཅན་གྱི་སྣང་བ་ཐམས་ཅད་ཆོས་ཉིད་སྤྱོས་མཐའ་བྲལ་བ་འཕོར་
འདས་དག་མཉམ་ཆེན་པོ་ཧྲར་སངས་པའི་དང་དུ་རྒྱ་ཡན་པ་ཆོས་སྐུ་ཀུན་ཏུ་བཟང་
པོའོ། །རིགས་ཀྱི་བུ་ཆུ་ཟླ་དང་ཆུའི་གཟུགས་བརྙན་ཐམས་ཅད་ཆུའི་རོལ་
པ་ཆུ་ལས་མ་འདས་པ་དང་། སྣང་བཅུད་བརྟན་གཡོ་ཐམས་ཅད་རྣམ་མཁའི་
རོལ་པ་རྣམ་མཁའ་ཉིད་ལས་མ་འདས་པ་དང་། འཕོར་འདས་ཐམས་ཅད་
ཆོས་ཉིད་གཅིག་གི་རོལ་པ་ཆོས་ཉིད་ལས་མ་འདས་པའོ། །དེ་ལྟར་གཞིའི་
ཆོས་སྐུ་གཏིང་གསལ་ཆེན་པོ་མཛོད་དུ་བྲུབས་པའི་དུས་དེར་རྫོག་འཕོར་འདས་དག
མཉམ་གྱི་ཆོས་སྐུ། རང་བཞིན་ཡེ་ཤེས་འོད་ཏན་གྱི་ལོངས་སྐུ། ཐུགས་
རྗེ་རང་གསལ་སྤྲུལ་གཡོག་དང་བྲལ་བའི་སྤྲུལ་སྐུ། དེའི་རོལ་པ་དོན་དམ་
པའོ། གཞི་ཀ་དག་གི་ངོ་བོ་མ་རིག་པ་ལ་ཀུན་གཞི། དེའི་གདངས་ལས་
སྣང་བ་རྩལ་སེམས་བྱུང་གི་རོལ་པ་ཀུན་རྫོབ་ཅེས་བྱ་བ་ཡིན་ནོ། །འདི་ལྟར

that is the ground of all ordinary experience (*kun-zhi*), like myriad dream images manifesting within a state of sleep. This is the basis, or source, of all samsara.

"All manifestations of phenomena are unrestricted within a state of wide-open clarity, the supreme equal purity of samsara and nirvana, the true nature of phenomena free of the limitations of conceptual elaboration. This is wholly positive dharmakaya (*chhö-ku*).

"Ah, son of spiritual heritage, all the reflections of the moon and other objects in water are the display of the water and do not go beyond the water. The entire animate and inanimate universe is the display of space and does not go beyond space itself. The whole of samsara and nirvana is the display of the single nature of phenomena and does not go beyond that nature.

"Thus, when the ground aspect of dharmakaya, supremely profound and lucid, has been made evident, its essence (*ngo-wo*) is dharmakaya as the equalness and purity of samsara and nirvana, its nature (*rang-zhin*) is sambhogakaya as timeless awareness and enlightened qualities, and its responsiveness (*t'hug-je*) is nirmanakaya, naturally lucid and free of obscuring overlay. The display of these constitutes ultimate reality.

The term 'ground of all ordinary experience' (*kun-zhi*) refers to nonrecognition of the originally pure essence of the ground of being. The term 'relative reality' (*kun-dzob*) refers to sensory appearances as the dynamic energy, and mental events as the display, that come from the radiance of this nonrecognition.

"Having come to an understanding of all the ramifications

༄༅། རོལ་པ་དང༌། ཆེངས་པ་དང༌། ཁྱབ་པ་དང༌། བརྡལ་
བའི་དང་ཚུལ་ཐབས་ཅད་ཤེས་པར་བྱས་ཏེ། ཆོས་ཉིད་རང་གར་འདུག་པ།
དང་བཞག་སྒྲོ་འདངས་རྒྱ་ཡན་ཆོས་ཉིད་ཅི་ཡང་མ་ཡིན་པའི་བརྟོད་བྲལ་ཆེན་པོ་ཉིད་
དུ་ལ་བཀླ་ཞིང༌། རྣམ་པ་ཐམས་ཅད་མཁྱེན་པའི་ཡེ་ཤེས་ཆེན་པོ་མ་འཕོབ་
ཀྱི་བར་དུ་བྱང་སྤྱོད་མེད་པའི་བཙོན་འགྱུས་དག་པོས་རྣམས་སུ་བྱུང་བ་ནི་གནད་
མཆོག་ཏུ་བྱུངས་ཤིག །ཅེས་གསུངས་ཤིང་ཆོས་ཉིད་ཀྱི་དབྱིངས་སུ་འབྱམས་
སུས་སོ།

༄༅། །ཞེས་པ་འདི་ཡང་སྐྱེ་བ་དུ་མར་ལས་དང་སྨོན་ལམ་གྱིས་འབྲེལ་
བའི་སྒྱལ་སྲུ་པདྨ་ལུང་རྟོགས་རྒྱ་མཚོ་དང་མཁྱེན་རབ་རྒྱ་མཚོ་གཉིས་ཀྱིས་ནན་
དུ་བསྐུལ་དོར། ཁྲག་འཐུང་བདུད་འཇོམས་རྡོ་རྗེ་གྲོ་ལོད་རྩལ་གྱིས་སྐུ་འཕུལ་
རོལ་པའི་སྐྱིང་མཛོད་ལས་གཏན་ལ་ཕབ་པ། ཆོས་ཀྱི་བདག་པོ་སྤྲེས་མཆོག་
དྲག་ཏུ་རྩ་བརྒྱུད་དུ་མཁའ་འགྲོས་ལུང་བསྟན་ནས་རྟེན་འབྲེལ་གྱི་དུས་ཚིགས་
ཕོག་མ་ཡིན་ཅེས་ཇོ་རྒྱུན་ཆེན་པོའི་བཀའས་གནང་བ་ཕེབས་པའོ། །རང་གི་
རིགས་སྲས་དྲ་པ་མཁས་མཆོག་བསོད་རྣམས་བསྟན་འཛིན་ རྡོ་གྲུབ་རིན་པོ་ཆེ་
གྱིས་ཞུས་དག་ནན་དུ་བགྱིས་པའོ།།

of the fundamental nature—its display, encompassing quality, pervasiveness, and extension—you reach the decisive experience of the true nature of phenomena that is immediately present, a supreme and inexpressible state that is nothing in and of itself, an unrestricted state of resting in the fundamental nature beyond ordinary consciousness. Hold this to be the most excellent key point—to practice with intense and unflagging exertion until you attain supreme timeless awareness, which is total omniscience."

Saying this, he expanded into the basic space of the true nature of phenomena.

This text was written in response to repeated requests by Padma Lungtog Gyatso and Khyenrab Gyatso, two incarnate teachers who have been connected to me for many rebirths through shared karma and aspirations. I, T'hrag-t'hung Dudjom Dorje Drolod Tzal, codified this from the treasury of the expanse of the display of magical illusion. The dakinis prophesied that sixty-eight sublime spiritual individuals would act as custodians of this teaching. On the first occasion when the auspicious circumstances came together, these teachings were written down by permission of the great Orgyan. My own holy son, the excellent scholar Sonam Tandzin (Dodrub Rinpoche), edited the manuscript meticulously.

༄༅། །དེ་ལྟར་ཀ་དག་རྫོགས་པ་ཆེན་པོ་ཁྲེགས་ཆོད་ཀྱི་གནས་ལུགས་ཆོན་པོར་སྟོན་པའི་ཁྲིད་རིམ་སྙང་སྙུང་དུ་བཀགས་པ་འདི་ལ། སྟོན་ཆད་རྗེ་རང་ཉིད་ཀྱི་སྐྱའི་སྲས་ཀྱི་བུ་པོ་རྟོ་གྲུབ་རིན་པོ་ཆེ་ནས་ལུས་དག་ཅུང་ཟད་གནང་བར་མཛོན་ཡང་ད་དུང་མ་ཕྱི་ནོར་བ་རྒྱུན་འབྱམས་སུ་སོང་བས་ཡིག་སློན་ཞིན་དུ་མང་བར་བརྟེན། དཔལ་མིའི་དབང་པོ་ཐབ་རྗེ་ཚེ་དབང་རིག་འཛིན་རྣམ་པར་རྒྱལ་བའི་ཕྱགས་བསྒྱེད་ཕྱིན་ལས་ཀྱི་ཆ་ལས་ཆོས་སྐྱའི་རིང་སྲེལ་ཆོས་སྦྱིན་མི་འཛད་པའི་གཏེར་དུ་བསྒྲུབས་པར་མཛད་དེ་ཡབ་གཞིས་བསམ་འགྲུབ་པོ་བྲང་གི་གཙོ་ལར་བཞུགས་སུ་གསོལ་བའི་རྒྱབས་སྒྱར་ཀྱི་ཕྱི་མོར་ལེགས་པར་དཔྱད་པའི་སློ་ནས་ཞུས་ཏེ་གཙང་དག་དུ་གཏན་ལ་འབེབས་པ་པོ་ནི་ཁྲག་འབྱུང་རིག་འཛིན་ཆོན་པོའི་སྐྱ་བའི་སྐྱ་གར་དུ་རྟོམ་པ་འཛིགས་བྲལ་ཡེ་ཤེས་རྡོ་རྗེ་སྟེ། །འདིས་ཀྱང་འོད་གསལ་རྫོགས་པ་ཆེན་པོའི་བསྟན་པ་ལ་བྱ་བ་རྒྱབས་པོ་ཆེར་སྒྱོད་པས་

Afterword

His Holiness Dudjom Rinpoche,
Jigdral Yeshe Dorje

THIS TEXT, KNOWN BY the short title *Refining One's Perception* (*Nang-jang*), is a developmental teaching which demonstrates that originally pure great perfection is the supreme way in which things abide, arrived at by "cutting through solidity" (*t'hreg-chhod*). It is evident that it was edited somewhat in the past by Dodrub Rinpoche, the eldest son of the lord [Dudjom Lingpa] himself. Later on, however, the text became rife with errors, so that at present there are many corrupt manuscripts. It is for this reason that through the aspirations and activities of the glorious ruler T'haiji Tsewang Rigdzin Nampar Gyalwa, this edition was prepared as an inexhaustible treasure trove of the gift of the Buddha's teachings, the relics of the dharmakaya.

When the blocks for printing the text were installed in the shrine room of the Samdrub P'hodrang palace on the family estate of the father of one of the Dalai Lamas, I edited this latest edition of the text with great attention to accuracy. I, Jigdral Yeshe Dorje, who presume to consider myself a dancer in the illusion, a rebirth of the great heruka and rigdzin, prepared this critical edition. May it be of enormous service to

༄༅། སྐལ་ལྡན་གྱི་གདུལ་བྱ་དཔག་ཏུ་མེད་པ་རང་དབྱིངས་གདོད་མའི་
གཞི་ཐོག་ཏུ་མཚོན་པར་གྲོལ་བའི་རྒྱུར་གྱུར་ཅིག །   ཤུ་བྷཾ།།   །།

the Great Perfection teachings of utter lucidity, and may it be a cause for innumerable fortunate beings—those to be tamed—to find actual freedom in the immediacy of inner basic space, the primordial ground of being. Good fortune!

༄༅། །རྫོགས་ཆེན་ཁྲེགས་ཆོད་སྣང་སྦྱང་གི་བསྡུས་དོན་ས་བཅད་བཞུགས།།

Structural Analysis and Outline

For Refining One's Perception (Nang-jang),
a Text on the Great Perfection Approach
of Cutting Through Solidity

༄༅། །ན་མོ་གུ་རུ་ཡེ། །འདིར་རྟོགས་པ་ཆེན་པོ་ཀ་དག་ཁྲེགས་ཆོད་ཀྱི་གདམས་པ་མ་བསྒོམ་སངས་རྒྱས་ཀྱི་ཁྲིད་རིམ་འཆད་པ་ལ་དོན་གསུམ། ཁྲིད་ལ་འཇུག་པའི་རྒྱ་བསྐྱན་པ། འཇུག་ཡུལ་གཞུང་གི་དོན་བཀྲོལ་བ། མཐར་ཕྱིན་མཇུག་གི་དོན་སྡོམས་པའོ།

།དང་པོ་ཁྲིད་ལ་འཇུག་པའི་རྒྱ་བསྐྱན་པ་ལ་གསུམ།
མཚན་སློས་པ། མཆོད་པར་བརྗོད་པ། བྱེད་སློང་བའོ།

I. དང་པོ་མཚན་སློས་པ་ནི།
རང་བཞིན་རྫོགས་པ་ཆེན་པོའི་རང་ཞལ༔

II. གཉིས་པ་མཆོད་པར་བརྗོད་པ་ནི།
ཁྱབ་བདག་བདོད་མའི་མགོན་པོ༔

III. གསུམ་པ་བྱེད་སློང་བ་ནི།
དུས་དེང་སང་སྐྱིགས་མ་ལྔ་བདོ་བའི༔

186

NAMO GURUYE: HOMAGE TO THE GURU!

This text, *Buddhahood Without Meditation,* contains advice on the Great Perfection approach of cutting through solidity (*t'hreg-chhod*) in order to realize original purity (*ka-dag*). To explain the stages of instruction, three major headings are employed: presenting the initial elements of the teaching; revealing the meaning of the main text as the purpose of the undertaking; and relating the conclusion that brings the text to an end.

PART ONE: PRESENTING THE INITIAL ELEMENTS OF THE TEACHING

This part has three sections: relating the title; showing reverence; and providing the background.

 I. **Relating the title**
 Buddhahood Without Meditation . . .

 II. **Showing reverence**
 With unwavering faith, I pay homage to the sublime citadel of the magical display of timeless awareness (ye-shey) . . . * [p. 3]

 III. **Providing the background**
 These days, when the five kinds of degeneration . . . [p. 3]

---

* Italicized portions appear in the main text.

187

གཉིས་པ་འདུག་ཡུལ་གཞུང་གི་དོན་བཀྲོལ་བ་དངོས་ལ་བཞི།

ལྟ་བས་ཐག་བཅད་པ། སྒོམ་པས་ཉམས་སུ་ལེན་པ། སྤྱོད་པས་བོགས་དབྱུང་
བ། འབྲས་བུ་མངོན་དུ་གྱུར་ཚུལ་ལོ།

I. དང་པོ་ལྟ་བས་ཐག་བཅད་པ་ལ་བཞི། ཚོས་ཐམས་ཅད་སྟོང་ཉིད་བརྗོད་དུ་
མེད་པར་གཏན་ལ་དབབ་པ། གཞི་དབྱིངས་རང་བྱུང་གི་ཡེ་ཤེས་གཅིག་པུར་
འགག་བསྡམ་པ། འཁོར་འདས་ཕྱལ་བ་བར་མེད་རྒྱུ་ཚད་ཕྱོགས་ལྷུང་དང་
བྲལ་བར་ཆེངས་སུ་བཅིང་བ། ཡེ་ནས་རྩོལ་མེད་རང་གསལ་ལྷུན་གྲུབ་ཆེན་པོར་
ལ་བཞག་བའོ།

A. དང་པོ་ཚོས་ཐམས་ཅད་སྟོང་ཉིད་བརྗོད་དུ་མེད་པར་གཏན་ལ་དབབ་པ་ལ་
གཉིས། གང་ཟག་གི་བདག་མེད་གཏན་ལ་དབབ་པ་དང་། ཚོས་
ཀྱི་བདག་མེད་གཏན་ལ་དབབ་པའོ།

1. དང་པོ་གང་ཟག་གི་བདག་མེད་གཏན་ལ་དབབ་པ་ལ་གསུམ། ཐོག་
མར་བྱུང་བའི་ཁུངས། བར་དུ་གནས་པའི་ས། ཐ་མར་འགྲོ་
བའི་ཡུལ་གཏན་ལ་དབབ་པའོ།

a. དང་པོ་བྱུང་བའི་ཁུངས་ལ་བཏག་པ་ནི།
དང་པོ་གང་ཟག་གི་བདག་ཅེས་བྱ་བ༔

b. གཉིས་པ་བར་དུ་གནས་པའི་ས་ལ་བཏག་པ་ནི།
བར་དུ་གནས་པའི་ས་བཙལ་བ༔

PART TWO: REVEALING THE MEANING OF THE MAIN
TEXT AS THE PURPOSE OF THE UNDERTAKING

This main part has four sections: reaching a decision through view;
practical application through meditation; enrichment through conduct; and how the fruition becomes evident.

I. Reaching a decision through view
This first major section has four subsections: reaching the definitive conclusion that all phenomena are inexpressible emptiness; discerning the implication of the ground of being as basic
space to be that of a single, naturally occurring timeless awareness; embracing samsara and nirvana within a paradigm of
openness, uninterrupted and free of restrictions or extremes;
and coming to a decisive experience within a supreme state of
spontaneous presence, forever effortless and naturally lucid.

A. Reaching the definitive conclusion that all phenomena are
inexpressible emptiness
This subsection has two divisions: reaching a definitive conclusion regarding the nonexistence of personal identity and
reaching a definitive conclusion regarding the nonexistence
of the identity of phenomena.

1. Reaching a definitive conclusion regarding the nonexistence of personal identity
This division has three subdivisions, which involve reaching definitive conclusions regarding the source from which
this supposed identity arises initially; the location in
which it dwells in the interim; and the destination to
which it finally goes.

a. Examination of the initial source
Let us begin by defining "personal identity"... [p. 9]

b. Examination of the interim location
*In searching for the place where this identity might
dwell...* [p. 11]

c. གསུམ་པ་ཐ་མ་འགྲོ་བའི་ཡུལ་ལ་བརྟག་པ་ནི།

དེ་བཞིན་དུ་ཐ་མ་འགྲོ་བའི་ཡུལ་དང་བདག་པོ༔

2. གཉིས་པ་ཚོས་ཀྱི་བདག་མེད་གཏན་ལ་དབབ་པ་ལ་བཞི། མིང་གི་
གདགས་གཞི་བཙལ་བ།   བདེན་དངོས་ཀྱི་རྟག་འཛིན་བཤིག་པ།
ཕན་གནོད་ཀྱི་མཚང་ལ་རྟོལ་བ། རེ་དོགས་ཀྱི་ཧྲུན་ཕུག་བརྟེབ་པའོ།

a. དང་པོ་མིང་གི་གདགས་གཞི་བཙལ་བ་ལ་གཉིས། ཚོས་ཐམས་
ཅད་མིང་དུ་བཏགས་པའི་དོན་བཙལ་ཏེ་སྟོང་པར་གཏན་ལ་དབབ་པ་
དང་།   སྟོང་པ་ལས་སྣང་ཕྱོགས་རྟེན་འབྲེལ་གྱི་རོལ་པར་འཆར་
ཚུལ་ལོ།

1) དང་པོ་ཚོས་ཐམས་ཅད་མིང་དུ་བཏགས་པའི་དོན་བཙལ་ཏེ་སྟོང་
པར་གཏན་ལ་དབབ་པ་ནི།

མིང་ཐམས་ཅད་བཏགས་དོན་བཙལ་ན༔

2) གཉིས་པ་སྟོང་པ་ལས་སྣང་ཕྱོགས་རྟེན་འབྲེལ་གྱི་རོལ་པ་འཆར་
ཚུལ་ནི།

སྣར་ཡང་ཨོ་རྒྱན་མཚོ་སྐྱེས་རྡོ་རྗེ༔

b. གཉིས་པ་བདེན་དངོས་ཀྱི་རྟག་འཛིན་བཤིག་པ་ལ་གསུམ། ཀུན་
ཁྱབ་འདུས་མ་བྱས་པའི་ནམ་མཁའ་ཚོས་བདུན་ཕྱུན་དུ་བསྟན་པ།

c. Examination of the final destination
   *Similarly, you should come to the decision that all fi-
   nal destinations ...* [p. 13]

2. **Reaching a definitive conclusion regarding the nonexistence of the identity of phenomena**
   This division has four subdivisions: searching for the basis of the designation of names; abolishing conceiving of
   things as permanent with true existence and substantiality; disputing the hidden flaws of benefit and harm; and
   collapsing the false cave of hope and fear.

   a. **Searching for the basis of the designation of names**
      This subdivision has two categories: searching for ul-
      timate objects to which the names of all phenomena
      are applied, thus reaching the definitive conclusion
      that they are empty; and showing how the manifest
      aspect of sensory appearances arises from emptiness
      as the display of interdependent connection.

      1) **Searching for ultimate objects to which the names
         of all phenomena are applied, thus reaching the
         definitive conclusion that they are empty**
         *To begin with, if you search for something with ul-
         timate meaning that underlies the application of
         all names ...* [p. 13]

      2) **Showing how the manifest aspect of sensory ap-
         pearances arises from emptiness as the display of
         interdependent connection**
         *On another occasion, when I encountered Orgyan
         Tsokyey Dorje—the embodiment of the magical
         illusion of timeless awareness ...* [p. 25]

   b. **Abolishing conceiving of things as permanent with
      true existence and substantiality**
      This subdivision has three categories: demonstrating
      that all-pervasive, uncompounded space is endowed

འདས་བྱས་ཀྱི་ཆོས་རྣམས་འགྱུར་བ་མེད་པའི་བདེན་དངོས་ཀྱིས་སྟོང་
ཚུལ། སྟོང་པར་ཤེས་དགོས་པའི་རྒྱུ་མཚན་དགོས་གཏོད་བསྟན་
པའོ།

1) དངོ་པོ་ཀུན་ཁྱབ་འདས་མ་བྱས་པའི་ནམ་མཁའ་ཆོས་བདུན་ལྡན་
དུ་བསྟན་པ་ནི།
ཡང་རིག་འཛིན་བདུད་འདུལ་རྡོ་རྗེས༔

2) གཉིས་པ་འདས་བྱས་ཀྱི་ཆོས་རྣམས་འགྱུར་བ་མེད་པའི་བདེན་
དངོས་ཀྱིས་སྟོང་ཚུལ་ལ་གསུམ། སྟོང་ཚུལ་དངོས་དང་།
དེ་ལ་རིས་ཤེས་བསྒྱེད་ཕྱིར་རྨི་ལྔང་དང་སྒྱུ་འཆིའི་འགྲོ་འོང་ལ་
བཏག་པ། གྲུབ་དོན་ལྔང་ཚམ་དུ་ཐག་ཆོད་ཀྱིས་འཛིན་པའོ།
    a) དང་པོ་སྟོང་ཚུལ་དངོས་ནི།
       རྫས་གཞན་གང་ལའང་མཚན་གྱིས༔

    b) གཉིས་པ་དེ་ལ་རིས་ཤེས་བསྒྱེད་ཕྱིར་རྨི་ལྔང་དང་སྒྱུ་འཆིའི་
       འགྲོ་འོང་ལ་བཏག་པ་ནི།
       དེ་ལྟར་གཏན་ལ་ཕབ་པས་སྣང་བ༔

    c) གསུམ་པ་གྲུབ་དོན་ལྔང་ཚམ་དུ་ཐག་ཆོད་ཀྱིས་འཛིན་པ་ནི།
       ཡང་བདག་གིས་ཏྟ་མ་ལགས༔

3) གསུམ་པ་སྟོང་པར་ཤེས་དགོས་པའི་རྒྱུ་མཚན་དགོས་གཏོད་
བསྟན་པ་ལ་གསུམ།

with seven attributes; showing how composite phenomena are empty of unchanging true existence and substantiality; and showing how to remove doubt concerning the necessity of understanding that phenomena are empty.

1) **Demonstrating that all-pervasive, uncompounded space is endowed with seven attributes**
   On another occasion, Rigdzin Duddul Dorje said to me ... [p. 33]

2) **Showing how composite phenomena are empty of unchanging true existence and substantiality**
   This category has three topics: showing how phenomena actually are empty; examining the coming and going of dream images and birth and death in order to give rise to certainty concerning this; and arriving at the level of deciding that objects that seem to exist are merely sensory appearances.

   a) **Showing how phenomena actually are empty**
   "Since all material substances can be damaged by weapons ..." [p. 33]

   b) **Examining the coming and going of dream images and of birth and death in order to give rise to certainty concerning this**
   Having come to such a definitive conclusion, I understood all sensory appearances ... [p. 41]

   c) **Arriving at the level of deciding that objects that seem to exist are merely sensory appearances**
   To this I responded, "My guru ..." [p. 47]

3) **Showing how to remove doubt concerning the necessity of understanding that phenomena are empty**

དངོས་འཛིན་སྐྱེ་གཞིའི་གཏོར་བོ་ལུས་ལ་ཞེན་པའི་ཉེས་དམིགས།

དེ་ལྟར་གཏན་ལ་འབེབས་པ་ལ་ལོག་རྟོག་བསལ་བ། རྟོགས་བྱེད་

ཤེས་རབ་ཀྱི་རྣམ་དབྱེ་དང་འབྲེལ་བར་གནད་ཀྱི་འགག་བསྡུ་བའོ།

a) དང་པོ་དངོས་འཛིན་སྐྱེ་གཞིའི་གཏོར་བོ་ལུས་ལ་ཞེན་པའི་ཉེས་

དམིགས་ནི།

ལུས་སུ་སྣང་བ་འདི་སྟོང་པར་མ་ཤེས༔

b) གཉིས་པ་དེ་ལྟར་གཏན་ལ་འབེབས་པ་ལ་ལོག་རྟོག་བསལ་

བ་ནི།

ཡང་འདི་ལྟར་སྟོང་པར་ཤེས་ཀྱང༔

c) གསུམ་པ་རྟོགས་བྱེད་ཤེས་རབ་ཀྱི་རྣམ་དབྱེ་དང་འབྲེལ་བར་

གནད་ཀྱི་འགག་བསྡུ་བ་ནི།

དེ་ལྟར་སྣང་བ་ཐམས་ཅད་སྟོང་ཉིད་དུ༔

c. གསུམ་པ་ཐབ་གཏོད་ཀྱི་མཚང་ལ་རྐོལ་བ་ལ་གསུམ། ཐབ་གཏོད་

མཚན་འཛིན་གྱི་རྟོག་པ་འབྱུང་བའི་རྒྱུ་རྫས་བཟུང་བ། ཐབ་གཏོད་

དུ་སྦྱང་བའི་ཡུལ་གྱི་རང་བཞིན་ལ་བཏགས་པ། དེ་ལྟར་རྟོགས་པའི་

ཆེ་བ་བསྟན་པའོ།

1) དང་པོ་ཐབ་གཏོད་མཚན་འཛིན་གྱི་རྟོག་པ་འབྱུང་བའི་རྒྱུ་རྫས་

བཟུང་བ་ནི།

ཡང་རེ་ཞིག་གི་དུས་སུ་གྲུབ་ཆེན་ས་ར་ཧའི༔

This category has three topics: showing the shortcomings of clinging to the body, the principal basis for giving rise to concepts of substantiality; dispelling wrong ideas concerning such a definitive conclusion; and focusing on the key point, in connection with a detailed analysis of sublime knowing, the means of realization.

a) **Showing the shortcomings of clinging to the body, the principal basis for giving rise to concepts of substantiality**
"It is an enormous flaw not to understand that what manifests as the body is empty..." [p. 49]

b) **Dispelling wrong ideas concerning such a definitive conclusion**
"In addition, even though you know things to be empty in this way..." [p. 51]

c) **Focusing on the key point, in connection with a detailed analysis of sublime knowing, the means of realization**
"Accordingly, the term 'discerning sublime knowing (so-sor tog-pai shey-rab)' refers to knowledge gained through analysis..." [p. 53]

c. **Disputing the hidden flaws of benefit and harm**
This subdivision has three categories: identifying the causes leading to the idea of ascribing characteristics of benefit and harm; examining the nature of objects that are perceived to be beneficial or harmful; and demonstrating the significance of such realization.

1) **Identifying the causes leading to the idea of ascribing characteristics of benefit and harm**
On yet another occasion, when I met the great siddha Saraha in a vision... [p. 59]

2) གཉིས་པ་ཐབ་གཏོད་དུ་སྐྱང་བའི་ཡུལ་གྱི་རང་བཞིན་ལ་བརྟག་
པ་ལ་གཉིས། ཚོ་ཕྱི་མར་ཐབ་གཏོད་དུ་སྐྱང་བ་དགེ་སྡིག་ལ་
བརྟག་པ། ཚོ་འདིར་ཐབ་གཏོད་དུ་སྐྱང་བ་སླ་འདྲེ་ལ་བརྟག་
པའོ།

a) དང་པོ་ཚོ་ཕྱི་མར་ཐབ་གཏོད་དུ་སྐྱང་བ་དགེ་སྡིག་ལ་བརྟག་
པ་ལ་གཉིས། བརྟག་ཚུལ་དངོས་དང་། བརྟག་དགོས་
པའི་རྒྱུ་མཚན་ནོ།

    i) དང་པོ་བརྟག་ཚུལ་དངོས་ནི།
    ཐན་བྱེད་ལུས་ངག་གི་དགེ་བ་ཐམས་ཅད༔

    ii) གཉིས་པ་བརྟག་དགོས་པའི་རྒྱུ་མཚན་ནི།
    འདི་ལྟར་དགེ་བ་གཏན་ལ་མ་ཐབ་ན༔

b) གཉིས་པ་ཚོ་འདིར་ཐབ་གཏོད་དུ་སྐྱང་བ་སླ་འདྲེ་ལ་བརྟག་པ་
ལ་གཉིས། བརྟག་ཚུལ་དངོས་དང་། འཁྲུལ་སྣང་
ཉམས་ཀྱི་ཐུན་རིས་སུ་བསྟན་པའོ།

    i) དང་པོ་བརྟག་ཚུལ་དངོས་ནི།
    ཡང་ཐན་སྐྱོབས་ཀྱི་སྨ་ཞེས་བྱ་བ་རྣམས༔

    ii) གཉིས་པ་འཁྲུལ་སྣང་ཉམས་ཀྱི་ཐུན་རིས་སུ་བསྟན་པ་ནི།

2) **Examining the nature of objects that are perceived to be beneficial or harmful**
This category has two topics: examining virtuous and harmful actions that manifest as beneficial or harmful in future lifetimes and examining gods and demons that manifest as beneficial or harmful in this lifetime.

a) **Examining virtuous and harmful actions that manifest as beneficial or harmful in future lifetimes**
This topic has two points: the actual manner of examination and the reasons the examination is necessary.

i) **The actual manner of examination**
"Where does all beneficial physical and verbal virtue abide? ..." [p. 59]

ii) **The reasons the examination is necessary**
"If you have not come to such a definitive conclusion regarding virtuous actions ..." [p. 61]

b) **Examining gods and demons that manifest as beneficial or harmful in this lifetime**
This topic has two points: the actual manner of examination and a demonstration that perceptions based on confusion are false impressions of fleeting experiences.

i) **The actual manner of examination**
"Furthermore, when you examine what are called 'helpful and protective gods' ..." [p. 63]

ii) **A demonstration that perceptions based on confusion are false impressions of fleeting experiences**

མི་རྟམས་འཁྲུལ་པའི་དབང་གིས་རང་ལུས་སྟོད་སྨད་ལ་འང༔

3) གསུམ་པ་དེ་ལྟར་རྟོགས་པའི་ཆེ་བ་བསྟན་པ་ནི། །

འདིའི་གནད་དོན་ནི་ཡིན་ལུགས་ཤེས་པ་ནི༔

d. བཞི་པ་རེ་དོགས་ཀྱི་རྟེན་ཕུག་བརྟིབ་པ་ལ་གསུམ། རེ་ཡུལ་སངས་

རྒྱས་ཞིང་ཁམས་དང་བཅས་པ་ལ་བདེན་ཞེན་གྱི་རྟེན་ཕུག་བརྟིབ་པ།

དོགས་ཡུལ་འཁོར་བའི་གནས་རིས་བདེ་སྡུག་དང་བཅས་པ་ལ་བདེན་

ཞེན་གྱི་རྟེན་ཕུག་བརྟིབ་པ། དེ་ལྟར་རྟོགས་པའི་བསྒགས་པ་མིང་

གི་ཆེ་བ་བརྗོད་པའོ།

1) དང་པོ་རེ་ཡུལ་སངས་རྒྱས་ཞིང་ཁམས་དང་བཅས་པ་ལ་བདེན་

ཞེན་གྱི་རྟེན་ཕུག་བརྟིབ་པ་ལ་གསུམ། སངས་རྒྱས་ཞིང་དང་

བཅས་པ་ལ་མཐར་འཛིན་ཞེན་པ་དགག་པ། དེ་ལ་སྐྱོ་ལྟ་ཡུལ་

ལྟ་དང་བཅས་པར་བཏག་སྟེ་བདེན་པའི་སྐྱོ་འདོགས་བཀྲོག་པ།

རེས་པ་དོན་གྱི་སངས་རྒྱས་རོས་བཟུང་བའོ།

a) དང་པོ་སངས་རྒྱས་ཞིང་དང་བཅས་པ་ལ་མཐར་འཛིན་གྱི་ཞེན་

པ་དགག་པ་ནི། །

ཡང་འོད་གསལ་དག་པའི་སྐྱང་དོར་དཔལ་ཆེན་ཕུག་ན་ཏོ་རྗེའི༔

b) གཉིས་པ་དེ་ལ་སྐྱོ་ལྟ་ཡུལ་ལྟ་དང་བཅས་པར་བཏག་སྟེ་བདེན་

པའི་སྐྱོ་འདོགས་བཀྲོག་པ་ནི། །

> *"Human beings, under the influence of con-*
> *fusion, regard the upper and lower parts of*
> *their bodies ..."* [p. 65]

3) Demonstrating the significance of such realization
   "The key point here—understanding this mode of
   being—constitutes the means to dispel ..." [p. 65]

d. Collapsing the false cave of hope and fear
   This subdivision has three categories: collapsing the
   false cave of investing buddhahood and its attendant
   pure realms with true existence, as objects of hope;
   collapsing the false cave of investing the states of samsara and their attendant pleasures and pain with true
   existence, as objects of fear; and describing in significant terms the praiseworthiness of such realization.

   1) Collapsing the false cave of investing buddhahood
      and its attendant pure realms with true existence,
      as objects of hope
      This category has three topics: negating fixation
      on conceiving of buddhahood and its attendant
      pure realms as something absolute; to that end, ex-
      amining the five senses and their attendant objects
      and refuting the exaggeration of ascribing true ex-
      istence to these; and identifying buddhahood in
      the ultimate and definitive sense.

      a) Negating fixation on conceiving of buddha-
         hood and its attendant pure realms as some-
         thing absolute
         On another occasion I met the great and glori-
         ous Vajrapani in a pure vision (dag-nang) of ut-
         ter lucidity (od-sal) ... [p. 71]

      b) To that end, examining the five senses and
         their attendant objects and refuting the exag-
         geration of ascribing true existence to these

199

དེ་བཞིན་གཤེགས་པ་ཕྱིར་རྒྱག་དང་བདེན་གྲུབ་ཏུ་ལྟ་བ༔

c) གསུམ་པ་ངེས་པ་དོན་གྱི་སངས་རྒྱས་ངོས་བཟུང་བ་ནི།

ངེས་པའི་དོན་དུ་རང་གི་གཞི་ཀུན་ཏུ་བཟང་པོ་ནི༔

2) གཉིས་པ་དོགས་ཡུལ་འཁོར་བའི་གནས་རིས་བདེ་སྡུག་དང་

བཅས་པ་ལ་བདེན་ཞེན་གྱི་རྟེན་ཕུག་བརྗེད་པ་ནི།

ཡང་འཁོར་བའི་གནས་རིས་གཞན་ཡོད་ཅིང་གྲུབ་སྟེ༔

3) གསུམ་པ་དེ་ལྟར་རྟོགས་པའི་བསྒྲགས་པ་མིང་གི་ཆེ་བ་བཙོད་

པ་ནི།

དེ་ལྟར་འཁྲུལ་སྣང་གཏན་ལ་ཕབ་ནས་བདེན་མེད་སྟོང་པ༔

B. གཉིས་པ་གཞི་དབྱིངས་རང་བྱུང་གི་ཡེ་ཤེས་གཅིག་པུར་འགག་བསྒྲུབས་པ་

ལ། འགག་བསྒྲུབ་ཚུལ་དངོས། དེ་ལས་གྲོལ་འཁྲུལ་གཉིས་སུ་

སྤྱང་ཚུལ། གནད་ཀྱི་དོན་བསྡུ་བའོ།

1. དང་པོ་འགག་བསྒྲུབ་ཚུལ་དངོས་ནི།

དེ་ལྟར་བདག་གིས་ཡུན་རིང་པོར་གཏན་ལ་ཕབས་ནས༔

2. གཉིས་པ་དེ་ལས་གྲོལ་འཁྲུལ་གཉིས་སུ་སྤྱང་ཚུལ་ལ་གཉིས། མདོར་

བསྟན་པ་དང་། རྒྱས་པར་འཆད་པའོ།

"However we label it, the view that a tatha-gata is something constant that can be found to have true existence ..." [p. 73]

c) Identifying buddhahood in the ultimate and definitive sense
"In the definitive sense, the wholly positive ground of your own being—Kuntuzangpo ..." [p. 75]

2) Collapsing the false cave of investing the states of samsara and their attendant pleasures and pain with true existence, as objects of fear
"Furthermore, it is illogical to think that other, separate states of being exist or have ever existed within samsara ..." [p. 77]

3) Describing in significant terms the praiseworthi-ness of such realization
"If you thus come to a definitive conclusion re-garding the sensory appearances that arise from confusion, realizing that they lack true existence, are empty ..." [p. 77]

B. Discerning the implication of the ground of being as basic space to be that of a single, naturally occurring timeless awareness
This subsection has three divisions: the actual manner of discerning this implication; how the two modes of freedom and confusion manifest from this ground; and a synopsis of the key points of this subsection.

1. The actual manner of discerning this implication
In this way, after a long time I reached a definitive con-clusion ... [p. 83]

2. How the two modes of freedom and confusion manifest from this ground

a. དང་པོ་མདོར་བསྟན་པ་ནི། །

དེ་ནས་ཡང་ལོ་ཁྲིམ་བདུན་གྱི་རྗེས་སུ་རྗེ་ལམ་དག་པའི་སྣང་དོར༎

b. གཉིས་པ་རྒྱས་པར་བཤད་པ་ལ་གཉིས། གྲོལ་བ་སྐྱང་འདས་ཕྱོགས་ ཀྱི་ཡོན་ཏན་རང་ཆས་སུ་ཡོད་ཚུལ། འཁྲུལ་སྣང་འཁོར་བའི་རོལ་ པ་སྒྲོ་བུར་དུ་མཆེད་ཚུལ་ལོ། །

1) དང་པོ་གྲོལ་བ་སྐྱང་འདས་ཕྱོགས་ཀྱི་ཡོན་ཏན་རང་ཆས་སུ་ཡོད་ ཚུལ་ལ་བཞི། གཞི་ལ་སྐུ་བཞི་ཡེ་ཤེས་ལྔ་རང་ཆས་སུ་རྫོགས་ ཚུལ། ལམ་ལ་སྐུ་བཞི་ཡེ་ཤེས་ལྔ་རང་བབས་སུ་འཆར་ཚུལ། དེ་ལྟའི་ཡིན་ལུགས་མ་རྟོགས་པའི་ཤེས་པ་བཟོ་མེད་ལམ་བྱེད་ གོལ་སར་བཤད་པ། རྟོགས་མ་རྟོགས་ཀྱི་རྣམ་དབྱེ་ཤེས་ཕྱིར་ ཤེས་རབ་དང་སེམས་སེམས་བྱུང་དོས་བཟུང་བའོ། །

a) དང་པོ་གཞི་ལ་སྐུ་བཞི་ཡེ་ཤེས་ལྔ་རང་ཆས་སུ་རྫོགས་ཚུལ་ནི། གཞི་གདོན་མའི་མགོན་པོ་ཀུན་ཏུ་བཟང་པོ་ཉིད་ནི༎

b) གཉིས་པ་ལམ་ལ་སྐུ་བཞི་ཡེ་ཤེས་ལྔ་རང་བབས་སུ་འཆར་ ཚུལ་ནི།

202

This division has two subdivisions: a brief presentation and an extensive explanation.

a. **A brief presentation**
Seven years later, while having a pure vision in a dream... [p. 89]

b. **An extensive explanation**
This subdivision has two categories: from the perspective of freedom, or nirvana, how enlightened qualities are present as naturally occurring attributes; and how the display of perceptions based on confusion in samsara evolves adventitiously.

1) **From the perspective of freedom, or nirvana, how enlightened qualities are present as naturally occurring attributes**
This category has four topics: how the four kayas and five aspects of timeless awareness are complete as natural attributes within the ground of being; how the four kayas and five aspects of timeless awareness arise as the natural condition of the path; explaining the point at which one goes astray when forging one's path with a passive state of consciousness that does not realize such a mode of being; and identifying sublime knowing as opposed to ordinary mind and mental events in order to understand the process of differentiation between realization and its lack.

a) **How the four kayas and five aspects of timeless awareness are complete as natural attributes within the ground of being**
"The ground of being itself, the primordial guide Kuntuzangpo..." [p. 89]

b) **How the four kayas and five aspects of time-**

དེ་ལྟར་རང་བྱུང་གི་སངས་རྒྱས་སུ་གྲོལ་བའི་ལམ་རིག་པ་ཡང་ཱ

c) གསུམ་པ་དེ་ལྟའི་ཡིན་ལུགས་མ་རྟོགས་པའི་ཤེས་པ་བཟོ་མེད་
ལམ་བྱེད་གོལ་སར་བཕད་པ་ནི།
འདིའི་ཡིན་ལུགས་ཇེ་ལྟ་བ་བཞིན་དུ་མི་ཤེས་ཤིང་ཱ

d) བཞི་པ་རྟོགས་མ་རྟོགས་ཀྱི་རྣམ་དབྱེ་ཤེས་ཕྱིར་ཤེས་རབ་དང་
སེམས་སེམས་བྱུང་དོས་བཟུང་བ་ནི།
འཁོར་འདས་ཀྱིས་བསྡུས་པའི་ཚོས་ཐམས་ཅད་ཱ

2) གཉིས་པ་འཁྲུལ་སྣང་འཁོར་བའི་རོལ་པ་སྒྱོ་བྱུང་དུ་མཆེད་ཚུལ་
ལ་གསུམ། ཕྱི་འབྱུང་བ་ལྟའི་སྣང་བ་མཆེད་ཚུལ། ནང་
ཚོགས་བརྒྱད་ཡུལ་སྣང་དང་བཅས་པ་མཆེད་ཚུལ། དེའི་
རོན་གྱི་གནད་བསྟུ་བའོ།

a) དང་པོ་ཕྱི་འབྱུང་བ་ལྟའི་སྣང་བ་མཆེད་ཚུལ་ནི།
གཞི་ལ་རང་དབང་བསྒྱུར་བ་དག་པ་གཞིའི་སངས་རྒྱས་ཱ

b) གཉིས་པ་ནང་ཚོགས་བརྒྱད་ཡུལ་སྣང་དང་བཅས་པ་མཆེད་
ཚུལ་ནི།

less awareness arise as the natural condition of the path
"In this way, the path of freedom within naturally occurring (rang-jung) buddhahood makes evident awareness..." [p. 91]

c) Explaining the point at which one goes astray when forging one's path with a passive state of consciousness that does not realize such a mode of being
"Many do not understand this mode of being just as it is..." [p. 93]

d) Identifying sublime knowing as opposed to ordinary mind and mental events in order to understand the process of differentiation between realization and its lack
"The term 'sublime knowing that knows the nature of things just as it is' refers to knowing..." [p. 93]

2) How the display of perceptions based on confusion in samsara evolves adventitiously
This category has three topics: how the appearances of the five elements evolve externally; how the eight modes of consciousness, and the manifest objects they entail, evolve internally; and a synopsis of the key points of these topics.

a) How the appearances of the five elements evolve externally
"When the true face of the ground aspect of buddhahood—a state of purity and mastery of the ground of being—is obscured by the nonrecognition of awareness (ma-rig-pa)..." [p. 95]

b) How the eight modes of consciousness, and the manifest objects they entail, evolve internally

འབྲུལ་པའི་གཞི་ལུ་དེ་དག་གི་རྩལ་དུ་འར་བ༔

c) གསུམ་པ་དེའི་དོན་གྱི་གནད་བསྡུ་བ་ནི།

འགགས་ཤིག་གིས་སྡུང་བ་སེམས་སུ་འདོད་ཅིང་༔

3. གསུམ་པ་གནད་ཀྱི་དོན་བསྡུ་བ་ནི།

དེ་ལྟར་སྡུང་སྲིད་འཁོར་འདས༔

C. གསུམ་པ་འཁོར་འདས་ཕྱལ་བ་བར་མེད་རྒྱུ་ཁད་ཕྱོགས་ལྡུང་དང་བྲལ་བར་

ཆེངས་སུ་བཅེང་བ་ལ་གཉིས། སྡུང་ཕྱོགས་ནས་སྡུང་ཚམ་སྐྱ་མ་ལྟ་བུར་

ཕྱལ་བར་བསྟན་པ། སྟོང་ཕྱོགས་ནས་རང་བཞིན་བདེན་མེད་དུ་ཕྱལ་

བར་བསྟན་པའོ།

1. དང་པོ་སྡུང་ཕྱོགས་ནས་སྡུང་ཚམ་སྐྱ་མ་ལྟ་བུར་ཕྱལ་བར་བསྟན་པ་ནི།

ཡང་དུས་རེ་ཞིག་གི་ཚེ་རིག་འཛིན་ཆེན་པོ་ཧཱུྂ་ཆེན་ཀུ་རའི༔

2. གཉིས་པ་སྟོང་ཕྱོགས་ནས་རང་བཞིན་བདེན་མེད་དུ་ཕྱལ་བར་བསྟན་པ་

ལ་གཉིས། ཚོས་ཉིད་གཅིག་གིས་ཆེངས་པའི་ཆུལ་གྱིས་མདོར་

བསྟན་པ། ཇེ་ལྟར་ཕྱལ་བའི་རྣམ་གྲངས་གསལ་བར་བསྟན་པས་རྒྱས་

པར་བཤད་པའོ།

a. དང་པོ་ཚོས་ཉིད་གཅིག་གིས་ཆེངས་པའི་ཆུལ་གྱིས་མདོར་བསྟན་པ་ནི།

མཚོ་ལ་གཟན་སྣར་ཇེ་ལྟར་མང་ཡང་༔

b. གཉིས་པ་ཇེ་ལྟར་ཕྱལ་བའི་རྣམ་གྲངས་གསལ་བར་བསྟན་པས་རྒྱས་

པར་བཤད་པ་ལ་གསུམ། ཕན་གཏོད་མཚན་མ་ལས་འདས་པའི་

> *"The following is a discussion of what arises as the dynamic energy of this fivefold basis of confusion. . . ."* [p. 97]

    c) **A synopsis of the key points of these topics**
    "Some people hold sensory appearances to be mind. . . ." [p. 103]

3. A synopsis of the key points of this subsection
"In summary, the world of all appearances and possibilities, whether of samsara or nirvana . . ." [p. 103]

C. Embracing samsara and nirvana within a paradigm of openness, uninterrupted and free of restrictions or extremes
This subsection has two divisions: from the perspective of sensory appearances, demonstrating their openness as mere appearances, like illusions; and from the perspective of emptiness, demonstrating their openness in having no independent nature.

  1. From the perspective of sensory appearances, demonstrating their openness as mere appearances, like illusions
  On yet another occasion, when I met the great rigdzin Hungchhenkara in a vision . . . [p. 107]

  2. From the perspective of emptiness, demonstrating their openness in having no independent nature
  This division has two subdivisions: demonstrating concisely how everything is embraced by the single nature of phenomena and explaining this extensively by clearly demonstrating the numerous ramifications of openness.

    a. Demonstrating concisely how everything is embraced by the single nature of phenomena
    "Consider the fact that no matter how many planets and stars are reflected in a lake . . ." [p. 109]

    b. Explaining this extensively by clearly demonstrating numerous ramifications of openness

དེ་བོར་ཕྱལ་བར་བསྒྲུན་པ། མཐའ་བཀྱད་སྤྱོས་གྲལ་གྱི་རང་

བཞིན་དུ་ཕྱལ་བར་བསྒྲུན་པ། རྣམ་ཐར་སྒོ་གསུམ་གྱི་བདག་ཉིད་

དུ་ཕྱལ་བར་བསྒྲུན་པའོ།

1) དང་པོ་ཕན་གནོད་མཚན་མ་ལས་འདས་པའི་དེ་བོར་ཕྱལ་བར་
བསྒྲུན་པ་ནི།

སེམས་ཉིད་བདེ་གཤེགས་སྙིང་པོ་ཞེས་བྱ་བ་ནི༔

2) གཉིས་པ་མཐའ་བཀྱད་སྤྱོས་གྲལ་གྱི་རང་བཞིན་དུ་ཕྱལ་བར་བསྒྲུན་
པ་ནི།

གཞི་ཡི་ཆོས་སྐུ་བདེ་བར་གཤེགས་པའི་སྙིང་པོ༔

3) གསུམ་པ་རྣམ་ཐར་སྒོ་གསུམ་གྱི་བདག་ཉིད་དུ་ཕྱལ་བར་བསྒྲུན་
པ་ནི།

ཡང་སྙིང་འོག་ཕྱོགས་མཚམས་བར་དང་དུས་ལས་འདས་པས༔

D. བཞི་པ་ཡེ་ནས་རྩོལ་མེད་རང་གསལ་ཡོན་ཏན་ལྷུན་གྲུབ་ཆེན་པོར་ལ་བརྒྱ་
བ་ལ་གསུམ། ཐབས་ཤེས་དང་རིས་ཀྱི་སྒོ་ནས་སྤྱིར་བསྒྲུན་པ། ལྷུན་
གྱིས་གྲུབ་པའི་ཡོན་ཏན་གྱི་རྣམ་གཞག་བྱེ་བྲག་ཏུ་བཤད་པ། དེ་ལྟར་རྟོགས་
པའི་ཚུལ་ལ་ཡོན་ཏན་གྱི་ཁྱད་པར་རྟོགས་ཚུལ་ལོ།

1. དང་པོ་ཐབས་ཤེས་དང་རིས་ཀྱི་སྒོ་ནས་སྤྱིར་བསྒྲུན་པ་ནི།

ཡང་འོད་གསལ་ནམས་ཀྱི་སྣང་དོར་འཛམ་དཔལ་སྤྱ་བའི་སེང་གིའི༔

This subdivision has three categories: demonstrating that openness is the essence of being, beyond being characterized by benefit or harm; demonstrating that openness is the nature of being, free of the elaborations of the eight limits; and demonstrating that openness is the epitome of the three doorways to liberation.

1) **Demonstrating that openness is the essence of being, beyond the characteristics of benefit or harm**
   "The nature of mind, referred to as 'buddha nature' (de-sheg nying-po)..." [p. 109]

2) **Demonstrating that openness is the nature of being, free of the elaborations of the eight limits**
   "The ground aspect of dharmakaya, buddha nature, is free of everything related to origination—any location, object, or creator..." [p. 109]

3) **Demonstrating that openness is the epitome of the three doorways to liberation**
   "Furthermore, it is empty in that it is beyond upper or lower, cardinal or intercardinal direction, interval or time frame...." [p. 111]

D. **Coming to a decisive experience within a supreme state of spontaneous presence in which enlightened qualities are forever effortless and naturally lucid**
   This subsection has three divisions: demonstrating in general by way of provisional skillful means and definitive sublime knowing; explaining in detail the categories of these spontaneously present qualities; and showing how specific kinds of qualities are perfect in such a manner of realization.

1. **Demonstrating in general by way of provisional skillful means and definitive sublime knowing**
   On yet another occasion, during a meditative experience of utter lucidity, I met Manjushri, the Lion of Speech ...
   [p. 117]

2. གཉིས་པ་བླུན་གྱིས་གྲུབ་པའི་ཡོན་ཏན་གྱི་རྣམ་གཞག་ཉེ་བརྒད་ཏུ་བཤད་
པ་ལ་ལྔ། སྐུ་ལྷ་བླུན་གྱིས་གྲུབ་ཚུལ། རིགས་ལྷ་བླུན་གྱིས་
གྲུབ་ཚུལ། ཞིང་ཁམས་ལྷ་བླུན་གྱིས་གྲུབ་ཚུལ། སངས་རྒྱས་
ལྷ་བླུན་གྱིས་གྲུབ་ཚུལ། མཁའ་འགྲོ་ལྷ་བླུན་གྱིས་གྲུབ་ཚུལ་ལོ།

a. དང་པོ་སྐུ་ལྷ་བླུན་གྱིས་གྲུབ་ཚུལ་ནི།
   འཁོར་བའི་སྦྱོར་བསྐུན་ནས་དོན་དམ་ཀུན་རྫོབ་ཏུ་བསྐུན་པ༔

b. གཉིས་པ་རིགས་ལྷ་བླུན་གྱིས་གྲུབ་ཚུལ་ནི།
   འགྲོ་བ་རྣམས་རིགས་ལ་མངོན་པར་ཞེན་པ་དེ་དང་བསྐུན་ཏེ༔

c. གསུམ་པ་ཞིང་ཁམས་ལྷ་བླུན་གྱིས་གྲུབ་ཚུལ་ནི།
   མི་རྣམས་ཡུལ་ལ་མངོན་པར་ཞེན་པའི་ཡུལ་དང་བསྐུན༔

d. བཞི་པ་སངས་རྒྱས་ལྷ་བླུན་གྱིས་གྲུབ་ཚུལ་ནི།
   གཞི་དབྱིངས་ཁྲབ་བཅལ་གྱི་རང་མདངས་ཁྲབ་བྱེད་ཀྱི་ཤེས་རབ༔

e. ལྔ་པ་མཁའ་འགྲོ་ལྷ་བླུན་གྱིས་གྲུབ་ཚུལ་ནི།
   དོན་གྱི་དྲོ་རྗེ་སྦྱོང་བ་ཉིད་ཀྱི་མཁའ་ལ༔

3. གསུམ་པ་དེ་ལྟར་རྟོགས་པའི་ཚུལ་ལ་ཡོན་ཏན་གྱི་ཁྱད་པར་རྟོགས་ཚུལ་ལ་
གསུམ། དོན་དམ་པའི་ཚེ་གའི་ཡན་ལག་རྟོགས་ཚུལ། ཐེག་པ་རང་
གི་མིང་གི་ཆེ་བ་རྟོགས་ཚུལ། རིམ་དགུའི་ཐེག་པའི་ཡོན་ཏན་ཡར་བླུན་
གྱི་ཚུལ་དུ་རྟོགས་ཚུལ་ལོ།

2. Explaining in detail the categories of these spontaneously present qualities
   This division has five subdivisions: how the five kayas are spontaneously present; how the five families are spontaneously present; how the five pure realms are spontaneously present; how the five buddhas are spontaneously present; and how the five dakinis are spontaneously present.

   a. How the five kayas are spontaneously present
      "The following is a demonstration of ultimate reality on the relative level, in accord with modes of samsaric experience...." [p. 119]

   b. How the five families are spontaneously present
      "The following is the basis on which deities are described in terms of families, corresponding to the identification of beings with their species...." [p. 123]

   c. How the five pure realms are spontaneously present
      "The following is a demonstration of pure realms as fivefold, which corresponds to the identification of human beings with their territory..." [p. 125]

   d. How the five buddhas are spontaneously present
      "When the natural glow of the pervasive and extensive ground of being as basic space has been made evident by sublime knowing that is supreme and pervasive..." [p. 127]

   e. How the five dakinis are spontaneously present
      "Ultimate vajra emptiness is the space..." [p. 127]

3. Showing how specific kinds of qualities are perfect in such a manner of realization
   This division has three subdivisions: how the components of rituals are perfect from the perspective of ultimate reality; how the perfection of this approach is expressed in the exalted terms for it; and how the qualities

a. དང་པོ་དོན་དམ་པའི་ཚོ་གའི་ཡན་ལག་རྟོགས་ཚུལ་ལ་གཉིས། ཇི་
ལྟར་རྟོགས་ཚུལ་དངོས་དང་། ཀུན་རྟོབ་ཐབས་ཀྱི་སྦྱོའི་བསྐྱེད་
རིམ་བསྟན་པའི་དགོས་པའོ།

   1) དང་པོ་ཇི་ལྟར་རྟོགས་ཚུལ་དངོས་ནི།
    དེ་ལྟར་གཞིའི་ཚོས་སྐུ་བདེ་གཤེགས་སྙིང་པོ༔

   2) གཉིས་པ་ཀུན་རྟོབ་ཐབས་ཀྱི་སྦྱོའི་བསྐྱེད་རིམ་བསྟན་པའི་དགོས་
པ་ནི།
    སྣར་ཡང་བར་སྣབས་ཤིག་ཏུ་དཔལ་ཨོ་རྒྱན་མཚོ་སྐྱེས་རྡོ་རྗེའི༔

b. གཉིས་པ་ཐེག་པ་རང་གི་མིང་གི་ཆེ་བ་རྟོགས་ཚུལ་ནི།
   ཡང་རེ་ཞིག་གི་ཚོ་དབྱིངས་ཀྱི་རྗེ་མོ་ཨེ་ཀ་ཛ་ཏིའི༔

c. གསུམ་པ་རིམ་དགུའི་ཐེག་པའི་ཡོན་ཏན་ཡར་ལྡན་གྱི་ཚུལ་དུ་རྟོགས་
ཚུལ་ནི།
   དེ་ལྟར་སྐྱེར་བཞད་ནས་བུ་བྲག་རིམ་དགུའི་ཐེག་པའི་ལམ་གྱི༔

II. རྩ་བའི་གཉིས་པ་བསྒོམ་པས་ཉམས་སུ་ལེན་ཚུལ་ལ་གཉིས། སྒོམ་པ་དམིགས་
གཏད་དང་བྲལ་བའི་ཚུལ་སྒྱིར་བསྟན་པ། མཚམ་རྗེས་ཀྱི་རིམ་པ་བྱེ་བྲག་ཏུ་
བཤད་པའོ།

of the nine developmental approaches are complete, with the higher incorporating the lower.

a. **How the components of rituals are perfect from the perspective of ultimate reality**
This subdivision has two categories: the actual way in which these components are perfect and the value of teaching the development stage as an avenue for skillful means on the relative level.

   1) **The actual way in which these components are perfect**
   "The ground aspect of dharmakaya, buddha nature ..." [p. 129]

   2) **The value of teaching the development stage as an avenue for skillful means on the relative level**
   On yet another occasion, I met the glorious Orgyan Tsokyey Dorje in a vision... [p. 139]

b. **How the perfection of this approach is expressed in the exalted terms for it**
On yet another occasion, when I met the queen of basic space, Ekajati... [p. 145]

c. **How the qualities of the nine developmental approaches are complete, with the higher incorporating the lower**
I will elaborate on her general explanation by illustrating the way in which all qualities of the paths of the nine developmental spiritual approaches (t'heg-pa rim-pa gu)... [p. 149]

II. Practical application through meditation
This second major section has two subsections: demonstrating in general how meditation is without any fixed frame of reference; and explaining in detail the stages of formal meditation and postmeditation experience.

A. དང་པོ་སྟོབས་པ་དམིགས་གཏད་དང་བྲལ་བའི་ཆུལ་སྒྲིར་བསྟན་པ་ནི། །
སྣང་ཡང་རིག་འཛིན་གྱི་རྒྱལ་པོ་ཕྲི་སེང་དའི༔

B. གཉིས་པ་མ་ནུམ་རྗེས་ཀྱི་རིམ་པ་བྲི་བྱག་ཏུ་བཤད་པ་ནི། །
དེའི་དང་ཆུལ་ཤེས་ཏེ་ལུས་ཀྱི་སྒྲོ་ནས་བཟང་ངན་བར་གསུམ༔

III. རྩ་བའི་གསུམ་པ་སྒྲོད་པས་བོགས་དབྱུང་བ་ལ་གསུམ། །ལྷ་སྒྲོད་ཕྱོགས་རེར་
མི་འཛོལ་བའི་ཆུལ་ལ་བསྐྱབ་པ། །ལས་ཀྱི་གོལ་ས་གཏོད་པ། །ཡང་དག་
པའི་སྒྲོད་ཆུལ་གཞན་བསྟན་པའོ། །

A. དང་པོ་ལྷ་སྒྲོད་ཕྱོགས་རེར་མི་འཛོལ་བའི་ཆུལ་ལ་བསྒྲབ་པ་ནི། །
སྒྲོད་པའི་གནད་ནི་ཐམས་ཅད་སྒྲོང་པ་ཉིད་ཡིན་པས༔

B. གཉིས་པ་ལས་ཀྱི་གོལ་ས་གཏོད་པ་ལ་གཉིས། ། རྣམས་ཀྱི་གོལ་ས་ངོས་
བཟུང་བ་དང་། །སྒྲོང་གི་གོལ་ས་གཏོད་པའོ། །

1. དང་པོ་རྣམས་ཀྱི་གོལ་ས་ངོས་བཟུང་བ་ནི། །
རྣམས་ཀྱི་སྣང་བ་ནི་སེམས་དང་ཤེས་རྒྱུད་སྤྱར་སྤྱར་མ་ཡིན༔

2. གཉིས་པ་སྒྲོང་གི་གོལ་ས་གཏོད་པ་ནི། །
གཞན་ཡང་ཕྱི་སྒྲོང་ལྟ་འདྲིའི་ཚོ་འཕུལ་ཐན་དང་ལྱས་ངན༔

A. Demonstrating in general how meditation is without any fixed frame of reference
Later, when in a vision I met Shri Simha, king of rigdzins . . . [p. 157]

B. Explaining in detail the stages of formal meditation and postmeditation experience
"Understanding this fundamental nature, you give up the three kinds of physical activity—good, bad, and neutral . . ." [p. 159]

III. Enrichment through conduct
This third major section has three subsections: training so that one does not make errors in judgment at the expense of either view or conduct; defining points of potential deviation from the path; and demonstrating other modes of authentic conduct.

A. Training so that one does not make errors in judgment at the expense of either view or conduct
"The key point of conduct is to renounce nonvirtuous physical and verbal activities as if they were poison . . ." [p. 161]

B. Defining points of potential deviation from the path
This subsection has two divisions: identifying points of potential deviation regarding ephemeral meditative experiences; and defining points of potential deviation regarding upheavals.

1. Identifying points of potential deviation regarding ephemeral meditative experiences
"Meditative experiences (nyam) occur in which your ordinary mind—the continuum of your consciousness—is different from what it was before. . . ." [p. 163]

2. Defining points of potential deviation regarding upheavals
"As well, you may encounter upheavals (long). External

C. གསུམ་པ་ཡང་དག་པའི་སྒྲུད་ཆུལ་གཞན་བསྟན་པ་ནི།

ཡང་རེ་ཞིག་གི་ཚེ་རང་སྡུང་དོན་གྱི་འོག་མིན༔

IV. རྩ་བའི་བཞི་པ་འབྲས་བུ་མངོན་དུ་གྱུར་ཆུལ་ལ་གཉིས། འབྲས་བུ་གཏན་
གྲོལ་གྱི་རིམ་པ་དངོས། དེའི་གནད་མི་འཁྲུག་པའི་གཟེར་ཤན་འབྱེད་ཀྱི་མན་
ངག་གོ།

A. དང་པོ་འབྲས་བུ་གཏན་གྲོལ་གྱི་རིམ་པ་དངོས་ནི།

དང་པོ་བསྐྱབ་པ་ལ་བརྟེན་ནས་ཤེས་པ༔

B. གཉིས་པ་དེའི་གནད་མི་འཁྲུག་པའི་གཟེར་ཤན་འབྱེད་ཀྱི་མན་ངག་ལ་བཞི།
སེམས་དང་རིག་པའི་ཤན་འབྱེད། ཡིད་དང་ཤེས་རབ་ཀྱི་ཤན་འབྱེད།
རྣམ་ཤེས་དང་ཡེ་ཤེས་ཀྱི་ཤན་འབྱེད། ཀུན་གཞི་དང་ཆོས་སྐུའི་ཤན་འབྱེད་
དོ།

1. དང་པོ་སེམས་དང་རིག་པའི་ཤན་འབྱེད་ནི།

རིགས་ཀྱི་བུ་གཞི་མ་རིག་པ་རྩལ་རྣམ་པར་རྟོག་པ༔

2. གཉིས་པ་ཡིད་དང་ཤེས་རབ་ཀྱི་ཤན་འབྱེད་ནི།

རྣམ་པར་རྟོག་པའི་ཚོ་འཕུལ་མཆེད་པའི་སྦྱང་བ༔

216

upheavals consist of various phantasmagoria that affect one's senses, such as negative portents and omens..." [p. 163]

C. **Demonstrating other modes of authentic conduct**
On yet another occasion, in a naturally manifesting vision of the ultimate pure realm of Akanishtha... [p. 169]

IV. **How the fruition becomes evident**
This fourth major section has two subsections: the actual stage of ongoing freedom as the fruition; and the heart advice that creates clear distinctions, unerringly pinning down the key points.

A. **The actual stage of ongoing freedom as the fruition**
"At first, you develop comprehension by relying on training..." [p. 171]

B. **The heart advice that creates clear distinctions, unerringly pinning down the key points**
This subsection has four divisions: making a clear distinction between ordinary mind and awareness; making a clear distinction between conceptual mind and sublime knowing; making a clear distinction between consciousness and timeless awareness; and making a clear distinction between the ground of all ordinary experience and dharmakaya.

1. **Making a clear distinction between ordinary mind and awareness**
"Ah, son of spiritual heritage, ordinary mind (sem) can be characterized as the nonrecognition of awareness (ma-rig-pa)—that is, of the ground of being—with conceptualization..." [p. 173]

2. **Making a clear distinction between conceptual mind and sublime knowing**
"The term 'conceptual mind' (yid) refers to consciousness that makes evident all sensory appearances, which

3. གསུམ་པ་རྣམ་ཤེས་དང་ཡེ་ཤེས་ཀྱི་ཁྱད་འབྱེད་ནི། །

འདོད་ཡོན་གྱི་སྣང་བ་མཆེད་པའི་སྣང་ཡུལ༔

4. བཞི་པ་ཀུན་གཞི་དང་ཆོས་སྐུའི་ཁྱད་འབྱེད་པ་ལ་གཉིས། །ཁན་འབྱེད་

དངོས་དང་། །གནད་ཀྱི་དོན་བསྡུ་བའོ། །

a. དང་པོ་ཁྱད་འབྱེད་དངོས་ནི། །

གཞི་མ་རིག་པའི་དབང་གིས་ལུང་མ་བསྟན་དུ་སོང་བ༔

b. གཉིས་པ་གནད་ཀྱི་དོན་བསྡུ་བ་ནི། །

འདི་ལྟར་རོལ་པ་དང་། །ཆིངས་པ་དང་། །ཁྲབ་པ་དང་༔

རུ་བའི་གསུམ་པ་མཐར་ཕྱིན་མཐུག་གི་དོན་སྟོས་པ་ནི། །

ཞེས་པ་འདི་ཡང་སྐྱེ་བ་དུ་མར་ལས་དང་སྨོན་ལམ༔

སོགས་ཀྱིས་ཡོངས་སུ་གྲུབ་པའོ། །ཞེས་པ་འདི་ཡང་སྐྱོབ་དཔོན་ཕྱུབ་བསྟན་རྒྱལ་

མཚན་གྱིས་བྱེད་དཔོན་སྐྲབས་སུ་གོ་བདེའི་གསལ་བྱེད་དུ་བྲིས་ཤིག་པར་བསྐུལ་བ་

བཞིན་འཇིགས་བྲལ་ཡེ་ཤེས་རྡོ་རྗེས་སོ། ། །།

proliferate through the intricate workings of conceptualization. . . ." [p. 173]

3. **Making a clear distinction between consciousness and timeless awareness**

   "The term 'consciousness' (nam-par shey-pa) refers to the unimpeded avenue for apparent sense objects to proliferate as the six kinds of sense objects. . . ." [p. 175]

4. **Making a clear distinction between the ground of all ordinary experience and dharmakaya**

   This division has two subdivisions: the actual clear distinction and a synopsis of the key points.

   a. **The actual clear distinction**

      "Due to the nonrecognition of awareness—that is, of the ground of being—a karmically neutral state results. . . ." [p. 175]

   b. **A synopsis of the key points**

      "Having come to an understanding of all the ramifications of the fundamental nature—its display, encompassing quality, pervasiveness . . ." [p. 177]

PART THREE: RELATING THE CONCLUSION
THAT BRINGS THE TEXT TO AN END

This text was written in response to repeated requests . . .
With this the text is brought to a complete finish.

This was written by Jigdral Yeshe Dorje [His Holiness Dudjom Rinpoche] in response to a request by the master T'hubtan Gyaltsan for a study guide that would be easy to understand, when he was serving as a director of instruction.

Glossary

THE GLOSSARY THAT appeared in the first edition has been expanded and revised to include alternative translations of Great Perfection terms by a number of authors and translators, as well as current terms used by the Padma Translation Committee.

While some of the entries have wider application in more general Buddhist thought, the emphasis here is on their Great Perfection usage. It is frequently said that the Great Perfection speaks its own words and has its own unique vocabulary and meanings. The evolution and use of Great Perfection translations in English have several obvious characteristics. First, the ongoing search for standardization of English terms is still in a formative stage. Second, readers are thus faced with a wide variety of translations for terms that are quite standardized in Tibetan, but they are rarely given tools for bridging that variety. Third, the inclusion of alternative translations is useful in bringing out the larger meaning of Great Perfection terms, which are better rendered by interpretive than by literal translation. A caveat that should never be forgotten is that no book or its scholarly apparatus is a substitute for study, contemplation, and meditation within the context of the teacher–student relationship.

Glossary

KEY TO SOURCES CITED

BM: *Buddha Mind,* trans. by Tulku Thondup

CDN: *The Cycle of Day and Night,* by Namkhai Norbu, trans. by John Reynolds

CS: *The Circle of the Sun,* by Tsele Natsok Rangdrol, trans. by Erik Pema Kunsang

DZ: *Dzogchen,* by Namkhai Norbu, trans. by John Shane

DZP: *Dzogchen and Padmasambhava,* by Sogyal Rinpoche

FG: *The Flight of the Garuda,* by Lama Shabkar, trans. by Erik Pema Kunsang

FRC: *From Reductionism to Creativity,* by Herbert V. Guenther

GL: *The Golden Letters,* trans. by John Myrdhin Reynolds

HTV: *The Holy Teachings of Vimalakirti,* trans. by Robert Thurman

KB: *Kindly Bent to Ease Us,* by Longchenpa, trans. by Herbert V. Guenther

LM: *Lamp of Mahamudra,* by Tsele Natsok Rangdrol, trans. by Erik Pema Kunsang

LS: *The Life of Shabkar,* by Shabkar Tsogdruk Rangdrol, trans. by Matthieu Ricard et al.

MD: *Magic Dance,* by Thinley Norbu

ME: *Meditation on Emptiness,* by Jeffrey Hopkins

MK: *Mother of Knowledge,* by Nam-mkha'i snying-po, trans. by Tarthang Tulku

MW: *Myriad Worlds,* by Jamgön Kongtrul, trans. by the International Translation Committee

NGP: *Natural Great Perfection,* by Nyoshul Khenpo, trans. by Surya Das

NJ: Thinley Norbu Rinpoche's oral teaching of the *Nang-jang,* trans. by Sangye Khandro

NS: *The Nyingma School of Tibetan Buddhism,* Vol. II, by Gyurme Dorje and Matthew Kapstein

PC: *Perfect Conduct,* by Ngari Panchen, trans. by Khenpo Gyurme Dorje and Sangye Khandro

PE: *Primordial Experience,* by Mañjuśrīmitra, trans. by Namkhai Norbu and Kennard Lipman

RP: *Rainbow Painting,* by Tulku Urgyen Rinpoche, trans. by Erik Pema Kunsang

RW: *The Rain of Wisdom,* trans. by the Nālandā Translation Committee

SGK: *The Small Golden Key,* by Thinley Norbu

SL: *Self-Liberation Through Seeing With Naked Awareness,* by Karma Lingpa, trans. by John Myrdhin Reynolds

VH: *Vajra Heart,* by Tulku Urgyen, trans. by Erik Pema Kunsang

WPT: *The Words of My Perfect Teacher,* by Patrul Rinpoche, trans. by the Padmakara Translation Group

WS: *White Sail,* by Thinley Norbu

Abhirati (Skt.; Tib. Ngonpar Gawa, མངོན་པར་དགའ་བ་): literally, "Manifest Joy"; the pure realm associated with the buddha Akshobhya and the eastern direction

Akanishtha (Skt. Akaniṣṭha; Tib. Ogmin, འོག་མིན་): literally, "Under Nothing"; the pinnacle pure realm, an epithet for the pure realm of Ghanavyuha, that of the buddha Vairochana

Akshobhyavajra (Skt. Akṣobhyavajra; Tib. Mikyod Dorje, མི་བསྐྱོད་རྡོ་རྗེ་): literally, "Unshakable Vajra"; among the buddhas of the five families, the buddha associated with the eastern direction; the name denotes the ground of being endowed with the seven vajra (*dor-je*) attributes and unwavering (*mi-kyod*) throughout the three times

Amitabha (Skt. Amitābha; Tib. Nangwa T'hayay, སྣང་བ་མཐའ་ཡས་): literally, "Limitless Illumination"; among the buddhas of the five families, the buddha associated with the western direction; the name denotes the unlimited manifest aspect of the ground of being

Amoghasiddhi (Skt.; Tib. Donyod Drubpa, དོན་ཡོད་གྲུབ་པ་): literally, "Accomplishment of Meaning"; among the buddhas of the five families, the buddha associated with the northern direction; the name denotes the fact that everything that has authentic meaning occurs naturally

anuyoga (Skt.; Tib. ཨ་ནུ་ཡོ་ག་): the fifth of six levels of tantra in the Nyingma school; an approach in which all phenomena are realized to be perfect in their supreme purity and equalness

atiyoga (Skt.; Tib. ཨ་ཏི་ཡོ་ག་): the sixth of six levels of tantra in the Nyingma school, also known as the Great Perfection approach (*see* Dzogchhen), within which are subsumed the meanings of the eight lower approaches (*see t'heg-pa rim-pa gu*). The great perfection is the nature of reality—the ground of being and its manifest aspect—spontaneously present and naturally occurring [yoga of the innermost essence (MW)]

Avalokiteshvara (Skt. Avalokiteśvara; Tib. Kyanrayzig Wangkhyug, སྤྱན་རས་གཟིགས་དབང་ཕྱུག་): literally, "Powerful Lord with Eyes Gazing Down"; the bodhisattva embodying the compassion of all buddhas and bodhisattvas; also referred to as the "Supremely Compassionate One" (Skt. Mahākāruṇika; Tib. T'hugje Chhenpo, ཐུགས་རྗེ་ཆེན་པོ་)

bag-chhag (Tib. བག་ཆགས་; Skt. *vāsanā*): habitual patterns; patterns established by physical, verbal, or mental actions carrying over from lifetime to lifetime [habitual tendencies (CS); unconscious propensities (GL); ingrained tendencies, sedimented (KB); instinct (MW); habitual propensities (NJ); karmic traces (SL)]

bardo (Tib. བར་དོ་; Skt. *antarābhava*): literally, "intermediate state"; four, or sometimes six, bardo states are enumerated in Tibetan Buddhist teachings; commonly, the term denotes the interval between death and rebirth

bodhisattva (Skt.; Tib. *jang-chhub sem-pa,* བྱང་ཆུབ་སེམས་དཔའ་): literally, one with "a courageous mind bent upon enlightenment"; one who follows or has accomplished the mahayana path, which leads to realization of the nonexistence of both personal identity and the identity of phenomena

chhö (*see* dharma)

chhö-ku (*see* dharmakaya)

chhö kyi dag (Tib. ཆོས་ཀྱི་བདག་): identity of phenomena

chhö-nyid (Tib. ཆོས་ཉིད་; Skt. *dharmatā*): the true nature of phenomena [ultimate nature (BM); the nature of phenomena and mind (FG); meaningfulness (KB); ultimate content of what is (PE); uncontrived essence nature (WS)]

chhö-nyid zad-pai ying (Tib. ཆོས་ཉིད་ཟད་པའི་དབྱིངས་): the basic space in which phenomena resolve within their true nature

chhö-ying ye-shey (Tib. ཆོས་དབྱིངས་ཡེ་ཤེས་): timeless awareness as the basic space of phenomena; one of the five aspects of timeless awareness (*see ye-shey nga*); the realization that samsara and nirvana are of one taste in the basic space of the true nature of phenomena [primordial wisdom of the ultimate sphere (BM); wisdom of absolute expanse (LS); awareness of the Expanse of Dharma (MK); primordial wisdom of the dharmadhatu (sphere of truth)

(NJ, PC); pristine cognition of the expanse of reality (NS); Wisdom of Dharmadhatu (SGK); wisdom of absolute space (WPT)]

chhod-pa (Tib. མཆོད་པ་): making offerings, a component of sadhana practice; the display of phenomena within the context of their true nature is the supreme offering

chig-pu (Tib. གཅིག་པུ་): literally, "oneness"; one of the four key points of samaya of the Great Perfection; discerning that all of samsara and nirvana are a single, naturally occurring timeless awareness [single, unique (GL); sole (MD)]

city of the gandharvas (Tib. *dri-zai drong-khyer,* དྲི་ཟའི་གྲོང་ཁྱེར་): a mirage occurring at sunset under certain atmospheric conditions, when the sky seems filled with ethereal shapes of palaces and great cities

Cutting Through Maras (Tib. Dudkyi Chodyul, བདུད་ཀྱི་གཅོད་ཡུལ་): a school of Tibetan Buddhism, most commonly referred to as "Chod" (literally, "cutting through"), founded by the Tibetan teacher Machig Labdron (མ་ཅིག་ལབ་སྒྲོན་) in the twelfth century as an extension of the Zhijed teachings (*see* Pacification school)

da-gyud (Tib. བརྡ་བརྒྱུད་): the lineage of transmission through symbols

dag (Tib. བདག་): identity

dag-dzin (Tib. བདག་འཛིན་): concept or perception of identity

dag-med tog-pai shey-rab (Tib. བདག་མེད་རྟོགས་པའི་ཤེས་རབ་): sublime knowing that constitutes realization of the ultimate nonexistence of both personal identity and the identity of phenomena

dag-nang (Tib. དག་སྣང་): pure vision [pure perception (DZP, PC, WPT); pure thereness (KB); sacred outlook (RW); pure phenomena (WS)]

dakini (Skt. *ḍākinī;* Tib. *kha-dro-ma,* མཁའ་འགྲོ་མ་): literally, "sky

goer"; sky dancer; the feminine embodiment of timeless awareness; in the ultimate sense, the term denotes emptiness as the space
in which all phenomena manifest

dal-wa (Tib. བརྡལ་བ་): extensive; extension; congruence

dang (Tib. གདངས་): radiance

dang-sal (Tib. དངས་གསལ་): pristinely lucid

de-sheg nying-po (Tib. བདེ་གཤེགས་སྙིང་པོ་; Skt. *sugatagarbha*): literally, "potential for reaching a state of bliss"; often rendered "buddha nature"; the nature of mind as the potential that accounts for
any being awakening to buddhahood

de-zhin-nyid (Tib. དེ་བཞིན་ཉིད་; Skt. *tathatā*): suchness

dharma (Skt.; Tib. *chhö*, ཆོས་): broadly, any phenomenon or event
in one's experience; in the context of dharmakaya, the term con-
notes the fact that all phenomena are present as uncontrived, natural attributes within the supreme emptiness of the ground of being
as basic space [concepts and meanings (KB)]

dharmakaya (Skt. *dharmakāya*; Tib. *chhö-kyi ku*, ཆོས་ཀྱི་སྐུ་): literally, "body of truth"; a dimension of enlightened being, direct realization of the true nature of phenomena [ultimate body (BM);
reality dimension of awakening (MW); body of reality (NS); primordial contact with the total field of events and meanings (PE);
completely pure formless form (WS)]

dharmapala (Skt. *dharmapāla*; Tib. *chhö-kyong*, ཆོས་སྐྱོང་): a protective deity that guards Buddhist teachings and practitioners
against obstacles

ding (Tib. གདིང་): indwelling confidence

don-dam (Tib. དོན་དམ་): ultimate reality; the final mode of being as
"meaningful" (*don*), which is "sacred" (*dam*) in that it is the foremost of what is to be realized

don-dam jang-chhub kyi sem (Tib. དོན་དམ་བྱང་ཆུབ་ཀྱི་སེམས་): literally, "ultimate awakening attitude"; the second of seven terms referring to the Great Perfection teachings as explained to Dudjom Lingpa by Ekajati (*see jang-chhub [kyi] sem*)

dor-je (Tib. རྡོ་རྗེ་; Skt. *vajra*): a term referring to seven attributes of space—invulnerability, indestructibility, authenticity, incorruptibility, stability, unobstructedness, and invincibility; one of the five buddha families, denoting the ground of being endowed with these attributes

Dorje Drolod (Tib. རྡོ་རྗེ་གྲོ་ལོད་): a wrathful manifestation of Padmakara, particularly associated with the revelation of hidden treasure teachings in the Nyingma tradition

drang-don (Tib. དྲང་དོན་): provisional meaning

dri-ma (Tib. དྲི་མ་): distortions

drib-pa (Tib. སྒྲིབ་པ་): obscuration, the most fundamental level of which is a lack of awareness of the ground of being as the essence of emptiness

drol-wa (Tib. གྲོལ་བ་): freedom; the equivalent of nirvana

Duddul Dorje (Tib. བདུད་འདུལ་རྡོ་རྗེ་): a famous teacher and revealer of hidden treasure teachings in the Nyingma school, who lived from 1615 to 1672; Dudjom Lingpa was a later incarnation in the succession of rebirths that included Duddul Dorje

dzin-pa (Tib. འཛིན་པ་): the subjective pole of experience; the perception of a subject [subject, that which apprehends (GL); reifying concepts (PT)]

Dzogchhen (Tib. རྫོགས་ཆེན་): the Great Perfection approach of Buddhist practice, so called because the modes of samsara, nirvana, and the spiritual path are "perfect" (*dzog*) within this approach, which is "great" (*chhen*) because it functions as the common ground of all spiritual approaches; the third of seven terms referring to the Great Perfection teachings as explained to Dudjom Lingpa by Ekajati [already self-perfected state (DZP); absolute completeness (KB); total completeness (PE)]

Ekajati (Skt. Ekajaṭi; Tib. Ekadzaṭi, ཨེ་ཀ་ཛ་ཊི་, or Ngagsrungma, སྔགས་སྲུང་མ་): wrathful feminine protective deity; the main protector of the Great Perfection teachings

gandharva (Skt.; Tib. *dri-za*, དྲི་ཟ་): literally, one who "feeds upon smells"; a class of gods in the desire realm

gang zag gi dag (Tib. གང་ཟག་གི་བདག་): personal identity

geg-trad (Tib. བགེགས་བསྐྲད་): banishing hindrances, a component of sadhana practice; discerning sublime knowing banishes dualistic mind into emptiness, in which nothing exists as some object

Ghanavyuha (Skt. Ghanavyūha; Tib. Tugpo Kodpa, སྟུག་པོ་བཀོད་པ་): literally, "Dense Array"; the pure realm associated with the buddha Vairochana and the central direction

gom-pa (Tib. སྒོམ་པ་): meditation; while the term may refer to any systematic means of developing one-pointed attention and insight, in the context of the Great Perfection it implies maintaining ongoing awareness of the primordial ground of being

gong-gyud (Tib. དགོངས་བརྒྱུད་): the lineage of the mind-to-mind transmission of enlightened intent

gyu-ma (Tib. སྒྱུ་མ་): illusory; a magical illusion; a traditional metaphor for the illusion-like nature of phenomena

gyud (Tib. རྒྱུད་): mindstream; the flow or "thread" of conscious awareness from moment to moment that is misapprehended as a discrete "self" or ego-entity

Hungchhenkara (Tib. ཧཱུྃ་ཆེན་ཀཱ་ར་): one of the eight great rigdzins of Buddhist India who taught Padmakara; Hungchhenkara was responsible for transmitting to him the lineage of the deity Yangdag Heruka

ja-(wa) drub(-pai) ye-shey (Tib. བྱ་[བ་]གྲུབ་[པའི་]ཡེ་ཤེས་): timeless awareness as spontaneous fulfillment; one of the five aspects of timeless awareness (*see ye-shey nga*); awareness as the natural accomplishment of activities in the purity and freedom of all phenomena [primordial wisdom of accomplishment of actions (BM); All-accomplishing Awareness (MK); Pristine Wisdom of accomplishing aims (MW); wisdom that accomplishes all actions (RW); all-accomplishing wisdom (SGK, WPT)]

jang-chhub (kyi) sem (Tib. བྱང་ཆུབ་[ཀྱི་]སེམས་; Skt. *bodhicitta*): literally, "awakened mind"; denotes the "refining away" (*jang*) of all flaws and distortions; the consummate state (*chhub*) of all qualities of the kayas, timeless awareness, the path, and the goal; and "mind" (*sem*) as the ground for the arising of everything in equal purity [heart of enlightened essence (DZP); thrust/intent toward pellucidity and consummation of the whole cognitive domain (FRC); inner potential for limpid clearness and consummate perspicacity (KB); mind of enlightenment (NGP); (primordial) state of pure and total presence (PE); Primordial State of the individual (SL)]

jar-med (Tib. བྱར་མེད་): literally, "nothing needing to be done"; a term used by Shri Simha to indicate that when resting in one's fundamental nature, one has given up all activities

ji-nyed-pa zig-pai ye-shey (Tib. ཇི་སྙེད་པ་གཟིགས་པའི་ཡེ་ཤེས་): timeless awareness of the multiplicity of things

ji-ta-wa khyen-pai ye-shey (Tib. ཇི་ལྟ་བ་མཁྱེན་པའི་ཡེ་ཤེས་): timeless awareness that knows the real nature of things

jin-beb (Tib. བྱིན་འབེབས་): bringing down blessings, a component of sadhana practice; infusing the supreme blessing of the recognition of timeless awareness into the darkness of nonrecognition constitutes the actual stage of bringing down blessings

ka-dag (Tib. ཀ་དག་): original purity [primordial purity (BM, DZP, MW, NGP, NS, SL, VH, WPT); pure from the beginning (DZ, DZP); diaphanous (FRC); absolutely pure (KB)]

kaya (Skt. *kāya;* Tib. *ku,* སྐུ་): literally, "body"; a dimension of enlightened being, functioning as a basis for the enlightened qualities and aspects of timeless awareness [gestalt (FRC); founding stratum (KB); aspect/form of the unconceivable qualities of Buddhas (WS)]

kha-dro (*see* dakini)

kham (Tib. ཁམས་): the fundamental nature of being

khor-day ub-chhub (Tib. འཁོར་འདས་ཟུབ་ཆུབ་): literally, "all-embracing consummation of samsara and nirvana," since all phenomena of samsara and nirvana (*khor-day*) are subsumed within the embrace (*ub*) of buddha nature and are totally consummated (*chhub*) therein; the sixth of seven terms referring to the Great Perfection teachings as explained to Dudjom Lingpa by Ekajati

khyab-pa (Tib. ཁྱབ་པ་): pervasiveness

khyag-tsal (Tib. ཕྱག་འཚལ་): the act of paying homage, a component of sadhana practice; to experience a great sense of wonder upon encountering one's true face—the primordial ground aspect of dharmakaya—is to pay homage by encountering the view

khyal-wa (Tib. ཁྱལ་བ་): openness; one of the four key points of samaya of the *t'hreg-chhod* approach of Great Perfection; the experience of samsara and nirvana as free of biased extremes [omnipresent (GL); continuous (KB); free (MD); openness (PT); all-pervasiveness (RP)]

kriyatantra (Skt. *kriyātantra;* Tib. *ja-wai gyud,* བྱ་བའི་རྒྱུད་): the first of six levels of tantra in the Nyingma school; an approach employing ascetic practices and ritual purity

ku (*see* kaya)

kun-dzob (Tib. ཀུན་རྫོབ་): relative reality; the level on which all (*kun*) phenomena manifest in a "false" (*dzob*) manner, as though they truly existed [superficial reality (MW)]

kun-zhi (Tib. ཀུན་གཞི་; Skt. *ālaya*): the ground of all ordinary experience; a karmically neutral state resulting from the non-recognition of awareness and functioning as the ground (*zhi*) of all (*kun*) samsara [all ground (CS); stratum of all things (KB); basis of all (NJ); fundamental structuring of all experience (PE); basis of samsara and nirvana, which is not unobscured (WS)]

kun-zhii nam-shey (Tib. ཀུན་གཞིའི་རྣམ་ཤེས་; Skt. *ālayavijñāna*): consciousness as the ground of all ordinary experience; rudimentary consciousness caused by the subtle energy of karma being aroused due to the nonrecognition of awareness [all-ground consciousness (CS); store consciousness (GL); stratum-bound perceptivity (KB); fundamental consciousness (MW); consciousness of the all-pervasive ground (NJ, PC); consciousness of the ground of all (NS)]

Kuntuzangpo (Tib. ཀུན་ཏུ་བཟང་པོ་; Skt. Samantabhadra): literally, "wholly positive"; the dharmakaya buddha embodying the primordial nature of mind; in the definitive sense, the wholly positive ground of one's own being is the meaning of buddhahood

kyab-dro (Tib. སྐྱབས་འགྲོ་): going for refuge, a component of sadhana practice; gaining true independence in the knowledge that awareness unites all spiritual principles is the ultimate refuge

kyan-dren (Tib. སྤྱན་འདྲེན་): the stage of invitation as a component of sadhana practice; the shift in perspective from the phenomena of samsara to the display of the single nature of phenomena, making the fundamental nature fully evident, is the ultimate stage of invitation

kyod-pa (Tib. སྤྱོད་པ་): conduct, in the sense of how one's view and meditation carry over into and influence daily activities [behavior, action (GL)] *lam* (Tib. ལམ་): path; the process that leads from the unenlightened state of an ordinary being to the awakened state of a buddha

lay (Tib. ལས་; Skt. *karma*): activity, action; one of the five buddha families, denoting the spontaneous fulfillment of all activities within the ground of being [evolutionary action (MW); actions and their effects (WPT)]

lay kyi lung (Tib. ལས་ཀྱི་རླུང་): the subtle energy of karma; refers to conceptualization that invests sensory appearances with reality

lha (Tib. ལྷ་): god, in the sense of a being reborn within the relatively highest realms of samsara; in other contexts, the term refers to a meditation deity embodying a particular quality of timeless awareness

lhag-t'hong (Tib. ལྷག་མཐོང་; Skt. *vipaśyanā*): profound insight

lhun-drub (Tib. ལྷུན་གྲུབ་): spontaneous presence; one of the four key points of samaya of the Great Perfection; refers to the fact that phenomena manifest naturally and that the qualities of buddhahood are timelessly perfect without having to be cultivated [spontaneous perfection (RP); spontaneously self-perfected (SL)]

lo-day (Tib. བློ་འདས་): literally, "beyond ordinary consciousness"; a term used by Shri Simha to indicate that when one rests in one's fundamental nature, there is no contrivance by ordinary mind

long (Tib. ལོང་): upheavals occurring as hallucinations due to outside forces, on an inner level as disease and physical pain, or on a secret level as emotional and mental instability

long-dhe (Tib. ཀློང་སྡེ་): the Category of Expanse; the second of the three categories of teachings in atiyoga, or Great Perfection

long-ku (*see* sambhogakaya)

Longchhenpa Drimed Odzer (Tib. ཀློང་ཆེན་པ་དྲི་མེད་འོད་ཟེར་): the greatest scholar of the Nyingma school, who lived from 1308 to 1364

lu-gu-gyud (Tib. ལུ་གུ་རྒྱུད་): interlinking; continuum

lung (Tib. ལུང་): subtle energy

lung-ma-tan (Tib. ལུང་མ་བསྟན་): karmically neutral

ma-rig-pa (Tib. མ་རིག་པ་; Skt. *avidyā*): nonrecognition of awareness; lack of awareness of the ground of being as the essence of
emptiness [unenlightenment (BM); low-level (cognitive) intensity
(FRC); loss of pure awareness (KB); unawareness, ignorance (MW);
non-recognition (NJ)]

mahayoga (Skt. *mahāyoga;* Tib. མ་ཧཱ་ཡོ་ག་): the fourth of six levels
of tantra in the Nyingma school; the approach in which all phenomena are viewed as the inseparability of the two levels of truth,
pure from the very beginning in supreme dharmakaya

Maheshvara (Skt. Maheśvara; Tib. Wangkhyug Chhenpo, དབང་ཕྱུག་
ཆེན་པོ་): an epithet of Shiva, regarded (especially in the Nyingma
school of Tibetan Buddhism) as a protector of the Buddhist teachings

man-ngag (Tib. མན་ངག་): pith instruction; heart advice [instruction
(CS); experiential instruction (DZP); pith instructions (LS, WPT);
oral pith instructions (NJ); secret oral instructions (SL); pith of
teachings (WS)]

man-ngag-dhe (Tib. མན་ངག་སྡེ་): the Category of Direct Transmission; the third of three categories of teachings in atiyoga, or Great
Perfection

mandala (Skt. *maṇḍala;* Tib. *kyil-khor,* དཀྱིལ་འཁོར་): literally, in Tibetan, "center and circumference"; the symbolic configuration de-
picting a pure realm with deities dwelling therein, expressing the
totality of the enlightened state of being [immeasurable existence
and wisdom energy (WS)]

Manjushri, Lion of Speech (Skt. Mañjuśrī Vādisiṃha; Tib. Jampal
Mrawai Seng-ge, འཇམ་དཔལ་སྨྲ་བའི་སེང་གེ་): a bodhisattva embodying
the wisdom and sublime knowing of all buddhas and bodhisattvas

mara (Skt. *māra;* Tib. དུད་): forces that bind one to samsara and obstruct the pursuit of virtue; four are usually enumerated—the afflictive emotions, the mind–body aggregates, mortality, and fascination with positive meditative experiences that impedes progress on the path to enlightenment

me-long (ta-bui) ye-shey (Tib. མེ་ལོང་[ལྟ་བུའི་]ཡེ་ཤེས་): mirrorlike timeless awareness; one of the five aspects of timeless awareness (*see ye-shey nga*); refers to the fact that emptiness is not an inert void, but is pristinely lucid and free of sullying factors, like a polished mirror in which anything can arise [mirror(-like) primordial wisdom (BM); Mirrorlike Awareness (MK); mirrorlike wisdom (RW, WPT); Mirror Wisdom (SGK)]

med-pa (Tib. མེད་པ་): ineffability; literally, "nonexistence"; one of the four key points of samaya of the Great Perfection; the definitive conclusion that the true nature of all phenomena is inexpressible emptiness, with no true existence or independent nature

mi-gyur dor-jei ku (Tib. མི་འགྱུར་རྡོ་རྗེའི་སྐུ་): literally, "unchanging vajrakaya"; the fifth kaya, explained to Dudjom Lingpa by Manjushri [body of indestructible reality (NS)]

mig gi dzin-pa sem (Tib. མིག་གི་འཛིན་པ་སེམས་): ordinary mind that reifies through vision

mig gi zung-wa yul (Tib. མིག་གི་གཟུང་བ་ཡུལ་): field for the perception of visual objects

mon-pa med-pa (Tib. སྨོན་པ་མེད་པ་): the absence of speculation; one of the three "doorways to liberation" (*t'har-pai go*); refers to the fact that in ultimate reality no context exists on which to base any speculation concerning the goal of enlightenment [absence of aspiration (NJ); aspirationlessness (NS)]

nam(-par) shey(-pa) (Tib. རྣམ་[པར་]ཤེས་[པ་]; Skt. *vijñāna*): consciousness; the unimpeded avenue for the manifestation of sensory objects [consciousness (CS, NJ, PC); perception (KB); modes of awareness or perception (PE)]

nam(-par) tog(-pa) (Tib. རྣམ་[པར་]རྟོག[་པ་]): conceptualization

nang-wa (Tib. སྣང་བ་): sensory appearances; perception; manifestation [appearances (CS, NJ, PC); display (CS); coming-into-presence (FRC); thereness, (self-)presentation, reflective-thematic (KB); how things appear, presence (PE); perceptions (WPT)]

nay-lug (Tib. གནས་ལུགས་): the way of abiding, the true nature of phenomena

ngag (Tib. སྔགས་; Skt. *mantra*): a formula, usually in Sanskrit, repeated aloud, the function of which is to protect the mind from erroneous views

ngang(-tsul) (Tib. ངང་[ཚུལ་]): fundamental nature

ngey-don (Tib. ངེས་དོན་): definitive meaning

ngö-med (Tib. དངོས་མེད་): insubstantiality

ngö-po (Tib. དངོས་པོ་): substance; substantiality

ngo-wo (Tib. ངོ་བོ་): essence (of being); emptiness as the dharmakaya aspect of the true nature of mind [essence (BM, DZP, GL, PC, VH); (open-ended) facticity (of Being) (KB, FRC); nature (MW); what it comes down to, at bottom, in fact (PE)]

ngo-wo-nyid (Tib. ངོ་བོ་ཉིད་): essence itself; denotes the ground of being as the essence of all samsara and nirvana

ngo-wo-nyid (kyi) ku (Tib. ངོ་བོ་ཉིད་[ཀྱི་]སྐུ་; Skt. *svabhāvikakāya*): literally, "body of the essence itself"; the fourth kaya, the totality of the three kayas as inseparable [founding stratum of pure facticity (KB); essential dimension of awakening (MW); embodiment of essential nature (NJ)]

nirmanakaya (Skt. *nirmāṇakāya;* Tib. *trul(-pai) ku,* སྤྲུལ་[པའི་]སྐུ་): literally, "emanation body"; the impermanent physical manifestation of enlightened being in response to the needs of ordinary beings [Manifested Body (BM); manifest dimension of awakening (MW); incarnate body (NGP); unobstructed miraculous emanation form (WS)]

nirvana (Skt. *nirvāṇa;* Tib. *nyang-day,* མྱང་འདས་): literally, "transcendence of sorrow"; the awakened state of buddhahood

nyam(-kyi nang-wa) (Tib. ཉམས་[ཀྱི་སྣང་བ་]): (ephemeral) meditative experience [experiences (CS); mystical experience (GL); apparent experiences (NJ); experiential sign of the development of practice (PE)]

nyam-nyid ye-shey (Tib. མཉམ་ཉིད་ཡེ་ཤེས་): timeless awareness as equalness; one of the five aspects of timeless awareness (*see ye-shey nga*); the awareness of samsara and nirvana as the display of equal purity in supreme emptiness [primordial wisdom of equanimity (BM); wisdom of sameness (LS); Awareness of Fundamental Sameness (MK); primordial wisdom of the nature of equality (NJ); pristine cognition of sameness (NS); All-equalizing Wisdom (SGK); wisdom of equality (WPT)]

nyam-par zhag-pa (Tib. མཉམ་པར་བཞག་པ་): (formal) meditative equipoise; a term used by Shri Simha to denote resting without contrivance in one's fundamental nature

nyan-gyud (Tib. སྙན་བརྒྱུད་): the lineage of oral transmission

nying-je (Tib. སྙིང་རྗེ་): compassion

nying-po (Tib. སྙིང་པོ་; Skt. *garbha*): heart essence; specifically, awareness abiding as the distilled essence of all phenomena [the heart of (BM); evolutionary dynamics, thrust toward it(self), the total system's energy (FRC); embryo (GL); nucleus (NS); energy pulse, core (PE); heart/essence (VH)]

Nyingma (Tib. རྙིང་མ་): the oldest school of Tibetan Buddhism; dating from the eighth century when Padmakara visited Tibet

nyon-yid (Tib. ཉོན་ཡིད་): emotionally afflicted consciousness; the perception of an "I," causing the mind to react on the basis of emotionality [emotionally toned ego-act (KB); defiled mind (MW); passion-based mental events (NJ); consciousness of the intellect endowed with conflicting emotions (NS)]

od-sal (Tib. འོད་གསལ་; Skt. *prabhāsvara*): utter lucidity; denotes the fundamental nature of awareness, buddha nature, as pristine and lucid, free of sullying factors [clarity, luminous absorption (BM); clear light (GL, MW, SL, WPT); sheer lucency, vibrant source of experience (KB); luminosity (LS, SGK, VH)]

od-sal dor-je nying-po (Tib. འོད་གསལ་རྡོ་རྗེ་སྙིང་པོ་): literally, "vajra heart essence of utter lucidity"; the fifth of seven terms referring to the Great Perfection as explained to Dudjom Lingpa by Ekajati [doctrine of the adamantine essence of the Clear Light (GL); clear light vajra essence (NJ, PC)]

Orgyan Tsokyey Dorje (Tib. ཨོ་རྒྱན་མཚོ་སྐྱེས་རྡོ་རྗེ་): literally, "Lake-Born Vajra of Oddiyana"; epithet of an aspect of Padmakara

Pacification school (Tib. Zhijed, ཞི་བྱེད་): a school of Tibetan Buddhism based on the teachings of the Indian master known to Tibetans as P'hadampa Sang-gyay (ཕ་དམ་པ་སངས་རྒྱས་), who traveled and taught in Tibet in the late eleventh and early twelfth centuries; the focus is the pacification of suffering through the realization of emptiness, and the main scriptural sources are the sutras of the Perfection of Sublime Knowing (Prajñāpāramitā)

pad-ma (Tib. པད་མ་; Skt. *padma*): lotus; one of the five buddha families, denoting the ground of being unsullied by flaws

Padmakara (Skt. Padmākara; Tib. པདྨ་ཀ་ར་): the master of the Indian Buddhist tradition who was primarily responsible for bringing the vajrayana teachings to Tibet in the eighth century; also referred to as Padmasambhava or Guru Rinpoche

pratyekabuddha (Skt.; Tib. *rang-gyal*, རང་རྒྱལ་, or *rang sang-gyay,* རང་སངས་རྒྱས་): literally, "self-made buddha"; one who follows or has accomplished the hinayana path, which leads to realization of the nonexistence of personal identity and partial realization that phenomena are interdependent and have no independent nature

rang-dang (Tib. རང་མདངས་): natural glow

rang-gyud (Tib. རང་རྒྱད་): in its own right

rang-jung (Tib. རང་བྱུང་): naturally occurring

rang-nang (Tib. རང་སྣང་): awareness's own manifestations; naturally manifesting; mind's own projections

rang-ngo (Tib. རང་ངོ་): very essence

rang-sa (Tib. རང་ས་): natural state; own context

rang-sem (Tib. རང་སེམས་): natural mind

rang-tsan-pa (Tib. རང་མཚན་པ་): independent existence

rang-wang gyur-wa (Tib. རང་དབང་སུ་རཔ་): (to gain) mastery; to gain true independence (in the sense of mastery of one's situation)

rang-zhin (Tib. རང་བཞིན་; Skt. *svabhāva*): nature (of being); the lucidity of mind that accounts for the realization and manifestation of sambhogakaya [nature (BM, DZP, GL, PT, SL, VH); actuality (of Being) (FRC, KB); natural (NJ, PC); natural expression (NS, WPT); actuality, essence (PE)]

rang-zhin med-pa (Tib. རང་བཞིན་མེད་པ་): without independent nature

Ratnasambhava (Skt.; Tib. Rinchhen Jungdan, རིན་ཆེན་འབྱུང་ལྡན་): literally, "Source of Preciousness"; among the buddhas of the five families, the buddha associated with the southern direction; the name denotes the ground of being as the source of all elements of the path and its fruition, and endowed with an abundance of positive qualities

rig (Tib. རིགས་): literally, "family"; a schema for describing deities in terms that correspond to the fixation of beings on their species; five such families are usually enumerated (*see dor-je; lay; pad-ma; rin-chhen; sang-gyay*)

rig-pa (Tib. རིག་པ་; Skt. *vidyā*): (the recognition of) awareness, whereupon the ground of being becomes evident, with the true nature of mind present as the dynamic energy of that awareness; its "ground aspect" is awareness of the fundamental nature of the ground of being; its "path aspect" is the ongoing experience of unsullied, lucid awareness [awareness (CS); cognitive excitation, wholeness in ecstatic intensity, cognitively intensificatory (FRC); immediate awareness, state of contemplation (GL); pure awareness (KB, NJ, PC); pure cognitiveness, non-representationally cognitive (KB); innate wisdom or wakefulness, pure presence, primordial being (NGP); awareness (NS, WPT); flash of awareness, flash of knowing that gives awareness its (illumining) quality (PE)]

rigdzin (Tib. *rig-dzin*, རིག་འཛིན་; Skt. *vidyādhara*): one who "holds" the realization of awareness

rin-chhen (Tib. རིན་ཆེན་; Skt. *ratna*): jewel; also, one of the five buddha families, denoting the ground of being functioning as the source all kayas and aspects of timeless awareness

rol-pa (Tib. རོལ་པ་): display [play (BM, FRC, NJ, PC); manifestation (GL); playfulness (KB); excitement (PE)]

rudra (Skt. *rūdra;* Tib. རུ་ད་): harmful influences due to ignorance and negativity, personified as a demonic figure

sadhana (Skt. *sādhana;* Tib. *drub-pa,* སྒྲུབ་པ་): formal techniques that promote spiritual development and accomplishment

samaya (Skt.; Tib. *dam-tsig,* དམ་ཚིག་): the principles to which a practitioner is personally committed in vajrayana practice

sambhogakaya (Skt. *sambhogakāya;* Tib. *long-kyod dzog-pai ku,* ལོངས་སྤྱོད་རྫོགས་པའི་སྐུ་): literally, "body of perfect enjoyment"; the pure form manifestation of enlightened being perceptible only to beings of advanced realization [enjoyment dimension of awakening (MW); body of perfect rapture (NS); primordial contact with total richness and all its satisfactions (PE); immeasurable qualities of flawless, inconceivable, desireless exaltation form (WS)]

samsara (Skt. *saṃsāra;* Tib. *khor-wa,* འཁོར་བ་): cyclic existence; the unenlightened state of an ordinary being

sang-gyay (Tib. སངས་རྒྱས་; Skt. *buddha*): buddha(hood); also, one of the five buddha families, denoting the ground of being whereby the distortions of habitual patterns are cleared away in basic space and the context of timeless awareness and positive qualities unfolds

sang-ngag dor-je t'heg-pa (Tib. གསང་སྔགས་རྡོ་རྗེ་ཐེག་པ་): literally, "secret mantra approach of vajrayana"; the first of seven terms referring to the Great Perfection teachings as explained to Dudjom Lingpa by Ekajati

sang-wa (Tib. གསང་བ་): secret, secrecy; there are two aspects: "concealment" (Tib. *bay-pai sang-wa,* སྦས་པའི་གསང་བ་), in that vajrayana teachings are kept very private and imparted only under certain conditions, and "self-secrecy" (Tib. *gab-pai sang-wa,* གབ་པའི་གསང་བ་), in that such teachings cannot be comprehended without preparation and personal instruction

Saraha (Skt.; Tib. ས་ར་ཧ་): a great vajrayana master and siddha of Indian Buddhism; Dudjom Lingpa was an emanation of Saraha

sem (Tib. སེམས་): mind in the ordinary sense, characterized by the nonrecognition of awareness, with thoughts subject to origination and cessation as the dynamic energy of this nonrecognition [cognitive act (CS); mentation (FRC); mind (GL, KB, NJ, PC, PE); thoughts, thought process (GL); intentiveness, operational cognitiveness (KB); the finite, dualistic rational mind/discursive, conceptual mind (NGP); experiencing, potential for experience (PE)]

sem-dhe (Tib. སེམས་སྡེ་): the Category of Mind; the first of the three categories of teachings in atiyoga, or Great Perfection

sem-kyed (Tib. སེམས་བསྐྱེད་): arousing awakening mind, or bodhichitta; deciding that samsara and nirvana are the phantasmagoria of a single awareness is the most sacred way of arousing awakening mind (*see jang-chhub kyi sem*)

sem-nyid (Tib. སེམས་ཉིད་): mind itself, or the nature of mind, as contrasted with the contents of mind as thoughts, perceptions, emotions, and so forth [Mind (BM); pure experience, experience-as-such (FRC); Mind-as-such (KB, LS); mind-essence (LM); nature of mind (NJ, PC)]

shey-drib (Tib. ཤེས་སྒྲིབ་): cognitive obscurations; obscurations concerning the true nature of phenomena

shey-pa (Tib. ཤེས་པ་): knowing

shey-rab (Tib. ཤེས་རབ་; Skt. *prajñā*): sublime knowing as the aspect of spiritual development that corresponds to the level of ultimate reality; its initial phase, or "ground aspect," is an understanding of the fundamental state of samsara and nirvana as supreme emptiness; its "path aspect" is the ongoing experience of that understanding, directly introducing one to the unimpeded avenue of relaxed and open awareness [wisdom (BM, DZP, MW, WPT); discriminative awareness (in the context of the three trainings) (DZP); critical analytical acumen (FRC); knowledge (LM); appreciative discernment (MW); gnosis, transcendental wisdom (NGP); knowledge (NJ, PC); discerning wisdom (SL); knowledge or intelligence; in particular, the knowledge that realizes egolessness (VH); discerning wisdom (WPT)]

shi-shed (Tib. ཤི་གཤེད་): literally, "murderous executioner"; the personification of the erroneous investment of one's body with true existence, since this misapprehension provides the link from death to the next birth in samsara

shravaka (Skt. *śrāvaka;* Tib. *nyan-t'hö,* ཉན་ཐོས་): literally, "one who hears or listens"; a practitioner of the hinayana path who realizes the nonexistence of personal identity but still holds phenomena to have an independent nature; the shravaka path leads to the realization of an arhat, one who has "conquered the inner foe" of afflictive emotions and no longer accumulates karma or experiences suffering as a result

Shri Simha (Skt. Śrī Siṃha; Tib. ཤྲཱི་སེང་ཧ་): the master of the Great Perfection lineage who codified the teachings of the Category of Direct Transmission into four cycles of outer, inner, secret, and most secret unsurpassable teachings

Shrimat (Skt. Śrīmat; Tib. Paldang Danpa, དཔལ་དང་ལྡན་པ་): literally, "Endowed with Glory"; the pure realm associated with the buddha Ratnasambhava and the southern direction

siddha (Skt. *siddhā;* Tib. *drub-t'hob,* གྲུབ་ཐོབ་): one who has gained siddhi, or spiritual attainment; a term for a realized saint of the vajrayana path

siddhi (Skt.; Tib. *ngö-drub,* དངོས་གྲུབ་): attainment gained through spiritual practice; two kinds are distinguished: relatively common powers and accomplishments, such as clairvoyance and telepathy, and the sublime siddhi of enlightenment itself

so-sor tog-pai shey-rab (Tib. སོ་སོར་རྟོགས་པའི་ཤེས་རབ་): discerning quality of sublime knowing; knowledge gained through analytical investigation leading to the definitive conclusion that all phenomena are emptiness

(so-)sor-tog(-pai) ye-shey (Tib. [སོ་]སོར་རྟོགས་[པའི་]ཡེ་ཤེས་): discerning timeless awareness; one of the five aspects of timeless awareness (*see ye-shey nga*); the unimpeded avenue for the expression of the lucidity of mind that understands each thing individually [discriminative primordial wisdom (BM); All-encompassing Investigating Awareness (MK); pristine wisdom of discernment (MW); discerning awareness-wisdom (RW); discerning wisdom (SGK); discerning wisdom (WPT)]

srog-chod (Tib. སྲོག་གཅོད་): literally, "cutter of life force"; a personification of the erroneous investment of one's body with true existence, since one is driven to seek happiness for the sake of the body, thus severing the lifeline of liberation by fixation upon attachment and aversion

srung-khor (Tib. སྲུང་འཁོར་): protection circle, a component of sadhana practice; making evident sublime knowing which realizes that things have no identity constitutes the actual protection circle

Sukarmapurna (Skt. Sukarmapūrṇa; Tib. Layrab Dzogpa, ལས་རབ་རྫོགས་པ་): literally, "Utterly Perfect Activity"; the pure realm associated with the buddha Amoghasiddhi and the northern direction

Sukhavati (Skt. Sukhāvatī; Tib. Dewachan, བདེ་བ་ཅན་): literally, "Blissful (Realm)"; the pure realm associated with the buddha Amitabha and the western direction

sung (Tib. གསུང་): enlightened speech

ta-wa (Tib. ལྟ་བ་): view; refers to the "worldview" or philosophical underpinnings of a given spiritual approach; in the Great Perfection approach, view is the understanding of the supreme common ground of samsara and nirvana—basic space, in which the three modes of samsara, nirvana, and the spiritual path are perfect and complete

tan la wab-pa (Tib. གཏན་ལ་དབབ་པ་): to reach a definitive conclusion

tathagata (Skt. *tathāgata;* Tib. *de-zhin sheg-pa,* དེ་བཞིན་གཤེགས་པ་):

literally, "(one) gone to suchness"; an epithet for a buddha, often Shakyamuni Buddha

ten-drel (Tib. རྟེན་འབྲེལ་): interdependent connection

t'ha (Tib. མཐའ་): limitation

t'hab (Tib. ཐབས་; Skt. *upāya*): skillful means as the aspect of spiritual development that corresponds to the level of relative reality, associated with the gaining of merit

t'heg-pa (Tib. ཐེག་པ་; Skt. *yāna*): a spiritual approach integrating principles of spiritual development into a practical system of application

t'heg-pa rim-pa gu (Tib. ཐེག་པ་རིམ་པ་དགུ་): the nine developmental spiritual approaches elaborated in the teachings of the Nyingma school; the three paths of the shravaka, pratyekabuddha, and bodhisattva, and the six levels of tantra—kriyatantra, upatantra, yogatantra, mahayoga, anuyoga, and atiyoga; the eight lower approaches are subsumed within the ninth yana of atiyoga, or Great Perfection

t'hig-le (Tib. ཐིག་ལེ་; Skt. *bindu*): sphere (of being); implies "beyond all the angles and corners of concepts" [sphere, circle (CS); creative essence (DZP); essence (WPT)]

t'hig-le nyag-chig (Tib. ཐིག་ལེ་ཉག་གཅིག་): literally, "unique bindu, or sphere (of being)," unique in the sense that samsara and nirvana are of one taste in bodhicitta; the fourth of seven terms referring to the Great Perfection teachings as explained to Dudjom Lingpa by Ekajati [single circle (CS)]

t'hod-gal (Tib. ཐོད་རྒལ་): literally, "surpassing the pinnacle"; one of two phases of Great Perfection practice and teaching (*see also t'hreg-chhod*) [Direct Approach (BM, DZP); Direct Crossing (CS, DZP); leapover (DZP); final leap (FRC); transcendence (NGP); crossing over (NJ, PC)] *t'hreg-chhod* (Tib. ཁྲེགས་ཆོད་): literally, "cutting through solidity"; one of two phases of Great Perfection practice and teaching (*see also t'hod-gal*); *Buddhahood Without Meditation* is a manual of *t'hreg-chhod* teaching [cutting through (BM, NGP, NJ, PC, VH); breakthrough, cutting through all attachment (DZP); barrier-free (FRC); Seeing Through (NGP)]

t'hug (Tib. ཐུགས་): enlightened mind; the direct experience of basic space as original purity, free of conceptual limitations

t'hug-je (Tib. ཐུགས་རྗེ་): responsiveness (of being); the union of emptiness as the essence of mind and lucidity as its nature [compassion (BM, DZP, NJ, PC, VH, WPT); energy (DZP, MW, SL); resonance (of Being) (FRC); responsiveness (KB); capacity (RP)]

ting-nge-dzin (Tib. ཏིང་ངེ་འཛིན; Skt. *samādhi*): meditative absorption; meditation in which the mind rests naturally [contemplation (BM, MW, PE, SL); meditative concentration (DZP, VH); meditative stabilization (ME, NJ, PC)]

tod-pa (Tib. བསྟོད་པ་): the act of praising, a component of sadhana practice; to feel a sense of wonder and conviction when one perceives the way in which samsara and nirvana abide as great perfection is the ultimate praise

tog-pa (Tib. རྟོགས་པ་): realization

tong(-pa)-nyid (Tib. སྟོང་[པ་]ཉིད; Skt. *śūnyatā*): emptiness, the absence of any independent nature; one of the three "doorways to liberation" (Tib. *t'har-pai go*); refers to the lack of true existence of anything external or internal, and the absence of differentiation due to dualistic perception [voidness (HTV); nature of emptiness (NJ, PC)]

trö-pa (Tib. སྤྲོས་པ་): (conceptual) elaboration

trul-ku (*see* nirmanakaya)

tsan-ma med-pa (Tib. མཚན་མ་མེད་པ་): the absence of characteristics; one of the three "doorways to liberation" (Tib. *t'har-pai go*); refers to the fact that buddha nature is free of characterization, comparison, or demonstration [absence of characteristics (NJ, PC); attributelessness (NS); signlessness (HTV)]

tsog-drug (Tib. ཚོགས་དྲུག་): the six modes of consciousness

tzal (Tib. རྩལ་): the dynamic energy of the ground of being, accounting for all qualities of the awakened state; when it is misperceived due to the nonrecognition of awareness, it gives rise to all aspects of ordinary experience [power, skill (BM); creativity (FRC, MW, PE, SL); display (NJ, PC); potency, the external manifestation of energy (SL)]

ub-chhub (Tib. ཡུབ་ཆུབ་): all-embracing consummation (*see khor-day ub-chhub*)

ug-len (Tib. དབུགས་ལེན་): literally, "stealer of breath"; a personification of the erroneous investment of one's body with true existence, in that this misapprehension robs one of the breath of lasting happiness

upayatantra (Skt. *upāyatantra;* Tib. *u-pa-yai gyud,* ཨུ་པ་ཡའི་རྒྱུད་): the second of six levels of tantra in the Nyingma school; the approach of gaining accomplishment, especially through mantra repetition and meditative absorption

Vairochana (Skt. Vairocana; Tib. Nampar Nangdzad, རྣམ་པར་སྣང་མཛད་): literally, "Distinct Manifestation"; among the buddhas of the five families, the buddha associated with the central direction; the name denotes the positive qualities of the nature of mind becoming fully evident

vajra (*see dor-je*)

Vajradhara (Skt.; Tib. Dorje Chhang, རྡོ་རྗེ་འཆང་): literally, "Bearer of the Vajra"; the dharmakaya buddha embodying the ultimate nature of mind; the form manifested by Shakyamuni when teaching tantra

Vajrapani (Skt. Vajrapāṇi; Tib. Khyagna Dorje, ཕྱག་ན་རྡོ་རྗེ་): literally, "Vajra in Hand"; the bodhisattva embodying the spiritual power of all buddhas and bodhisattvas

vajrayana (Skt. *vajrayāna;* Tib. *dor-je t'heg-pa,* རྡོ་རྗེ་ཐེག་པ་): the path of Buddhist practice based on principles expounded in the tantras

wang gyur-wa (Tib. དབང་བསྒྱུར་བ་): (to gain) mastery

yana (*see t'heg-pa*)

ye-shey (Tib. ཡེ་ཤེས་; Skt. *jñāna*): timeless awareness; awareness (*shey*) that is so from the beginning (*ye*), having always been the true nondual nature of mind [primordial wisdom (BM, NJ, PC); wisdom (DZP, RW); existential awareness (FRC); pristine cognition (KB); ever fresh awareness (PE); primal wisdom (SL, WPT); wakefulness (VH)]

ye-shey nga (Tib. ཡེ་ཤེས་ལྔ་): the five aspects of timeless awareness—timeless awareness as the basic space of phenomena (*chhö-ying ye-shey*); mirrorlike timeless awareness (*me-long ta-bui ye-shey*); timeless awareness as equalness (*nyam-nyid ye-shey*); discerning timeless awareness (*so-sor tog-pai ye-shey*); and timeless awareness as spontaneous fulfillment (*ja-wa drub-pai ye-shey*)

yid (Tib. ཡིད་): conceptual mind; consciousness that perceives all sensory appearances—the five physical senses and the realm of mental constructs

yid (kyi nam)-shey (Tib. ཡིད་[ཀྱི་རྣམ་]ཤེས་): consciousness based on conceptual mind; the unimpeded avenue for the six kinds of sensory objects, which integrates this information into a coherent picture of the phenomenal world

yogatantra (Skt.; Tib. *nal-jor gyi gyud,* རྣལ་འབྱོར་གྱི་རྒྱུད་): the third of six levels of tantra in the Nyingma school; the approach of calm abiding and profound insight undertaken to perceive basic space, devoid of characteristics

yon-tan (Tib. ཡོན་ཏན་): enlightened or positive qualities

yul (Tib. ཡུལ་): (sensory) object; field for objectification; field; objective environment [cognitive domain (FRC); object (NJ, PC)]

yul-med (Tib. ཡུལ་མེད་): nonexistent as an object

za-dre (Tib. ཟ་འདྲེ་): literally, "consuming demon"; a personification of the erroneous investment of one's body with true existence, in that effort made for the sake of the body eats away at, or undermines, the fruit of omniscience that results from spiritual attainment

zhal-yay-khang (Tib. གཞལ་ཡས་ཁང་): immeasurable mansion (of a deity); refers to the fact that the qualities of the ground of being cannot be measured and completely fill samsara and nirvana

zhi (Tib. གཞི་): the ground (of being); the fundamentally uncontrived nature of being; the Great Perfection teachings state that this ground is already endowed with all qualities of enlightened being, perfect and complete without having to be sought or brought into being deliberately; the process of the spiritual path is one of making the ground evident as the fruition, rather than fundamentally altering it in any way [basis (BM); Being (FRC); ground-basis (NJ, PC); base, foundation (SL)]

zhi-nay (Tib. ཞི་གནས་; Skt. *śamatha*): calm abiding

zhi-nyid (Tib. གཞི་ཉིད་): the ground (of being) itself; the very ground

zhi-ying (Tib. གཞི་དབྱིངས་): the ground of being as basic space

zhing-kham (Tib. ཞིང་ཁམས་): pure realm; denotes the "field" (*zhing*) of basic space as the fundamental nature of being (*kham*) from which there is no wavering

zhon-nu bum-ku (Tib. གཞོན་ནུ་བུམ་སྐུ་): literally, "youthful vase body"; the fundamental nature of awareness is "youthful" (*zhon-nu*), since it is free of all birth, death, and decay; like a "vase" (*bum*), since there is no violation of its encompassing spontaneous presence; and referred to as "body," or "kaya" (*ku*), since it supports an amassing of all qualities of buddhahood; the seventh of seven terms referring to the Great Perfection teachings as explained to Dudjom Lingpa by Ekajati

zhug-sol (Tib. བཞུགས་གསོལ་): the request to remain, a component of sadhana practice; holding to the natural state in all its immediacy, free of transition or change, is the ultimate request to remain

zung-dzin (Tib. གཟུང་འཛིན་): the dualistic framework of object and subject; dualistic perception

zung-wa (Tib. གཟུང་བ་): the perception of objects; the manifestation of sensory appearances as visual forms [object (GL)]

Zurchhung Sheyrab Dragpa (Tib. ཟུར་ཆུང་ཤེས་རབ་གྲགས་པ་): famous teacher of the Nyingma school of Tibetan Buddhism who lived from 1014 to 1074

SOURCES CITED

Dorje, Gyurme, and Matthew Kapstein. *The Nyingma School of Tibetan Buddhism,* Vol. II. Boston: Wisdom Publications, 1991.

Guenther, Herbert V. *From Reductionism to Creativity: Dzogchen and the New Sciences of Mind.* Boston: Shambhala, 1989.

Hopkins, Jeffrey. *Meditation on Emptiness.* London: Wisdom Publications, 1983.

Kongtrul, Jamgön (Lodrö Tayé). *Myriad Worlds: Buddhist Cosmology in Abhidharma, Kalachakra, and Dzogchen.*

Trans. by the International Translation Committee. Ithaca, NY: Snow Lion Publications, 1995.

Lama Shabkar. *The Flight of the Garuda*. Trans. by Erik Pema Kunsang. Kathmandu: Rangjung Yeshe Publications, 1986.

Lingpa, Karma. *Self-Liberation Through Seeing With Naked Awareness*. Trans. by John Myrdhin Reynolds, Barrytown, NY: Station Hill, 1989.

Longchenpa. *Kindly Bent to Ease Us*. Trans. by Herbert V. Guenther. Emeryville, CA: Dharma Publishing, 1976.

Mañjuśrīmitra. *Primordial Experience: An Introduction to rDzogs-chen Meditation*. Trans. by Namkhai Norbu and Kennard Lipman. Boston: Shambhala, 1987.

Nālandā Translation Committee. *The Rain of Wisdom . . . The Vajra Songs of the Kagyu Gurus*. Boulder, CO: Shambhala, 1980.

Nam-mkha'i snying-po. *Mother of Knowledge: The Enlightenment of Ye-she mTsho-rgyal*. Trans. by Tarthang Tulku. Berkeley, CA: Dharma Publishing, 1983.

Ngari Panchen Pema Wangyi Gyalpo. *Perfect Conduct: Ascertaining the Three Vows*. Trans. by Khenpo Gyurme Samdrub and Sangye Khandro. Boston: Wisdom Publications, 1996.

Norbu, Namkhai. *The Cycle of Day and Night*. Trans. by John Reynolds. Barrytown, NY: Station Hill, 1987.

Norbu, Namkhai. *Dzogchen: The Self-Perfected State*. Trans. by John Shane. Ithaca, NY: Snow Lion Publications, 1996.

Norbu, Thinley. *Oral Teaching on Nang-jang*. Trans. by Sangye Khandro, Pema Odsal Ling, Watsonville, CA, 1996.

Norbu, Thinley. *Magic Dance*. Boston: Shambhala, 1995.

Norbu, Thinley. *The Small Golden Key to the Treasure of the Various Essential Necessities of General and Extraordinary Buddhist Dharma*. Trans. by Elisabeth Anderson. New York: Yeshe Nyingpo, 1977.

Norbu, Thinley. *White Sail*. Boston: Shambhala, 1992.

Nyoshul Khenpo. *Natural Great Perfection*. Trans. by Surya Das. Ithaca, NY: Snow Lion Publications, 1995.

Patrul Rinpoche. *The Words of My Perfect Teacher*. Trans. by the Padmakara Translation Group. San Francisco: Harper-Collins, 1994.

Rangdrol, Shabkar Tsogdruk. *The Life of Shabkar: The Autobiography of a Tibetan Yogin*. Trans. by Matthieu Ricard et al. Albany: State University of New York Press, 1994.

Rangdrol, Tsele Natsok. *The Circle of the Sun*. Trans. by Erik Pema Kunsang. Kathmandu: Rangjung Yeshe Publications, 1990.

Rangdrol, Tsele Natsok. *Lamp of Mahamudra*. Trans. by Erik Pema Kunsang. Boston: Shambhala, 1989.

Reynolds, John Myrdhin. *The Golden Letters: The Three Statements of Garab Dorje, the First Teacher of Dzogchen, Together with a Commentary by Dza Patrul Rinpoche Entitled "The Special Teaching of the Wise and Glorious King."* Ithaca, NY: Snow Lion Publications, 1996.

Sogyal Rinpoche. *Dzogchen and Padmasambhava*. Berkeley, CA: Rigpa Fellowship, 1989.

Thurman, Robert, trans. *The Holy Teachings of Vimalakirti: A Mahayana Scripture*. University Park: Pennsylvania State University Press, 1976.

Tulku Thondup. *Buddha Mind: An Anthology of Longchen Rabjam's Writings on Dzogpa Chenpo*. Ithaca, NY: Snow Lion Publications, 1989.

Tulku Urgyen Rinpoche. *Rainbow Painting*. Trans. by Erik Pema Kunsang. Kathmandu: Rangjung Yeshe Publications, 1995.

Tulku Urgyen Rinpoche. *Vajra Heart*. Trans. by Erik Pema Kunsang. Kathmandu: Rangjung Yeshe Publications, 1988.

Pronunciation Guide to Tibetan Terms

THE FOLLOWING CHART provides general guidelines to pronouncing the transliterated Tibetan words used in this book. The phonetics are based on a system developed by H.E. Chagdud Tulku Rinpoche, which gives the approximate pronunciation of a syllable while retaining certain elements of its actual spelling in Tibetan.

INITIAL CONSONANTS

Phonetic	Pronunciation	Example
b	baby	*bag-chhag*
ch	lunch	*chig*
chh	church (more aspiration than the preceding consonant)	*rin-po-chhe*
d	door	*dor-je*
dh	hardhat (more aspiration than the preceding consonants)	*long-dhe*
dr	drive	*drang-don*
dz	fads	*dzog*
g	get	*gu-ru*
gy	energy	*sang-gyay*
h	happy	*hung*
j	jump	*dor-je*
k	calypso	*ku*
kh	buckhorn (more aspiration than the preceding consonants)	*nam-kha*

Pronunciation Guide

Phonetic	Pronunciation	Example
khy	church (more aspiration than the preceding consonants)	*khyen-pai*
ky	lunch	*lay-kyi*
l	lucky	*lung*
lh	lhasa apso (aspirated "l," almost sounds like "hl")	*lha*
m	mother	*pad-ma*
n	nothing	*nang*
ng	sing a song	*ngang*
ny	canyon	*nyam*
p	jump	*rig-pa*
p'h	slaphappy (more aspiration than the preceding consonants)	*p'hun-tsog*
r	river (note: "r" is not "rolled" in Tibetan)	*rol-pa*
s	simple	*sang-gyay*
sh	short	*ye-shey*
sr	simple ("r" is silent)	*srog-chod*
t	tallyho	*nam-tog*
t'h	rabbit hole (more aspiration than the preceding consonants)	*t'hab*
tr	trap	*trö-pa*
ts	flotsam (more aspiration than the preceding consonants)	*khyag-tsal*
tz	rats	*tzal*
w	wind	*wa*
y	yellow	*ying*
z	grasses (not quite a "z" sound)	*gang-zag*
zh	vision	*zhing-kham*

FINAL CONSONANTS

Phonetic	Pronunciation	Example
-b	shop	*lhun-drub*
-d	lead	*chod*
-g	soak	*tsog*
-l	ball	*yul*
-m	ham	*sem*
-n	pen	*dag-dzin*
-ng	sing	*zhing*
-r	far	*bar-do*

VOWELS AND DIPHTHONGS

a	father (alone or before final -b, -g, -m, -ng)	*wang*
	made (before final -d)	*pad-ma*
	let (before final -n)	*yon-tan*
ai	chain	*tog-pai*
ay	say	*sang-gyay*
e	say	*dor-je*
ei	(approx.) ay-ee (almost two syllables)	*t'hug-jei*
ey	say	*ye-shey*
i	pin	*ding*
ii	bean	*kun-zhii*
iy	season	*lhun-gyiy drub*
o	so (alone or before final -g, -b, -m, -ng)	*gom-pa*
	woman (before final -d, -n)	*kyod-pa*
ö	(approx.) thorough (= German o)	*chhö*
oi	soy	*gya-tsoi*
u	futon	*gyu-ma*
ü	(approx.) put (= German ü)	*lü*
ui	fluid	*ta-bui*

.